Managing
Information
and Statistics

Frances Bee read mathematics at Somerville College, Oxford before going on to take a postgraduate diploma in statistics at London University. She has worked not only as a statistician and a corporate planner but also in the personnel, training and finance functions. Her experience has included local government and a major building society, a stint as the general manager of a large department store, a period as a university lecturer and, on a consultancy basis, as course director of the 'Training the Trainer' portfolio of courses for the IPD.

Roland Bee had a very different career, initially as an industrial chemist, then as a navigator in the RAF before spending several years in human resource and management service roles. His career has included time as a chief personnel officer in local government and senior posts in the Housing Corporation and the electricity supply industry. Roland, too, has experience of teaching in further and higher education.

Frances and Roland are now directors of Time for People Ltd, a time management, personnel and training consultancy and work with a wide range of organisations. They met while undertaking the Masters' Programme at the Management College, Henley-on-Thames. They operate from a converted barn in the grounds of their late medieval/early Tudor farmhouse in Suffolk.

IPD

Other titles in the series:

*Core Personnel and
Development*
Mick Marchington and
Adrian Wilkinson

Employee Development
Rosemary Harrison

Employee Relations
John Gennard and
Graham Judge

Employee Resourcing
Stephen Taylor

Employee Reward
Michael Armstrong

Managing Activities
Michael Armstrong

*Managing Financial
Information*
David Davies

*Managing in a Business
Context*
David Farnham

Managing People
Jane Weightman

Personnel Practice
Malcolm Martin and
Tricia Jackson

The Institute of Personnel and Development is the leading publisher of books and reports for personnel and training professionals, students, and all those concerned with the effective management and development of people at work. For details of all our titles, please contact the Publishing Department:

tel 020 8263 3387
fax 020 8263 3850
e-mail publish@ipd.co.uk

The catalogue of all IPD titles can be viewed on the IPD website:

www.ipd.co.uk

ℙ𝔹

PEOPLE AND ORGANISATIONS

Managing Information and Statistics

ROLAND AND FRANCES BEE

INSTITUTE OF PERSONNEL AND DEVELOPMENT

Design by Curve

Typeset by Fakenham Photosetting Ltd, Fakenham, Norfolk

Printed in Great Britain by
the Cromwell Press, Trowbridge, Wiltshire

British Library Cataloguing in Publication Data
A catalogue record of this book is available from
the British Library

ISBN 0-85292-785-1

INSTITUTE OF PERSONNEL
AND DEVELOPMENT

IPD House, Camp Road, London SW19 4UX
Tel: 020-8971 9000 Fax: 020-8263 3333
Registered office as above. Registered Charity No. 1038333
A company limited by guarantee. Registered in England No. 2931892

Contents

Dedication

In memory of our beautiful and beloved
daughter Elizabeth Alice Bee
5 April 1988

Foreword

Welcome to this series of texts designed to complement the Core Management syllabus. The role of the personnel and development practitioner has become an important part of the total management of all types of organisation in the private, public and voluntary sectors. A fundamental element of that role is the ability to comprehend and contribute to the overall goals, performance and outcomes of organisations. This is the purpose of the Core Management syllabus: to equip personnel and development practitioners to understand and appreciate complex business and managerial issues and to develop their skills so that they can play a full role in that process.

The issue of understanding and handling the information on which all organisations depend has become both important and critical to business performance. Managers are increasingly required not only to deploy and apply the information affecting their roles, but to specify and define the kinds of information which they work with. In this sense there has been a blurring of the line between the information specialist on the one hand and the manager on the other, with new and vital expectations placed on managers to perform competently. This text provides the technical support for personnel and development professionals to cope with these demands and provides an excellent introduction to the techniques and approaches that underpin this essential area.

Professor Ian J Beardwell
Head, Department of HRM
Leicester Business School
De Montfort University
Leicester

Introduction

When we wrote *Management Information and Statistics* (Bee and Bee, 1990) we said we were living in a time of great change and, if anything in the intervening years, the pace of change has accelerated. Managers and specialists have to assimilate masses of data, convert that data into information, form conclusions about the information and make decisions leading to the achievement of business objectives – all in double-quick time. All of this is taking place against the background of a fiercely competitive environment and increasingly global markets! In these days of sophisticated computer technology, with distributed networks and software programs that have made even the most technical subject accessible to the lay person, it is vital that today's managers and specialists are able to take advantage of the technology on offer rather than be its prisoner. Experience and judgement are vital attributes, but in the fast-moving world of business today the successful manager and specialist will need to manage information effectively and have a portfolio of quantitative techniques to deploy in his or her decision-making processes.

In this book, we have moved away from the term *management* information to talking about information generally. Also, we use the terms *managers* and *specialists* to recognise the fact that it is not only managers who use information systems, but there are also a wide range of specialist professionals who are not managers but who routinely use business information in the course of their work.

Part 1 of this book is about the concepts and applications of information systems. We would make the point that information systems now are so sophisticated and complex, that writing about them can, and does, fill the pages of many, very thick textbooks. We have the space only to provide an introduction to information systems. We are not aiming to turn you into an information systems expert but to provide you, as a non-IT specialist, with sufficient knowledge of systems and systems theory to allow you to play the fullest part in the design, development and use of *your* information system. In places we have tried to simplify the concepts and to do this we may have drifted slightly away from the purist in the IT and information systems fields. We believe that this is preferable to absolute adherence to IT jargon and dogma, in the interests of wider understanding of the subject.

In Part 2, the section on statistics, we draw on examples from across the general business world, with some concentration on human resource management, to look at a range of quantitative approaches to managing your information. Our approach is to assume that you know little about the subjects, other than being able to cope with the basic mathematical functions, and to take you gently through to a reasonable level of understanding. We will not try and convert you into professional statisticians but hope to share with you an awareness of, even an excitement with, the value of the numbers in this world of business and organisation management. We aim to give you sufficient understanding of some of the most useful statistical techniques to enable you to recognise when they might be helpful in your business or professional activities and to be sufficiently knowledgeable to use the output from statistical packages. Some of the techniques are straightforward enough for anyone to apply themselves, others may require the help of a friendly neighbourhood (or in your case, organisation) statistician.

We are not going to blind you with jargon. We shall try and explain the terms as we go along, using **bold** type for emphasis when we introduce a term in its relevant section for the first time, then provide the definition in the Glossary of Statistical Terms at the end of the book. There may be occasions when, for the sake of simplicity in our explanations, we will offend the pure statistician and mathematician or IT specialist. We make no apology for this. When you get to the final line where the professional statistician or the computer package has calculated 'x' equal to something and therefore served his or her purpose, you the aspiring business manager and specialist will continue to use this computed or calculated value of 'x' to make your inferences about what is happening in your business.

The techniques are only a means to an end – they are not an end in themselves. They are a means of taking you from the chaos of the Dark Ages of data through to the renaissance of information. Data on its own is meaningless, it must be converted into information before it can be used in the decision-making process. We suggest that you think of the techniques as an engine converting raw fuel into usable energy and then into power. As you will appreciate, information is power and that is what statistics, properly applied, can give you. The core philosophy of our approach is that information systems, statistics and information technology are not theoretical subjects, ends in themselves, but the means to a greater understanding of the business process.

A final word of explanation, sometimes in the book we have used the word *business* to describe the organisation in which the information system works and in which the quantitative methods are used. We mean the word to include both the profit-making part of the economy and the not-for-profit sector, local government, charities, schools, hospitals, etc.

We would like to thank John Bevan of the Canterbury Business School at the University of Kent for his help on the statistical sections.

Roland and Frances Bee
Newsons Farm
June 1999

Part 1

INTRODUCTION TO INFORMATION SYSTEMS

'WHAT YOU NEED TO KNOW'

Information Systems

This sounds like a very grand title for a very basic but vital concept. Information is the lifeblood of any business or organisation. It can range from simple reports on sales and profits for a small company through to complex systems covering all aspects of a vast conglomerate. Information is in essence what you, whether a manager or specialist in your profession, need to know to run your business (or part of it) successfully. The system is merely the mechanism to ensure that information is available to you in the form you want it and when you need it.

Chapter 1 is an overview of information systems. It examines the content, form and timing of the information we need to make decisions and the management of information in the context of the organisation – its structures and cultures, the different levels of need, the decision-making processes. In Chapter 2 we explore some of the major systems concepts – the features of a systems approach, system boundaries, open and closed systems, holism, emergent properties, hard and soft properties and systems entropy. In Chapter 3 we move to look at how information systems can help us in our planning processes – discussing levels of planning, types and sources of information for planning, modelling and simulation, and sensitivity analysis. Chapter 4 then examines the information requirements for monitoring and control – the use of information in controlling, monitoring/reviewing and revising the plan. Chapter 5 is about the processing and storage of the data, the structure of databases and database management systems and various types of computer-assisted activity. In Chapter 6 we look at some of the issues that are considered important in the design, development and maintenance of information systems – we go through the basic project model for designing information systems and focus on the key area of requirements analysis. This chapter includes some of the proprietary systems used in the design and development of information systems, some words of wisdom about data protection, data security and when the seemingly inevitable worst thing happens, some thoughts on disaster recovery to help get your organisation back on its feet. Chapter 7 looks specifically at information systems for the Human Resource (HR) professional and we conclude in Chapter 8 with a glance into the future.

1 The philosophy of managing information

INTRODUCTION

Developments in computer technology, and the way this technology is used by organisations, has taken us from the twentieth century – where personal computers (PCs) performing simple tasks on individuals' desks have been used to improve local efficiency – into the twenty-first century where managing information effectively will make the difference between successful achievement of objectives and organisational failure.

Effective management of information is critically dependent on three main factors:

1. the content of that information

2. the form in which it is presented

3. the timing of its presentation.

For our purposes we choose to define management information as the right information in the right form and at the right time, to enable the manager or specialist effectively and efficiently to do his or her job. We support the definition of a management information system (MIS) as one emphasising the *use* to which the information is put, rather than the way it is produced, ie:

> A system to convert data from internal and external sources into information and to communicate that information, in an appropriate form, to managers (and others) at all levels in all functions to enable them to make timely and effective decisions for planning, directing and controlling the activities for which they are responsible.
>
> (Lucey, 1997, p2)

While we will be concerned in this book with *formal*

information systems, we need to be careful not to ignore the capture and integration of *informal* information derived from, for example, networking within and outside the organisation. When we are operating at a more strategic level, or in situations of uncertainty, information from informal systems can assume a greater profile.

CONTENT OF INFORMATION SYSTEMS

The starting point for understanding *what* information is required is the realisation that it is dependent on who requires it and for what purpose, ie who *owns* the information. Also, we are living at a time of great change and this will be reflected in continually evolving needs for information. Any system for delivering management/specialist information must be flexible and allow for easy updating and amendment. In an ideal world an information system would be tailored to the needs of the individual manager/specialist. In the past this has not always been possible. Managers and other users often had to make do with data that was produced for other purposes and convert it as best they could to meet their own requirements. However, developments in computer technology have increasingly made it possible for managers and specialists to select the information they require, in the form best suited to their needs and when they want it.

Identifying the needs of the *user* is a vital part of the development of any information system and we discuss approaches to exploring and codifying information requirements in Chapter 6.

PRESENTATION OF INFORMATION

We believe that getting the presentation of information right lies at the heart of designing an information system. Let us take a simple example of a company that manufactures glass bottles in 20 factories across the country. Consider the information needs, say, of the supervisor of a particular production line, and compare these with the information needs of the managing director (MD). The supervisor will need detailed information on the production line for which he or she is responsible. The MD will be more concerned with total production for the whole company and will probably not need to have information broken down to less than factory level. So both managers will need information on production – but at quite different levels of detail. The MD's powers of understanding, analysis and decision-making will be completely swamped by the sheer volume of information provided if it comes to him or her in the same degree of detail needed by the supervisor. On the other hand, the supervisor would find that the lack of detail provided for the MD would be totally inappropriate for his or her needs.

Lucey describes the different levels of management decision-making as strategic, tactical and operational. The characteristics of the decisions taken at the different levels will be discussed later but as the spectrum shifts from operational to strategic, the characteristics of the information needed change from being:

> operational information – largely internal, mainly historical, detailed, often quantitative, high precision, instant availability, often critical, narrow in scope, comprehensive.

> strategic information – largely external, informal sources are important, forward looking, qualitative information is important, precision is unimportant, instant access not vital, wide ranging, incomplete.
>
> (Lucey, 1997, p142)

So we can see that there are important issues affecting the way in which information is assembled and presented. Also, we can see that there can be as much danger in having too much information as in having too little. Indeed, with the use of computers in the routine operation of business processes we have the ability to produce masses of information, often as a by-product, and the problem often becomes one of too much information rather than not enough. It is easier to churn it out than to think about how it should be modified to meet the needs of individual managers. Ackoff (1967), in a classic article 'Management Misinformation Systems' argued that most MISs were designed on the assumption that managers lacked the relevant information whereas he believed that most managers suffered from an over-abundance of irrelevant information! Casual observation of the offices and desks of managers today suggests that Ackoff's message has still not been heard. Even in these days of the so-called electronic offices we still see evidence of the massive piles of computer printout that hit managers' desks from time to time. When we shift the emphasis from *supplying* relevant information to *eliminating* irrelevant information, then the two most important activities become *filtration* and *condensation* – we filter out the irrelevant and condense the relevant into manageable form.

The use of statistical techniques, described in Part 2 of this book, is also key to the successful conversion of data into information and to its presentation in a useable format. These techniques can be used to summarise data and present them in a form highlighting the significant points of interest, thereby aiding their use in decision-making.

Let us look at another simple example. Suppose we are interested in the number of working days lost through employee absenteeism. The basic data would be in the number of days lost, perhaps broken down by department. This can be pretty meaningless on its own. However, we can use statistical techniques to present information in a way which means something immediately to the user, for example, by presenting the absentee figures as a proportion of days lost compared with working days available. If these proportions were to be broken down by department we could compare the figures and take appropriate action. For example:

> We have two departments, A and B. A has 200 days lost through absence during the year while department B has only 75 days lost. Which department has the better absence figures?

> At first sight we might be tempted to say that department B has the better figure because 75 is less than 200.

> However, as suggested, compare the absences with the possible working days available. Let us assume that department A had

20,000 working days while department B had 5,000 working days available. The comparison looks like this:

Department A   *Department B*

$$\frac{200}{20,000} = 0.010 \ (1\%) \qquad \frac{75}{5,000} = 0.015 \ (1.5\%)$$

Department B, far from being better, is now shown as half as bad again (1.5 per cent:1 per cent) in percentage terms as department A, so management would probably decide to concentrate attention on Department B. By presenting the absence figures in this way we actually produce information on which management can take action. In the above example, the absence rates expressed as a proportion (or percentage) of days lost against employee availability give a much more useful picture of the absence levels in the two departments than the raw absence figures.

Often an item of information is meaningless on its own. For example, suppose we are interested in the productivity of a sales representative measured in terms of sales per year. Let us imagine Ms X achieves sales of £100,000 per year. Is this a good, bad or indifferent performance? We just do not know. How can we possibly tell? Well, we could compare her results with the other sales representatives. However, if there are 100 sales reps, it could be a bit difficult to compare 100 sales per year figures and make much sense out of it all. So what do we do? Perhaps we could:

• rank the results of all the sales people – in order from the highest results at the top, down to the lowest sales per year at the bottom – and see where Ms X's result falls

• compare her performance with the average performance of all sales representatives

• as a complete alternative, compare her performance over time. What sales results did she achieve last year, or over the last five years? Are her sales increasing or decreasing? How does this compare with the other reps?

As is evident managing information is a vast and complex

subject. However, as we have seen, the basic principles are fairly simple and so long as these are kept in mind we will be neither overwhelmed nor disappointed in our quest to manage information effectively. So far we have looked at what information is required and how it should be presented. We look next at the third key issue – when it is required.

TIMELINESS OF INFORMATION

Timeliness is often something that can be overlooked in the search for the right information in the right form but no matter how good the information is or how well it is presented, if it is presented too soon it will be ignored; too late and it is useless. A good example of the timeliness of information is the difference between financial accounting and management accounting. The distinction between them is that financial accounting gives a very accurate historical record of the results of the previous year's trading activities, while management accounting gives an up-to-date comparison with how the business is performing against budgeted targets. Management accounting aims to give information to managers in time for them to take corrective action, where necessary, to secure the results they are aiming for.

The frequency with which the information is presented to users is also very important. If it arrives too frequently it can overload the user. If the intervals between its arrival are too long then it is possible that it may arrive too late for its purpose. For example, if we are concerned about meeting a weekly target then we will probably want information on a daily basis. We will also want the latest information on our desk when we get into work in the morning. If it is yearly sales that are particularly important then monthly reports will probably suffice and the timing of their arrival will not be critical, at least at the beginning of the yearly cycle. A particularly good example for considering both the timeliness of information and the need for flexibility in information systems would be, in the final two months of the year the interval of reporting may well be reduced to weekly and in the final weeks, to daily reports. This change in interval is because there is so little time left for the manager to take corrective action to ensure that targets are met.

So, we have looked at what information is needed, in what form and when it is required. We now look at how the managers of information receive their information – the different types, or classes, of report that are generally used.

CLASSES OF MANAGEMENT INFORMATION REPORT

There are usually considered to be four main classes of report through which information may be made available to management. We shall consider them in turn. They are:

1. routine reports

2. exception reports

3. request reports

4. special reports.

As the name suggests, *routine reports* are the regular reports that are the bedrock of any management information system. They are characterised by the fact that they will usually arrive at regular, predetermined time intervals and contain the same type of information presented in exactly the same format on each occasion. Examples would be weekly sales reports, monthly reports on absenteeism, half-yearly reports on staff turnover, annual reports to staff and shareholders, etc.

The second class of report, the *exception report* is generated as the result of some exceptional situation. For example, it could be that as production manager we are interested in the performance of each production line. But are we? In fact, we may only be interested in receiving reports from those production lines that, by exception, do not achieve their targets. By asking only for these exception reports we would cut down the amount of information we have to study and concentrate our attention on those parts of the operation which are not going according to plan. Another example could be where we are managing a shop or a store with a vast number of product lines. We are clearly interested to know from time to time exactly how many items we have in each stock line but we would want to know immediately the details of any item that is about to go out of stock. Hence we would probably want, by exception, daily reports only on low or out-of-stock items. If we are conscious of the costs of overstocking we would probably also want exceptional, weekly reports on those item lines which exceed particular limits.

Alternatively, you might be a personnel manager responsible for a number of factories or premises. Suppose absenteeism is a concern. We would probably be inundated with information if we received reports from all factories. So we would seek exception reports only from those factories where the absentee rate (expressed as the number of days lost through absenteeism as a proportion of possible working days available – see earlier) is greater than a particular level, say, 5 per cent. What we have decided is that we are not worried about those premises with absentee rates below 5 per cent – they require no action to be taken by us at the present time. However, we are worried about all those premises with absentee rates over 5 per cent and we will wish to take action on them or at least monitor closely what is going on.

The finance professionals are always interested in variances from budget – be they on the income or on the cost side. With detailed budgets, there can be a vast range of variances to look at; so it makes sense to report on exceptional variances – perhaps those that are, say, more than 5 per cent above or below the budgeted figure.

Exception reports are really a more sophisticated version of routine reports. They have the advantage that they focus on the problem areas – the areas where action or decisions may be required. They take a lot more effort to set up but can be worth their weight in gold!

Request reports are those produced as a result of a specific request for information thought to be available but not usually included in a routine report. They may provide information in more detail, for example, staff turnover shown by the factories in a group rather than as an overall figure.

They may provide information required for a specific timescale, for example, we might be interested in one particular month's figures on profitability rather than waiting for the half-yearly report. A request report could be a report that other people receive as a routine report but we do not. An example of this could be where, as the finance manager, we might not routinely receive information on market trends whereas the marketing manager would – however, we could find such information invaluable at certain times, perhaps when we are putting together the budget for next year.

Of course, computers have the flexibility to produce request reports much more easily than was the case even a few years ago. In parallel with the developments in computing, there is a growing school of thought that most reports should be request reports and that routine reports should be kept to a minimum. Advances in computer technology, with the prospect and indeed the reality of most managers and specialists having immediate access to a computer or computer terminal, is making this more and more likely. Moves in this direction will necessarily be accompanied by a shift away from what might be thought of as the more traditional MIS, to the concept of the corporate database. More of this later.

Finally, we come to the *special report*. As the name implies, the need for this type of report usually arises out of some special or unusual situation. It may also require information which is not readily available from our database and which may require some special exercise in data capture. By their very nature, the need for special reports should arise infrequently, at least in those organisations that have sorted out their information requirements! Special reports will usually be designed from scratch specifically for the particular requirement and can be expensive to produce.

A typical example could be when a factory puts out a particularly poor production result one month. There could be a call for a lot of detailed information on that factory, for example, details of employees, the condition of plant and equipment, specific production line figures, etc. Another example could be where an opportunity has arisen to sell our product for the first time in a foreign country. We will want information on that country – its economy, its markets, its import regulations. That information will almost certainly not be available within our organisation and considerable external research will be required.

In this section we have looked at the types or classes of reports through which information is made available to managers and specialists. You will be getting a feel both for the potential for managing information and the sort of choices that have to be made in designing your information system.

IMPACT OF ORGANISATIONAL FACTORS ON INFORMATION SYSTEMS

When an organisation is a small, simple set-up the need for sophisticated information can be virtually non-existent. In a small firm with an owner/manager, a small number of staff and customers, that manager will probably know every aspect of the business in detail and will probably keep his or her own records of useful information in his or her informal information system. The situation becomes trickier if within this one business there are two different types of activity, for example, suppose the manager runs a decorating business and also has a shop selling paint, wallpaper, etc. Add to this a further dimension, say a redevelopment is planned of the premises where the business is located – and now the manager could really start to think that things are getting a little out of hand. The manager might begin to feel the need for some formal systems for managing information in order to allow him or her to prioritise the use of time and concentrate on the important indicators of business success.

This is a very simple and obvious example, but we have used it to introduce the very important concept that *the need for management information increases with the complexity of the organisation, the complexity of the tasks carried out and the rate of change in the environment of the organisation.* From this statement it can be readily understood why there is an increasing emphasis on managing information today. We have seen the growth of large complex organisations – vast conglomerates of many different, disparate businesses. We have also seen that companies that we normally associate with one particular activity are actually engaging in a variety of others. Take, for example, gas and electricity suppliers. They are now selling each other's products, as total energy suppliers. Similarly the supermarkets – at first they diversified out of food into other products such as petrol and then into different business areas altogether, such as financial services.

Another important factor is that we are now in a period of great change. Let's look at some of these changes:

- technological, for example, increasing use of computers, robot production lines, etc

- demographic, an ageing population in the UK, smaller families, rapid population growth in the developing world

- international, the breakdown of national barriers, for example, the growth of international companies or companies with worldwide interests, the emergence of global markets

- social values, for example, a greater concern for protecting the environment.

So not only are organisations becoming more complex and their activities more varied, but this is against a background of enormous changes in their environment. Hence there has come a burgeoning need for information and more emphasis on effectively managing that information. So what influences the type of management information system required? In part it will be the type of business the organisation is operating, for example, manufacturing, services, etc, but equally important will be the management structure and the culture within the organisation itself. By structure we mean the way in which an organisation is physically arranged in departments and/or locations. By culture we subscribe to the definition that:

> It is the set of traditional and habitual ways of thinking, feeling, reacting to opportunities and problems that confront an organisation.
>
> (Stonich, 1982)

Both structure and culture will influence the way information flows through the organisation.

There are one or two clear principles that apply in the development of all information systems. Generally, the simpler the structure and the culture, the more straightforward it is to work out the information needs and develop an overall information system. Organisations where responsibilities are clearly defined and understood will also find it much easier to set up effective information systems, as will those where the structure and culture are not in conflict. In practice, it is a rare organisation that achieves these. There will always be some blurring of the edges so far as managers' or departmental responsibilities are concerned. Indeed, some organisations that operate in very dynamic environments adopt looser styles of organisation structure to cope with their ever-changing environments, for example, moving towards multidisciplinary project teams. So, there will need to be a very different approach to developing an information system depending on how an organisation is structured – whether it has a traditional structure, a matrix management structure or whatever.

In the past, the traditional and probably most common organisational structure was that based on functional lines. Consequently, information systems have tended to develop within each function. For example, the director of personnel might have under his or her control payroll and information relating to all aspects of the staffing of the organisation. The director of finance might have systems for budgetary control, treasury function, etc. These systems will usually have been developed with only one purpose in mind – to suit their particular departmental or functional needs. They are known as *dedicated systems*, in that they are dedicated to one specific purpose and may have been developed independently of each other. As the organisation has grown both in size and complexity, so will the individual systems have grown and developed, often putting an almost impossible burden on an outdated computer system. Always assuming, that is, that there is one computer system in the organisation – it is just as likely that, as the separate information needs have been identified, they will have been met by the development of information systems on different types of computer hardware and computer software. Many organisations have rued the detrimental effects on their efficiency of this type of sporadic development of their overall information system's strategy. As well as being inefficient in meeting the traditional departmental needs, this functional approach to information is ineffective in meeting the needs of today's structures with their emphasis on multidisciplinary project team working.

So, what is the alternative to this *ad hoc* approach to the development of different types of information systems? The answer is the development of more sophisticated database systems – with the aim of providing a common pool of data to meet the information needs of all users in the organisation. More of this in Chapter 5 which covers the development of *database structures*. Database structures organise records and their structures in a logical way. For now just accept that there is a database management system that allows access to all the data in the database and permits the analysis of all the data against all the other data regardless of which files they are stored in. The advantages of this approach are enormous and will be discussed in detail in Chapter 5.

MANAGING INFORMATION FOR COMPETITIVE ADVANTAGE

So far we have discussed information systems and the management of information as a fairly abstract concept and we need to come down to earth and ask *why* managing information is so important as to justify the cost and attention we suggest is needed!

To this extent, all organisations exist for a purpose:

• in the commercial sector – to survive and grow, thus providing returns to investors over time

• in the not-for-profit sector – to provide services at the lowest cost.

In both sectors there is fierce competition for resources (human, financial, plant and equipment), suppliers and most of all, customers – in every meaning of that word. In recent years there has been an understanding that the way in which information is used can make the difference between the survival and growth of the organisation, and the total failure of that organisation to survive. One book on competitive strategy (Porter, 1980, p35) breaks down the total strategy into three generic, non-exclusive strategies that might be used in any sector:

- *overall cost leadership* – the ability to decrease production costs and/or to increase productivity. An example would have been the first marketing firm to sort the information in its customer database into specific interest segments for targeted mail shots – thus securing the same response but at lower mailing costs.

- *differentiation* – the ability to add value or some unique feature(s) to a product or service to improve its image and/or quality. An example of this would have been the market research information that allowed the first bank to decide to offer 24-hour banking over the telephone. This gave customers instant access to the information about their accounts so allowing them to pay bills, transfer money, etc, at any time of the day or night. A further differentiation was to allow access to customers to make the changes themselves direct from the PC in their own home or office.

- *focus (sometimes regarded as a combination of cost leadership and differentiation)* – specialisation and concentration on a particular market or product niche. According to Porter, focus can embrace both overall cost leadership and differentiation. Organisations analyse market information in order to focus on being the lowest-cost supplier to that segment or to meet a particular requirement of the segment that allows a premium to be added to the 'normal' price. Examples are businesses that specialise in certain vehicle repairs such as exhaust systems or tyres, or farmers that have opted for the organic markets, perhaps in specialist areas as well, eg supply of asparagus. These organisations develop their operational information as they move along their specialist learning curves through the repetitive nature of their activities. They become big fish in their small pools.

Porter's generic strategies are applied so as to overcome the strategic competitive threats faced by organisations. These threats are two-sided depending on whether we see them as applied to us or to our competitors. The four main competitive forces at work have been described as:

- *threat to entry* – barriers due to, for example, strict government legislation and high cost of setting up.

- *the power of suppliers and buyers* – a monopoly supplier can, in theory, charge a high premium; if there is only one customer for your goods and services that customer can drive a hard price and quality bargain.

- *threat of substitutes* – whether goods or services, if our customers can obtain supplies from sources other than ourselves.

- *rivalry between competitors* – possibly leading to setting off a price war.

Each of these factors will generate its own information requirements and if we are to succeed against our competitors we will need to be effective in managing the information on all four forces.

DECISION-MAKING AND INFORMATION SYSTEMS

The only purpose for having an information system is to support the decision-making processes. This process can be set out in a simple way:

- formulating the problem

- constructing a model to represent the problem

- using the model to generate the solution.

In a business environment there is a range of very different problems depending where on the spectrum of operational decisions to strategic decisions we are working. The decision characteristics, therefore, will follow the same spectrum:

> operational: repetitive, short time scale, small scale resources, usually structured, clear objectives and decision rules, little or no discretion

> strategic: long time horizons, large-scale resources, much creativity and judgement, usually unstructured, problems difficult to define, infrequent, much uncertainty.
>
> (Lucey, 1997, p142)

Also, it is often helpful to consider the purpose of the decision-making process in terms of the traditional activities of managers:

• planning and organising

• reviewing and controlling.

We look at the different information needs of these activities in Chapters 3 and 4 respectively.

In the classic decision-theory view the choices of action available to organisations can be linked to possible outcomes from the decisions taken. However, the nature of the link may vary according to the degree of certainty in our knowledge and understanding of the problem. Our range is from certainty to uncertainty:

> Certainty: where each choice of action is linked with only one particular outcome. Thus in a simple stock control situation ... we know there is a certain link between the amount of stock we decide to issue and the amount that will be left.

> Risk: where each choice of action may result in one of several identified possible outcomes. Thus in the Black Wednesday mini-case, a decision by the Bank of England to spend £2 billion intervening in the currency market might have maintained the value of the £ within the Exchange Rate Mechanism or not. Whatever the *probabilities* associated with either outcome, neither of them was *certain*.

> Uncertainty: where the possible outcomes resulting from each

choice of action are not necessarily known, and in any case we cannot assign probabilities to them. Thus the wider implications of the Black Wednesday decisions for the whole process of European integration, enlargement of the European Community, world trade, etc, cannot be neatly listed as a series of possible outcomes whose probability can be estimated.

(Harry, 1997, pp58–59)

Despite the obvious issues surrounding risk and uncertainty there is still some inclination on the part of designers of information systems to assume that all decision-making takes place in a *rational* way. By this we mean that there is:

- a single clear objective which can be described in positivist numerical or financial terms

- complete and perfect information

- all the possible outcomes are known, can be quantified and described in relation to the objectives

- the outcomes are ranked against the specific criteria describing the objectives

- the best outcome is chosen.

While this rational approach in its pure form may suit lower levels of decision-making, ie operational and some tactical occasions, where there is more certainty and structure, it is not always appropriate at the strategic level. Here, as we have shown, there is less certainty, there may be conflicting objectives and all the outcomes are not known. It is likely that other qualitative factors such as political, social and psychological issues will probably be included in the decision-making process. Indeed, when we were involved in the relocation of a business some years ago, the deciding factor was the extent to which the managing director felt the proposed locations would meet his family's requirements!

These fuzzy, uncertain situations we face, so lacking in clarity of objective and having incomplete and imperfect information, probably respond best to the *limited rationality* model. In these cases a comprehensive analysis is either not worth doing or is impossible. Possibly the best use of the busy manager/specialist's time here is to make a start searching for a possible solution and stop searching when we find something that appears to work. We then refine this decision as we go along through a series of incremental steps – known as *logical incrementalism.*

This *conflict* between objectives *and* between the socio-political issues surrounding them often continues after the decision has been made into and through the implementation stages, so that our decisions need to be thought of as processes rather than as single events. In fact, particularly in strategic decision-making, we often make our decisions in a piecemeal and unstructured manner. In other words, rather than being deliberate and rational the decisions are *emergent.*

In practice, this is probably the situation that faces most of us in the real world. We rarely analyse the problems we encounter, generate all the possible options for its solution and then scientifically identify the best solution. There is so much disorder in our decision-making processes – the problems are not clear-cut and discrete, they interact with each other and we vacillate between the problems and their possible solution(s). The level of *disorder* can be such that, instead of simply having a problem in need of a solution, the solution of one problem causes other problems (or opportunities) for us to solve. For example, the introduction of our personnel information system (see Chapter 7) may lead to a speedier, more efficient administration of personnel records, but where can we redeploy the clerks who previously worked on the paper files?

Sometimes the situation in which we are trying to make our decisions is such that, unlike the rational decision-making model where the decision itself is seen as all-important, there can be cases where the way in which we are seen to make the decisions is more important. For example, when we are trying to win the hearts and minds of our stakeholders, we might consult them and involve them in the decision-making process. When we are trying to persuade people to decide that we regard training as an important part of performance management, we conduct the training in light airy and well-equipped training rooms. In other words, the way in which we are seen to be arriving at our decision is *symbolic* of the degree of importance we attach to the decision itself.

All of these factors, and others, demonstrate the complexity of decision-making and the distance, in reality, between where we find ourselves and the structured, rational model. This is not to say that we ignore the rational model but that we need to identify which, if any, of the aspects surrounding our decision-making respond to the rational model and how best we can cope with those that do not.

In Chapter 18 we discuss *decision theory* – an approach to structuring our decision-making processes.

CONCLUSION

It is perhaps self-evident that the purpose of your information system is to support the organisation's objectives, at the strategic, tactical and operational levels. There needs to be an information strategy that helps answer the questions:

- Which business or businesses should we be in?

- How should these businesses be financed?

- How should the organisation be structured?

- How should resources be allocated?

- How should we organise these resources?

- How should people be rewarded for their performance?

- How should we integrate with others in the supply chain, our suppliers and customers?

In this chapter we have covered some of the important issues that affect the development of information systems. We have emphasised the requirement for information to be timely, in the right form and directly relevant to the users' needs. The principles we have covered are equally relevant to manual and to computer-based information systems although we believe that the large volumes of data generated in even the smallest organisations today suggest that computerised information systems are likely to be the norm. We have considered the different types of report through which information can be made available. We have concentrated on the information needs of the individual users because, by and large, most people work as part of an organisation, we have considered how the structure and culture in an organisation can influence the development of its information system.

We have discussed how the more traditional, dedicated information systems are giving way to the more flexible and robust database systems. We focused briefly on the way information can give competitive advantage and finally we have introduced some of the concepts of decision-making, touching on risk and uncertainty. One final point that some people might argue is that the cost of getting the right information in the right form at the right time is very high. We believe the cost of not doing so could be much higher.

In the next chapter we will consider some of the key systems concepts involved in designing an information system.

2 Information systems concepts

INTRODUCTION

Before we go much further in describing the processing and uses of information, or the design and development of systems for managing that information, it will be useful to set out some of the key concepts, and the terms used to describe them, which are common to all systems. As key players in the specification of requirements for the system and end users, it is essential that we understand and speak the language of the IT specialist. The key concepts and terms we cover are:

- the definition of a systems approach
- the key principles of a systems approach
- system boundaries
- open and closed systems
- hard and soft properties
- holism
- emergent properties
- systems entropy.

DEFINITION OF A SYSTEMS APPROACH

It is generally agreed that systems are made up of various parts that are connected together in a particular way in order for the parts to interact so as to achieve a specific purpose. Using this as a basis, a systems approach to information systems is one where we explore and analyse the component parts making up the total information in our environment *as well as* the impact of the interaction of the parts on each other. An example of a systems approach to the human body would be to consider the combined effects of high and low temperature and plenty or scarcity of food on human activity, rather than considering the separate impact. Separately low temperature, *per se,* might not have a bad effect on the human body but, when combined with a lack of appropriate food, could spell disaster.

THE KEY FEATURES OF A SYSTEMS APPROACH

The key features of a systems approach are:

- all systems are made up of component parts and/or subsystems and can only be described in terms of the whole

- the subsystems are arranged in a hierarchy where moving up the structure provides a wider view and descending the structure provides greater detail

- no part of the system can be changed without some effect being felt throughout the whole system

- systems are made up of hard and soft properties (see pages 25, 26).

SYSTEM BOUNDARIES

System boundaries define the scope of the system itself. In a business context a production manager will be responsible within the boundary of motivating, controlling and rewarding production staff in the effective performance of their duties. A sales manager will have similar responsibilities for the sales force. These boundaries are clear and well defined. Problems can arise where there is ambiguity and responsibilities overlap. Boundaries may change, for example, when there is organisation restructuring, takeovers, etc.

OPEN AND CLOSED SYSTEMS

Firstly, we wish to clarify our view of what open systems are *not* in the context of this book. We are not describing the open *architecture* systems of computing that can run any form of software. (Peppard, 1993, Ch5; Ward, 1995, pp196–197.) When the business applications of computers first started to develop, different hardware required its own dedicated operating systems and software. The open systems movement grew during the late 1980s and great strides have been made towards standardisation of computer operating systems as we move into the twenty-first century.

For our purposes:

- *open systems* are those that interact with the external environment, outside the system boundary

- *closed systems* are self-contained and neither influence, nor are influenced by, the external environment.

> Open systems operate in an external environment and exchange information and material with that environment. The external environment consists of the activities external to the system boundary with which the system can interact ... For example, a marketing system, which is an open system, operates in an environment of competition. If a competitor introduces new technology by providing customers with on-line order entry terminals, the marketing function must adapt to the change in the environment or remain at a competitive disadvantage.
> (Schultheis and Sumner, 1995, p30)

Schultheis and Sumner go on to wonder why closed systems which do not interact with their environment exist at all and surmise that they exist largely by accident in that the 'participants in a system become closed to external feedback without being fully aware of it'. (Schultheis and Sumner, 1995, p31)

In the strictest sense, while it is possible to visualise mechanical systems as being isolated from their environment it is difficult to imagine social systems, with all their complex interactions, as ever being 'closed'. However, in organisations there may be some attempts to keep some systems separate, for example, those concerned with the audit function and those concerned with authorising expenditure.

HARD AND SOFT PROPERTIES

Most business or organisational problems are made up of

both hard and soft properties. Whatever sector we work in, some of the issues we face can be precisely measured, eg the cost of an item, the strength of a particular piece of material, the number of employees. We define these as *hard* properties. 'A property which can be defined, measured, or assessed in some way that does not depend on someone's personal sense of value is called hard.' (Harry, 1997, p41)

On the other hand, we may face issues that are not capable of such precise measurement, contain at least an element of judgement or are subject to taste. Information such as whether a material looks attractive, whether we should recruit a particular person, what the average rate of price inflation will be over the next ten years, we call *soft* properties. They are 'Questions which depend on personal values, opinions, tastes or ethics (which) cannot be resolved by counting, measurement or some kind of proof.' (Harry, 1997, p41)

Hard properties are the very heart of rational decision-making, whereas soft properties and 'soft systems are characterised by more vagueness and irrationality'. (Lucey, 1997, p43)

HOLISM

We have already explained that under systems theory, all systems are made up of component parts and/or subsystems and can only be described in terms of the whole. To be effective an information system as a whole must be greater than the sum of its parts. This holism is fostered by the integration of the hard, measurable properties with the soft properties – the intuition and judgement of the people who interpret and use the information system.

EMERGENT PROPERTIES

In the previous section we talked about *holism* as being greater than the sum of the parts. This implies that from the whole emerges something that the component parts themselves do not possess. One example is the exquisite taste of a gin and tonic – the sharpness of the gin and the bitterness of the tonic promote the emergence of that gastronomic experience, the G&T. In a business context, where there is good research and development (R&D) allied to efficient manufacture the emergent property could be a competitive product. Also, teamwork is the emergent property of many things such as good leadership, high levels of motivation, as well as the specialist knowledge and skills of the individual team members. Other examples are:

> *Taste* is a property of water, not the constituent hydrogen and oxygen atoms.

> *Growth* is a property arising from the combination of seeds and soil.
>
> (Lucey, 1997, p30)

SYSTEMS ENTROPY

Later in this book we have set out some thoughts about dealing with, among other things, maintaining your information system. All systems whether they are mechanical, social, biological or information systems can deteriorate if they are not maintained. Business environments are subject to great change and our information systems need to be sufficiently robust to cope with this change. Like the planned maintenance of our cars we need to include maintenance of our information systems in our design or they will cease to do the things we designed them for, possibly even breaking down on the information highway! This running down of information systems leads to systems entropy.

> Systems entropy corresponds roughly to chaos and disorder – a state that occurs without maintenance ... The process of maintaining a system is a process of decreasing entropy or increasing orderliness ... Orderliness can be achieved through preventive maintenance checks, such as a yearly physical examination for an employee ... and then taking action as a result of these regular checks.
>
> (Schultheis and Sumner, 1995, p33)

It is possible to draw parallels between having diagnostic tools for plant and equipment – with the consequent reduction in downtime and avoidance of delays in production with its associated costs – and having similar tools for reviewing our information systems. While there is a cost to having such a process for the information systems maintenance, there is potentially a much bigger cost in terms of business performance if the system is allowed to deteriorate.

CONCLUSION

In this chapter we have set out some of the key concepts for consideration when thinking about a systems approach to managing information. They are all examples of the concepts that the experts, the information systems professionals, take into account when designing, developing and maintaining information systems.

3 Management information systems for planning

INTRODUCTION

In Chapter 1 we set out some of the traditional activities of management as:

• planning and organising

• reviewing and controlling.

In this chapter we concentrate on the planning function which Lucey defines as:

> All activities leading to the formulation of objectives or goals and deciding on the means of meeting them.
>
> (Lucey, 1997, p97)

We look at levels of planning, problems of planning and finally some of the typical planning tools provided by our sophisticated computer technologies.

LEVELS OF PLANNING

We stated previously that there are three levels of management decision-making – strategic, tactical and operational. Clearly there are also parallels in the planning processes. As we move up the spectrum from operational to strategic planning the planning horizon shifts from being very focused, very narrowly centred on the immediate, the day-to-day activities of the organisation, to being very broadly spread across the whole organisation as well as far into the future. The distinguishing features at the ends of the spectrum of the information requirements for planning are that:

Table 1   Levels of Planning. Based on Lucey, 1997, p125

		Increasing scope →	
LEVEL 1 (Current operations)	LEVEL 2 (Operational planning)	LEVEL 3 (Tactical planning)	LEVEL 4 (Strategic planning)
What operations need to be carried out by existing personnel with existing facilities to meet specified outputs in the coming operational period?	What finance, materials, plant and equipment are needed for the immediate future? Manning levels? Incentives?	What changes are due from our strategic plans? What interventions for motivation and morale?	What business(es) should we be in?
What is the quality of our management?	What are the best methods of organising these to meet operational requirements?	What new plant, equipment, information systems and working methods are needed to implement the new plans?	How should we organise/ structure/ finance the new plans and allocate resources?
Time: The present	Time: 1 to 12 months	Time: 12 months to 5 years	Time: From as far as we can see into the future, and beyond
←	Increasing detail		

- for operational planning we will usually focus internally and on accurate, historical data, with a high degree of detail

- for strategic planning we will be less concerned with absolute accuracy but will focus on external sources and build up our total information from all our environment.

Table 1 sets out in a clear diagrammatic way the implications of the three planning levels in terms of:

- the type of information required

- the time horizon

- the characteristics of the information in terms of scope and detail.

PROBLEMS WITH PLANNING

Our experience of consulting with, and running training workshops for, a wide range of managers and specialists in a variety of organisations for the past 15 years has led us to conclude that few of us are natural planners. We seem ready to let all sorts of excuses deflect us from settling down and formulating our plans. It is almost as though we do not see planning as the *real* job. Examples of the reasons we give are:

- planning is a time-consuming task and I do not have the time at present

- there are more urgent tasks to be done

- planning requires a clear head and I need to get all these small jobs done to clear the decks

- even when I do plan, the future is so dynamic and uncertain that I have to keep changing the plan – it's not worth planning

- taking action on our tasks feels better than thinking about them – at least I am achieving something

- having a plan reduces my freedom of action and restrains my creativity

- nobody takes notice of plans once they are written

- I don't know enough about where the organisation should be going

- having a plan can tie me to targets which might prove difficult to meet

- planning looks like and feels like hard mental exercise

- I do not have the information to plan properly.

Whether we recognise these as excuses or call them reasons we need to address them. Planning is the key to the efficient and effective running of an organisation. If we think of the analogy of a holiday – first we need to decide where we want to go (our objective). This is planning at a strategic level and for which will need information on issues such as:

- what we want from our holiday (market research on customer needs)
- availability of different types of holiday and what they can offer (information on suppliers)
- other environmental factors that might affect the decision, eg political turmoil in countries, value of currency, etc (environmental information).

The next stage in the planning process is at the tactical level, involving issues such as:

- Do we go for a package holiday, a tailored holiday or a do-it-yourself holiday?
- How might we finance the holiday – use existing savings, set up a specific savings account and save towards the holiday, take out a loan, etc?
- What is the most appropriate timing, taking into account school holidays, work commitments, etc?
- Do we have the right equipment, eg suitcases, skis, snorkels, etc?

The final planning stage, the operational level, deals with issues such as:

- What clothes do we need to take?
- How much currency do we need?
- How will we get to the airport, for example by train (train times), car (car parking sites and costs) or taxi (availability)?
- Do we have the right documentation, passport, tickets, etc?

None of us (we think) would choose to skimp on this planning if we wanted to have the holiday of our dreams. Although some people might say 'Oh no, I never plan my holiday. I just set off or take a cheap, last-minute package.' However, we all realise that this approach involves a certain risk. Now, a poor holiday or a holiday that was not quite up to standard may not be too serious. However, in the organisational context, we try to minimise risk. Not quite achieving our objectives, meeting customers' expectations or realising our quality standards may make all the difference between success and failure for the organisation. It could jeopardise the survival of the organisation and, of course, our own jobs.

TYPES AND SOURCES OF INFORMATION FOR PLANNING

It goes without saying that without the right information our planning will be fatally flawed. Short-term operational plans need accurate, historical, internal information. The longer-term plans need the more comprehensive external, environmental information. The tactical planning stage often combines both, but usually needs broader-brush internal information.

The types of external information we need are to answer questions such as:

• What is happening in the sectors and markets that interest us? What are the forecasts for growth within the sector and our markets? Is the market new or is it close to maturity? Can the market be segmented? What should be our size/place in the market? What are the barriers to entry into the sector and the markets? What competition already exists or might we face in the foreseeable future? What are their plans and their likely counters to our initiatives? Are they growing, shrinking or stable? Does a single organisation or small group of organisations dominate the sector? Are smaller organisations joining with others or are larger organisations demerging?

• What are the demographic changes we might encounter during the currency of our plan? Are there any geographical movements of population that are of interest to us? How might the age profile change in our population(s) of interest? What are the implications of changing employment structures?

- What is happening to society as a whole? Will there be changes in the role of the family? Will there be significant changes in consumption, eg in the consumption of organic food, convenience foods, etc? Will there be a growth in ethical investment?

- What will be the political changes in our market countries? Will we be operating in a stable political climate? Will there be trends towards political combination or political separation?

- What are the implications of future legislation, for example on safety, working practice, currency, etc?

- What impact will *information technology* (IT) have on our plans? Do we have the skills available to take advantage of IT? Can IT be harnessed as a positive competitive force? What will be the impact of technological change on our manpower plans?

Typical sources of external information are government and trade association statistics; company reports; commercial organisations set up for the purpose of collecting and selling business information; scientific and technical papers; specific research investigations; conferences and working parties; meetings and discussions; as well as informal business and social contacts.

The types of internal information we need are to answer questions such as:

- What is the production performance when compared with capacity? What are the delivery times and finished stock levels? What are the quality standards we are working to and how well do we meet them? How up-to-date are our plant, machinery and equipment? What marketing information do we have? How big are our markets? What is our market share? How do our distribution and logistics systems compare with our competitors? How do sales compare with targets?

- What information do we have on personnel employed and associates? How many people and with what skills do we need to recruit? What training and development needs are there? How well do our manpower plans and succession plans support business development needs? How effective is our personnel information system? How do our salary structures compare with the market? How do we measure personal performance and manage performance results that do not meet expectation? What is the state of labour relations when compared with the rest of our industry/sector?

- How up-to-date and accurate is our information on the financial state of the organisation – costs, margins, profits, cash flows, investment of surplus cash, etc?

- What is the state of our research and development activities? How do they compare with the industry/sector norms? To what extent are we leaders in products and technology?

- What is the state of our information technology and information systems? To what extent do they provide the business information support needed for the achievement of our objectives?

Typical sources of internal information are everything that comes out of the organisation's formal information system. These can range from:

- the results of the statistical treatment of raw business data

- modelling and simulation exercises where used

- special investigation reports

- budgets compared with actual performance

- intra-company comparison

- inter-company comparison

- plus all the informal sources, eg walking the floor to get a feel for the state of organisational morale, networking to pick up new ideas, etc.

Even a cursory comparison of the above types and sources of information with what information is actually available in your organisation for planning could reveal some interesting results!

MATHEMATICAL MODELLING

Most of us have heard about the use of physical models in business processes. Management services officers and others use models of factories and offices to enable them to plan efficient workplace layouts. These scale models are often called *iconic* models, ie created in the image of something. Aeronautical engineers use models of aeroplanes in a wind tunnel to give data on how the real aeroplane will fly and chemical engineers use models of chemical plants to try out their process before going to the expense of building the real thing. However, in addition to physical models there are mathematical models that are being used increasingly by managers and other professionals to help in their business planning. They use mathematical equations and algebra to model situations. These models are often known as *symbolic* models. The ability of computers to cope with thousands of mathematical calculations per minute has made it possible to model very complex situations and has extended the use of the technique of modelling to ordinary mortals, well beyond the realm of the mathematician. Because of this we now have available to us the means by which we can improve our decision-making through mathematical modelling. Two well-known examples of this type of model are:

- econometric models

- financial models.

Econometric models are a set of mathematical equations, which attempt to describe, or model, the economy. They try to set out the many complex relationships that exist within the economy. Economists use econometric models to test out different policy alternatives and to forecast the future economic situation based on different views or scenarios of the future. The techniques have been extended to other economic planning activities and even to areas outside economics.

Financial models represent the financial intricacies of an organisation showing what might happen to its finances against a range of different assumptions such as trading levels, interest rates, input costs and prices. A computerised spreadsheet is an application which represents a simple financial model of a part of an organisation's finances, often the cash flow. The spreadsheet can help us with our financial planning, for example, what cash flows to expect at different levels of sales, or show what will happen to profit with changes in the price of raw materials.

SIMULATION

We discussed above the use of mathematical models to help our planning by providing forecasts in dynamic, complex situations. The idea is to develop a set of equations describing how the information variables interact with each other. This technique is fine, so long as we know all the variables and are able to describe them mathematically. Much of the time our variables defy precise mathematical description and, even when we can so describe them, we cannot always represent their interaction with each other in mathematical terms. Simulation techniques have been designed to get around these problems. The techniques simulate the results or outcomes of operations that we are trying to model.

One of the most common simulation techniques, the Monte Carlo method, relied in the past on the use of thrown dice (hence its name) to generate random quantities representing the incidence of certain events. Let us say, for example, that we are managing the refuelling of airliners at a major airport. The arrival intervals of the aeroplanes for refuelling and the volumes of fuel they require are the random variables. (Read more about these in Chapter 12.) We can generate values of these variables for our simulation from random number tables.

Let us assume that our capacity to meet the refuelling needs of the aircraft depends on the availability of refuelling tankers, their capacity to carry fuel and the speed with which we can refill the tankers when they are emptied and get them back to their refuelling duties. In order to find the best combination of refuelling tankers to meet their task we can construct a model of the relationship between the constraints, for example, the rate of arrivals of the aircraft and the refuelling demands made upon the tankers. We can build into the model the capacities, etc, of the fuel tankers and, by throwing the dice time and time again and, by varying the constraints, find by trial and error which combination of tanker sizes and other factors produces the least delay in refuelling the aircraft. This is, at best, a very lengthy and frustrating process and could take days or weeks of constantly throwing the dice to get the optimum result. Our salvation is in the ability of the computer to allow us to design a model of the whole process, have programmed in a random number generator and ask it to simulate all the schedules and produce the optimum schedule to give the best fit within all the constraints.

So, by processing the available data through our simulation we produce information on which to base our planning.

There can be several reasons for using models. Lucey (1997, p138) tells us that 'The model is cheaper. Manipulation of the model may (also) be quicker, safer and less hazardous than trying out the real thing.' A good example of this would be the use of simulators for training pilots to fly complex airliners or warplanes. He also tells us that models further help us by 'the insight they give management into the working of the real system ... The proper use of models enables time scales to be compressed so that the results of several years' operations can be studied in a few hours.' Modelling and simulation are such integral parts of managing information for our planning processes that, together with the developments in IT, they have led to the creation of specific simulation languages to assist the programming process.

SENSITIVITY ANALYSIS

Before we leave the subjects of modelling and simulation we would like to say just a few words about the technique called sensitivity analysis and its use in managing information. In sensitivity analysis we hold constant all the variables in our model except one, in turn, and by altering that variable by steady incremental steps observe the effect on the outcome. The object of this analysis is to determine which of the variables are sensitive, ie relatively small changes in them having a disproportionate effect on the end result.

A good example of the use of sensitivity analysis could be in our HR planning model. We could test the sensitivity of the variables, eg changes in wastage rates and changes in production levels on our forecasts of the need for different classes of manpower. Another example would be to explore the sensitivity of a capital investment decision – perhaps to build a new department store – on different assumptions about interest rates, demand forecasts, etc.

CONCLUSION

'Fail to plan means plan to fail' goes the old adage, and this is one old adage that really is true. In this chapter we have looked at why we should plan, levels of planning, types of information needed and some of the reasons why we often find planning an onerous activity. We have also considered how information technology and mathematics can help our planning by modelling and simulating the real environment. We end with the thought that, while planning can often be a challenging activity, the advantages of formulating an appropriate plan lead to:

• greater personal effectiveness

• better use of resources of all types

• greater flexibility to respond when the real world turns out to be different from the one we had forecast, and hence

- consistently higher chances of meeting organisational objectives.

So, what happens next? Having produced our well-thought-out plans the next key issue is whether we are achieving them. The next chapter looks at issues of review and control.

4 Information systems for review and control

INTRODUCTION

We have completed our plans and set in progress the activities needed to achieve our objectives that have been agreed. Now, if we had used perfect information in terms of accuracy and relevance in our planning, used appropriate statistical techniques to process the information, and operated in a *certain* environment, we could sit back and await the achievement of our objectives. However, we rarely have perfect information even at the operational level because, for example, our plant and equipment require maintenance and resetting and our employees are subject to a whole raft of variability that affects their performance. Add to this the tactical and strategic actions of our competitors in response to our plans, the unpredictability of local and global economies and we have what Harry calls '*environmental disturbances*'. Harry goes on to say, 'Any attempt to predict and affect these will never be completely successful.' To emphasise the point he comments 'In fact, the existence of environmental disturbances is the only reason we need control at all.' (Harry, 1997, p68)

So, to ensure the achievement of our objectives and plans, we need to have information systems to *review* and *monitor* how well we are meeting our targets, etc and then take action in the event that there is a variance, to *control* the process involved. That action might be in the form of minor adjustments – perhaps the resetting of our machines, changing the hours worked, the quality of supervision, the layout of the workplace. Or, if there is a more serious variance it may require a revision of the plan itself or even of the objective(s). In this chapter we will discuss the information systems that support the review and control function.

ELEMENTS OF CONTROL SYSTEMS

All control systems are made up of a basic set of elements. These are:

• some form of performance standard or target that has resulted from our planning process

• a measure of the level of performance achieved

• the calculation of the effect of environmental disturbances, variance or performance gap between expected and actual results

• the feedback of these variances to the control system

• action by the control system to return to the plan

• the opportunity to feedback to a higher control unit if the environmental disturbances are so great that the original plan and/or objectives are no longer appropriate.

FEEDBACK LOOPS

In the above list of elements a *sensor* of some sort reports the actual level of performance. The sensor can be human or inanimate but whatever it is, it generates the feedback that is measured against the *comparator* – the objective, perhaps a target or a standard. When the feedback acts on the control system to return the performance to plan it is known as *single-loop feedback*. When the variance is so great that the feedback goes to some higher level for revision of the plan or the objectives themselves it is known as *double-loop* or *higher-order* feedback. See Figure 1.

Closed- and open-loop systems

Two other terms used to describe these feedback loops are whether they are *open* or *closed*. Closed feedback loops exist as integral parts of the control system. Feedback, based on measurement of performance and comparison with the target or standard, is used to make appropriate changes to the system inputs – a closed-loop system. The alternative, the open-loop system, exists where no feedback loop exists and control is exercised from outside the system.

Figure 1 Control and feedback cycle. Based on Lucey, 1997, p154

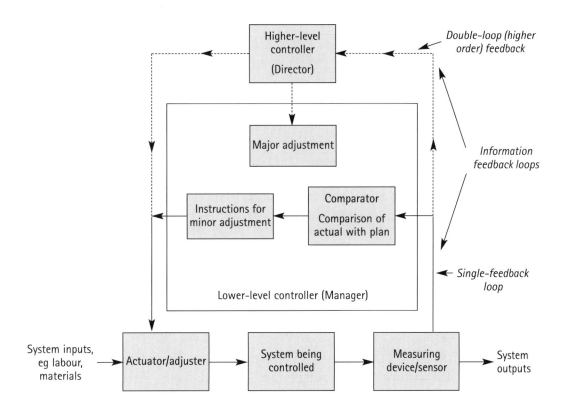

A simple example of a closed-loop system is the thermostat on our central heating system – it measures the temperature against a pre-set standard and turns the heating system on or off accordingly. A similar example, but with an open-loop system is where we might have a thermometer in our greenhouse and at a certain temperature we intervene and take action – perhaps to open a window or put in a heater. An example of how these loops can work to advantage or disadvantage is in the computer systems used for trading stocks and shares. Some years ago the traders' systems in the stock exchange were closed systems, programmed to sell a particular share when its value had dropped by a particular percentage or to a particular level. On *Black Monday,* when shares crashed worldwide, the systems were blamed for exacerbating an already difficult situation. The computers were reprogrammed to allow external control to be exercised by the traders when share values generally were in decline – they were made into open-loop systems.

Negative and positive feedback

In most situations, fluctuations in our systems around a norm are regarded as normal. Let us take again the example of our heating system, where a temperature-sensing device monitors the environment. Once the thermostat is set to a given level, fluctuations in temperature are controlled by applying heat when the temperature falls below this norm and applying cooling when it rises above the norm. The tendency is to dampen down wide fluctuations in temperature and in this situation, the feedback is known as *negative feedback* – corrections are applied in the opposite direction to the original deviation. Another example would be levels of stock in your warehouse – if stocks are high you reduce your orders. If they are low, you increase your orders. Figure 2 shows the oscillations damping down sooner with negative feedback.

Positive feedback, on the other hand, acts in the same direction as the deviation and reinforces the direction of movement caused by the environmental disturbance. We would rarely plan to have positive feedback in an automatic closed-loop system, as this would cause instability in the system, possibly leading to loss of control.

Positive feedback needs human intervention via an open-loop system. An example would be where a publisher is launching a range of books and knows from the market research information that there is only room for one of them to be a worldwide success. Initial sales information would show which of the books was likely to be the number one best-seller leading to the publisher increasing the promotion efforts on this book. The effects of positive feedback in maintaining the oscillation are shown in Figure 3.

Figure 2   Negative feedback. Based on Lucey, 1997, p157

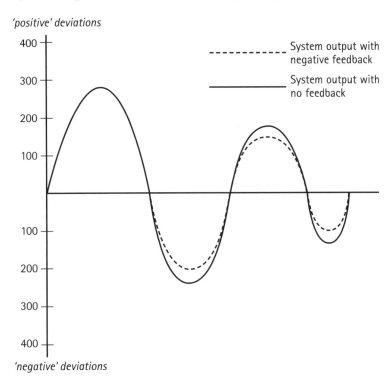

'positive' deviations

400 — System output with negative feedback

300 — System output with no feedback

'negative' deviations

MONITORING/CONTROLLING/REVISING THE PLAN

We saw in Chapter 3 that planning was defined as all the activities leading to the formulation of objectives and deciding on the means of meeting those objectives. So for monitoring and controlling the plan, the first prerequisite is to have clear, unambiguous and measurable objectives. Next, we need to implement the plan itself, linking strategic, through tactical and operational levels. Each level will have its yardsticks or milestones at an appropriate degree of detail so that we can measure progress against plan. Our feedback loops will convey this comparator information to the *actuator* who will make adjustments to maintain or regain the plan on target. If it is acceptable and achievable, the plan may be revised to achieve results above target. If the environmental disturbance is so great that we cannot achieve the objective

Figure 3 **Positive feedback**

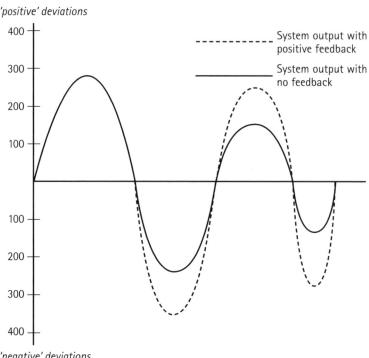

'positive' deviations

400	- - - - - - - - - - System output with positive feedback
300	_____ System output with no feedback

'negative' deviations

we may even abandon the plan and set new objectives, going round the system until we achieve a degree of stability which we can sustain with the resources that are available.

Monitoring, control and revision at the operational level may well be built into the plan as an automatic activity, for example, sensing of temperature variance from the norm and getting feedback via a closed loop. This would lead to the automatic application of heat or cooling to maintain the norm. However, in most cases at the tactical level and almost certainly in even more cases at the strategic level where the environmental disturbance and the degree of judgement needed is less predictable, the feedback will be via an open loop. This requires/allows control to be exercised externally to the system itself by human intervention.

One of the factors we discussed in Chapter 1 was the timeliness of information. We saw that too frequent or infrequent and too early or late information was not conducive to effective decision-making. Similarly, once we have feedback on how our processes are performing against target, the timing of our control action can seriously affect the size and effectiveness of the action taken. For example, when the American space shuttles have climbed just a few miles they can often be seen to make some minor corrections to their attitude before they leave the atmosphere. This small correction at the beginning of the flight is instrumental in them reaching the exact spot in space where they are planning to do their work. Leaving the attitude correction until later could require a much bigger correction or even make it impossible to reach the target position at all. The same principle applies to our earthbound activities – the sooner we take action on a variance the smaller corrective action we need to take and the more effective the correction will be. For those of us involved in the management of people and their performance, this principle is all too easily recognisable. The sooner we provide feedback on performance the more likely it will be effective. Wherever we have delays in the receipt of information there will be delays:

- in formulating decisions about employing control inputs

- about implementing those control actions

- getting the benefit of moving towards our objective.

The human aspects of control
We have already mentioned the importance of human intervention in taking control action where we have open-feedback-loop systems. Human intervention can also be used to override automatic control mechanisms where it is clear that all is not well with the control system. It is known for pilots to take over manual control of the aircraft when a *bug* gets into the autopilot. The so-called millennium bug is another example where human control is used to sort out computerised systems before the new millennium or to

manage the effects of any remaining bugs at the moment of changeover. Another example is a company pension scheme where the benefits are habitually increased year on year by five per cent or the rate of inflation, whichever is the lower. From time to time the pensions manager may make a calculation to determine the extent to which the scheme is affecting the real value of the pensions, with a view perhaps to making an additional increase – human intervention controls the effects of a company policy. We use this example in Chapter 17 on index numbers.

Yet another example will be of particular interest to those interested in the motivation of people in organisations. The objectives and performance measures we develop in our planning phase are used to monitor and control our processes and provide guidance as to what activities are needed to achieve the objectives. Clearly motivation will be present when control induces behaviour in the employee to work positively towards the objective(s). Also, there is plenty of evidence to show that people tend to be more motivated when they are involved in the setting of their objectives. This comes, in part, from the quality of the communication between the manager and the managed, leading to an understanding by all the parties of the relevance of the objectives to individuals and to the organisation. This means that the design of incentive schemes needs to be considered at the same time as we design our control systems, if the control systems are not to be ignored or at least ineffectively used. Conflicting objectives can also have an impact here. We know of a number of customer call centres where a target is set (expressed in number of calls taken per hour) for the staff to meet. This can cause conflict with standards for customer care as the operator concentrates on meeting the target rather than customer needs.

We must mention one final aspect of human activity in the control field. We could be accused of previously suggesting that information flow for control is only available in terms of what has already happened. However, this would be well wide of the mark so far as human activity is concerned. We refer in particular to the information that is known as *feedforward*. This is where the operators of our information systems scan their horizon to determine *in their judgement* how the environmental disturbances in the future will affect the operation of their present activities and gather information as feedforward rather than feedback – taking action in anticipation of environmental disturbances.

CONCLUSION

In this chapter we have looked at several terms used widely in describing the monitoring and control process of our information systems. We have seen that automatic systems can review and control our environmental disturbances but have been made aware that there can be instances where the disturbance is so great or our automatic treatment (electromechanical or otherwise) of the variance can be inadequate or exacerbate the situation. In these areas we need to build in the manual override that allows human intervention in the control process. We ended by discussing the importance of taking human factors such as motivation into account in the design of our information systems for review and control.

5 Processing data

INTRODUCTION

So far we have looked at some of the underlying concepts of information systems and the crucial role they play in helping managers and specialists make decisions in the areas of planning and control. In this chapter we look at some of the operational and technological aspects of information systems before going on in the next chapter to address the very important subject of designing your information system. So, in this chapter we will discuss issues such as the collection and storage of data, and the use of databases. Additionally we will look at some of the computer-assisted activities and software applications in the information management field.

COLLECTION AND STORAGE OF DATA

Data are all round our organisations as we measure, count, observe activities, read dials and scales, etc and then record this data as 'facts'. These compilations of facts relating to our activities give us the basic or *raw* data, as it is most often known, about our organisations. We can produce our data from internal sources by capturing it automatically as a part of the process or activity to which it relates, or as the result of some special data capturing activity. Similarly, data can be produced for us from external sources by specialist researchers, banks, etc and presented to us in a readily usable form without any further processing. This data produces all the building blocks for our information systems. Consequently the quality of data is crucial and this can be far more important than the technical mechanics of processing. If the raw data is flawed, then however sophisticated our processing, the eventual information produced will be worthless.

In a sense, the data within and around our organisations is almost limitless and, as we said in Chapter 1, it is more a case of filtration and condensation so that the user is presented with information that is relevant to his or her needs. We discuss in Chapter 6 this key issue of clearly specifying the information requirements.

Storage devices have come on a long way since we wrote *Management Information and Statistics* (Bee and Bee, 1990). Developments in technology since then have led to the miniaturisation of components allowing massive amounts of data to be stored in the smallest pieces of hardware. Computers for processing business information have come down in size from the mainframe to the personal computer, to the laptop and now to the palmtop. We can store masses of data in the smallest of boxes which, when combined with satellite technology, puts information processing and storage, and communication worldwide into the hands (literally) of the average 'person in the street'.

However, the principles of data storage remain largely unchanged. Computer disks are still in wide use as storage devices. They receive data that are no longer required to be worked on within the computer itself. Rather than losing this data when the computer is switched off at the end of a shift, or losing it by overwriting it with the next set of data, it can be stored for safekeeping or archiving. Storage can be on a variety of media but the most commonly used are:

• *magnetic hard disk form* – the disk is capable of storing ever greater amounts of data and software. Hard disks have grown in size from many megabytes (1MB = 1 million characters or bytes) to gigabytes (1GB = 1 billion characters or bytes) and will go further.

• *magnetic disk in floppy form* – available to most computers for backup and use of external software. Industry standard maximum capacities of floppy disks are currently around 1.5MB.

• *magnetic tape* – mainly used these days for backup purposes, that is, the storage of huge amounts of data and software. They take the entire contents from hard disks as a security process in case the hard disk is damaged in some way or the data or software held on it are corrupted and become unusable.

- *optical disks* – where the data are stored by laser light rather than by magnetic sensing. This technology is a development of the compact disc with read-only memory (CD-ROM) and has given us enough space on external disks to allow us to store such huge amounts of data as are contained, for example in encyclopaedias and directories, and the complete national census data. There are currently two types of optical disk available:
  - write once, read many times (WORM) which means exactly what it says, we can only write data once to the optical disk but we can read from it many times
  - erasable optical disks (EODs) which, like the traditional magnetic disks, allow data to be written to them, erased and rewritten many times.

- *floptical drives* – using a combination of magnetic and optical technology. The optics gives greater precision and allows more data to be stored on a traditional sized floppy disk than previously but they are much faster. The disks can be read by conventional disk drives.

- *flash 'disks'* – really memory chips that do not require power to retain the data stored on them. Because of their physical size (about the size of a credit card) and data capacity the flash disks are used with the newer palmtop computers. Once the technology has developed to allow overwriting and erasure byte-by-byte it is likely that these chips will replace components in conventional computer systems, leading to even smaller and more powerful computers.

- *glass disks* – one of the newer types of memory device. As the name suggests, glass is the storage mechanism and is a very stable medium. They may, in the future rival the flash disks because of small size and huge memory capacity.

The inventiveness of IT scientists and the pace of development means that we will constantly be having the benefit of improved storage devices and the future holds no bounds. The wristwatch-sized powerful computer and communication device may be just beyond the horizon as we write this book!

DATABASES

Before the advent of computers, those organisations that required information on customers, suppliers, etc tended to use card index systems to hold the data. These systems were very good but required considerable clerical work to keep them up to date. It was also a slow process to get at the data and convert it into the information needed for decision-making – and therefore an obvious case for computerisation. So, in the early days of computing, databases were largely electronic card index systems. They made life considerably easier for the holder of large volumes of data on clients, customers, spare parts, etc that were subject to regular amendment and updating. For example, staff records or customer information might be filed by surname in alphabetic order, or by salary record number, or customer number, or by some sort of code to indicate department, location, etc.

However, all was not perfect, even with this ability to update the records, sort and re-sort them, and to print out the records or parts of the records selectively. The main problem was that the records could only be sorted or accessed according to the actual file (the unique storage area for data) or database in which they were held and usually without reference to information held in other files. For example, details about an employee might be spread across several files – salary on the payroll file, age and length of service in the pension file, etc, effectively all in different databases. Particular applications or management reports made it necessary to interrogate every database separately to bring together all the data about one person, held in different files. Also it was usually necessary to amend the details of that person on every file in the system whenever a single piece of data changed. Without doubt this was a tedious and often long-winded process and frequently would be the cause of the information system falling into disrepute because no one could guarantee that all the files had been updated and were accurate. Apart from any other reason for requiring accurate data, the Data Protection Act 1984 (see Chapter 6) places a legal obligation upon computer users to ensure that the data they hold on living individuals is accurate.

Also, with the early systems it was necessary to be very specific about the reports that were to be output from the database and obtain the help of the systems designer and/or programmers to design these reports. Because of this, any changes in requirements for information from a database necessitated reprogramming to obtain the new report or the new report format. This was often a long and costly business and not one beloved by computer programmers and systems analysts who would much rather be developing new applications than maintaining old ones!

Fortunately, developments in computer technology have come to our rescue with the development of *database management systems* (DBMSs) and *database structures*. We will discuss each of these concepts in turn.

Database management systems (DMBSs)

Not surprisingly we use a DBMS to manage our database, constructing, expanding and/or maintaining it as required. A typical DMBS:

> ... is a collection of software programs that:
> - stores data in a uniform way
> - organises data into records in a uniform way
> - allows access to the data in a uniform way.

(Schultheis and Sumner, 1995, p196)

To explain what this actually means we need to consider how data was traditionally accessed from dedicated databases in the past. The user would probably have had his or her reports programmed for them by a computer specialist and would be stuck with the report in that form until the system was reprogrammed for a new report. With a DBMS the user can become independent of the computer specialist and can call for his or her own reports with a structured query language (SQL). In fact one of the most popular query languages is called SQL and is a set of about 30 English-sounding commands. These languages:

> ... provide – in a single command – the ability to do complete system tasks such as producing a printed report, updating a computer file, or merging different files together.
>
> (Edwards, Ward and Bytheway, 1995, p145)

Harry (1997, p187) draws the analogy between two types of coffee vending machine. The first machine, rather like the dedicated database, produces a beverage according to some expert's opinion of what premixed combinations of ingredients we find desirable. The coffee cup, if we have selected *coffee*, falls down the chute to have water added to mixture. The second machine, where there is a 'DBMS' in control, will produce a beverage according to whatever ingredients we select from the totality of its stored ingredients. Each ingredient falls down the chute after the empty coffee cup is in place to form our own uniquely selected mix, to which the water is added.

With the DBMS, our application software does not obtain the data needed direct from the storage media. Instead it requests the data first from the DBMS. The DBMS retrieves the data from the specific database or databases and provides them to the application we are using. In other words the DBMS operates between our software and the data in the database.

Database structures
Database structures, on the other hand, assist us in the task of organising large databases logically into records and establishing the relationships between these records. This can be a complex and time-consuming process, as even the smallest businesses will have large numbers of records, each having relationships with other records in the database. For example, a mail-order firm will have records relating to the customer who bought a particular item, the distribution company which transported the item, the picker who drew down the item from the store and the company that

manufactured the item. However, this example – showing only single relationships, eg *the* distribution company who transported *the* item to *the* customer – is not realistic. The reality is that there is a range of customers who bought a range of items, transported by one or more distribution companies. The items had been picked by several pickers from a range of items manufactured by several companies. In other words there could be a very complex set of relationships between the data that we might need to access in order to analyse the transactions.

We can represent the different types of relationships in our database using family relationship terminology as shown in Figure 4:

- one-to-one

- one-to-many

- many-to-one

- many-to-many.

Traditionally there have been three commercial approaches to organising the records and their relationships logically. These are the database structures we mentioned earlier. Each has its advantages and disadvantages and are known as the:

- hierarchical database structure

- network database structure

- relational database structure.

All records in the *hierarchical database* are called *nodes*. The structure starts from the top with what is known as the *root* record. The root record is the most generalised record and each layer in the hierarchy becomes progressively more specific. Records that are at a higher level in the hierarchy are known as the *parents* of those in the next layer down and those in this layer are known as the *children* of those in the layer above them. The parents are said to *own* the children. See Figure 5.

Figure 4 Relationships

1 One-to-one relationships

2 One-to-many relationships

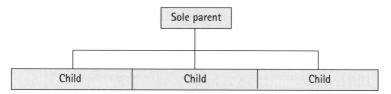

3 Many-to-one relationships

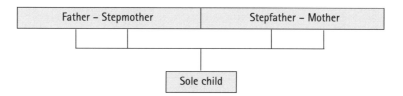

4 Many-to-many relationships

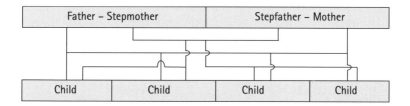

The relationships are fixed by the structure and this tends to make hierarchical databases relatively less flexible than the other two structures. They are relatively quick to process the day-to-day large batch, operational data, such as payroll or

Figure 5 **Organisation/hierarchy – hierarchical database showing relationships**

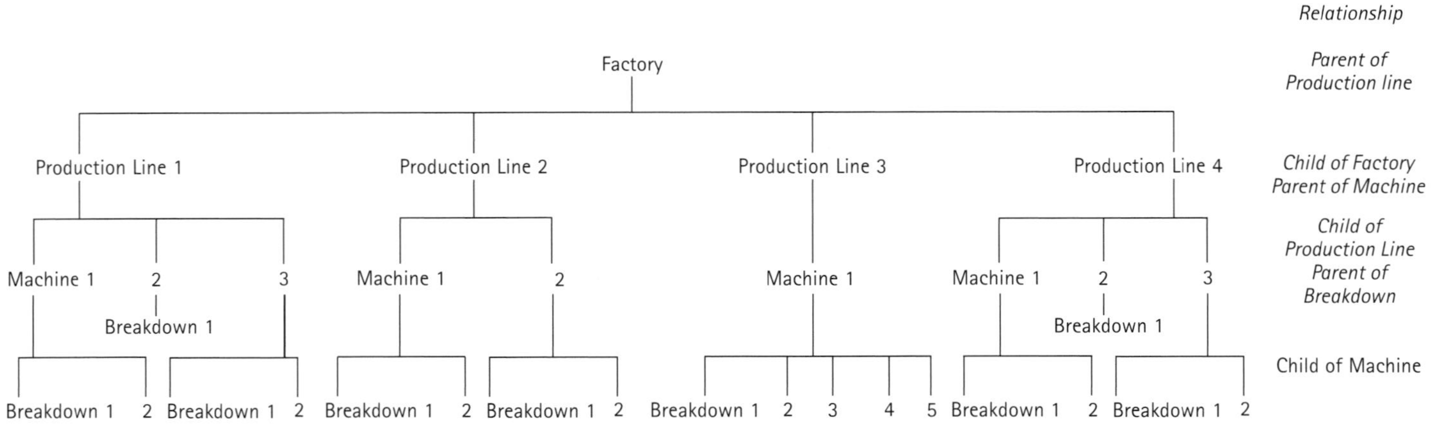

invoicing. However, managerial or non-IT specialist use of one of the query languages is cumbersome and slow and does not easily lead to the production of *ad hoc* reports.

Our next structure is the *network database* that views all its records in *sets*. Each set has an *owner* record and one or more *member* record, analogous to our sole parent to several children type of relationship, (see page 57). A record in this structure may be a member of more than one set, ie a record may have more than one owner, so allowing us to implement one-to-one, one-to-many, many-to-many and many-to-one relationships. However, these relationships need to be decided in advance because they are physically established by the DBMS when storage space is allocated on the hard disk. Because of the way the relationships are installed in advance, large batch processing and the production of routine reports is fairly quick. However, the production of *ad hoc* reports requiring relationships not established in the structure may take a long time and may not even be possible at all in some situations.

The final database structure we wish to discuss is the *relational database*. This differs from the previous two discussed in that it does not need the installation of the explicit relationships between the records nor is it necessary to process the records one at a time. Data is stored as individual records in files of like records. The user can select a single record, specific records or all records from each file to analyse with a single record, specific records or all records from any other file, and save them into a third, combined file. This process may be repeated as often as required until the user has examined all the data necessary to provide the answer(s) to the information queries posed. Thus, the relational database structure is much more flexible than the hierarchical or network database structures but, because the relationships between data are not decided in advance, large batch processing is likely to be relatively slow. You 'pays your money and takes your choice' but the flexibility given to the non-IT specialist and the freedom from the need to constantly re-engage the IT expert will make this option attractive to many managers/specialists.

Before we leave database structures there is one final point we wish to mention briefly. None of the structures we have mentioned so far are particularly well suited to many business applications, particularly those in engineering, where data in the form of images, drawings, videos, etc cannot be stored in the same way as data in the text form. *Object-orientated database* (OODB) technology has been developed to meet this need. This technology is substantially different from that which we have described earlier. It results in large libraries of objects that can be used time and again. New business applications can use these off-the-shelf objects in the same way that different machines can be assembled using off-the-shelf parts.

In our view one of the key advantages of database management systems concerns what is known as *data independence*. This is because with the DBMS, the data is kept separate from the applications that use it. Thus, when an item of data changes, for example when a new salary scale is introduced, the changes in the payroll file are automatically carried into the applications files, eg personnel records, pensions.

Our new style databases, therefore, are capable of easy amendment, capable of being used by lay professionals and managers with minimum intervention from the computer expert and, through the use of local area networks and wide area networks, are available to all users at most times of the day. With the use of modems, we can escape from the physical boundaries of our office buildings and access the data from other sites by telephone. Developments in communication technology such as the use of optical fibres and satellites have made worldwide access to these databases a practical proposition.

So what we have are information systems which are very flexible and very robust to change. They are admirably suited to an environment where change is the order of the day. They are also tailor-made to make use of the technological advantages of networked computer systems which, in turn, means that managers have direct access into *their* information system. By such devices our information systems have really come of age.

END-USER COMPUTING

Easy to use programming languages have been developed that allow the non-IT specialist to retrieve, manipulate, analyse data – the so-called fourth generation (4GL) languages. Arising out of the combination of use these 4GL (and later) languages, database management systems and a personal computer or terminal on every desk, is the developing trend for users to be directly involved in their own computing rather than indirectly via the computer professionals. This is called *end user* computing. At one level it has been facilitated by the provision of user-friendly software for common tasks such as word processing, basic database manipulation and spreadsheet activities all within the same 'environment', for example, the current industry standard Windows™ software. Once the busy executive has managed to learn one computer package all the others within the environment are relatively easy to use because of the common commands. There is a single learning curve and each new application is a small increment in computing knowledge over the previous applications.

However, it is at the second level of end-user activities that the greatest strides have taken place and will continue to develop. The list of end-user activities is already long and growing all the time. Some of the current types of computer-assisted end-user activity are:

- *computer-aided design* (CAD) – where computers are used to design products, buildings, components.

- *computer-aided manufacture* (CAM) – where computers are used to assist in the control of the manufacturing process.

- *computer-integrated manufacturing* (CIM) – a form of CAD/CAM where the entire industrial process from design to manufacture is controlled by computers.

- *computer numerical control* (CNC) – where the process of resetting machines is controlled by computer, thereby making small batch manufacturing more economic.

- *desktop publishing* and *text-handling* (DTP) – the ability to create visually interesting and attractive documents containing both text and pictures, for example, for brochures and in advertisements.

- *computer-based and multimedia training* (CBT/MMT) – the 'trainees' interact with the data stored on the computer to feel their way through the learning material at their own pace, receiving feedback visually and aurally as they go.

- *decision support systems* (DSSs) – designed to support managers and specialists in their decision-making processes. The emphasis is on the word *support* as the DSS does not take over the role of decision-making but allows the manager/specialist to play their 'what-if' games and use their judgement in deciding where to go next. DSSs assist the decision process best where there:
  - is a large database
  - is the need for a large amount of computer processing
  - are complex relationships between the data
  - is staged analysis of the problem requiring iteration between the human operator and the machine
  - is a requirement for human judgement in the definition of the problem and in selecting between the range of acceptable solutions
  - are several people involved in tackling the problem and each one contributes their special expertise which can be co-ordinated by the computer.

- *executive information systems* (EISs) – the provision of a wide variety of summarised information that enables executives, usually top management, to plan strategically and monitor the strategic plan, *drilling down* only to the level of detail required. Typical information '... might relate to competitor performance, the legal context, the economic environment or market preferences.' (Harry, 1997, p89)

Spreadsheets, modelling and simulation, sensitivity and risk analysis (mentioned earlier), and expert systems (described below) are all examples of decision support systems.

EXPERT SYSTEMS

Harry (1997, p89) describes *expert systems* as 'attempts to model the human ability to use reasoning and acquire knowledge'. Similarly, Lucey (1997, p231) describes an expert system as 'a computer system which embodies some of the experience and specialised knowledge of an expert or experts'. So an expert system is a computer system which can mimic our ability to reason and acquire the knowledge we learn from doing something. It will follow the expert through a process using not only the knowledge of the expert (from a huge professional or technical database) but also the reasoning processes of the expert when converting this data to information. This allows the non-expert operator to approximate to the performance of an expert in the particular specialism. There is also the possibility that over a period of time (because the system continues to learn the more it is used) the expert system will outperform many of the so-called experts in its field.

The list of applications is growing all the time and some of the following are examples:

- medical diagnosis
- personal tax planning
- product pricing
- selection of selling methods
- statutory sick pay entitlement and claims
- credit approval in banking
- air crew scheduling
- geological exploration.

(Lucey, 1997, p232)

ELECTRONIC DATA INTERCHANGE (EDI)

We have left EDI until last in these applications of computer-assisted activities. EDI allows 'computer to computer' exchange of data electronically, without human intervention and replaces traditional paper-based exchange of information activities. EDI is widely used in retailing, is spreading rapidly in manufacturing and is a perfect example of the use of IT to gain competitive advantage. In EDI, the systems can be supplier-focused or customer-focused. Where they are the former, for example, the supplier's computer regularly interrogates the buyer's inventory database(s) to determine whether stocks are at reorder levels. Where they are, the supplier's computer automatically generates an order and arranges the delivery within the agreed timescale. In this way, EDI passes the burden and cost of holding large inventories to the supplier and greatly reduces the administrative workload. Where just-in-time systems exist in manufacturing, the buyer's bins are constantly replenished with raw materials in the right quantity, according to material usage as measured by the buyer's computer.

It is not only the transfer of physical goods that have benefited from EDI – it is also used widely for financial transactions. Although the banks have generally been slow to take up the opportunities of the technology, it has been available to them for years. Most of the UK banks have been using *Bankers Automated Clearing Systems* (BACS) since the early 1970s to settle regular payments. A more recent financial system that has gained wide acceptance is the *Electronic Funds Transfer at Point of Sale* (EFTPOS). With EFTPOS, the customer has a plastic card containing details of his or her bank account encoded on a magnetic strip. The plastic card is 'swiped' through the retailer's card reader, the amounts and other transaction details are fed in via a small computer at the point of sale and the details are automatically passed overnight to the purchaser's bank to effect the transfer of the funds.

ELECTRONIC MAIL (E-MAIL)

It would not seem appropriate to leave this chapter without a few words about e-mail. For many of us, this form of communication now seems as commonplace as the fax and we tend to forget that it is one of the major changes in the way we communicate as the twentieth gives way to the twenty-first century. E-mail is a system that allows us to send and receive messages and images electronically using our computer terminals. This provides instant communication within our organisations through an Intranet. Using a modem and via a remote *service provider* this communication is worldwide through the Internet. Not only can we send memos, letters, etc but attach whole documents. For example, we sent the manuscript of this book, now published, via e-mail to our editor. We say communication is instant; it is on the part of the sender, but of course it relies on the receiver actually to pick up the messages. To help with this, many systems now indicate that e-mail messages are waiting.

To many business users the most important part of the Internet is the *World Wide Web* (WWW). The 'web' is the multimedia publishing side of the Internet. 'Pages' on websites are interactive documents using print, graphics (moving and still), pictures and sounds that can be called up by our computer. By using a unique website address enquirers can find out details about an organisation, its products, services and even its people. Also, many software providers now send their programs and updates via the web.

CONCLUSION

In this short chapter we have tried to do justice to what is becoming a massive field of activity. Commercial pressures and customer convenience is causing most organisations to examine carefully how best they can maximise the information that is available to them through the effective management of their data. As computer power grows and our ability to interchange vast amounts of information quickly and directly into others' computers develops, those that harness these capabilities to their business will discover substantial competitive advantage over those who trail behind.

6 Designing, developing and maintaining your information system

INTRODUCTION

Designing and implementing information systems in large organisations is a major and complex activity and, in the past, has often been the sole province of the IT specialist. However, when we carried out our research for *Project Management: The people challenge* (Bee and Bee, 1997) we found that there is a healthier variant of this, the multidisciplinary team approach. The simple point is that information systems are too important *to us* to leave them to the specialist. As a manager, specialist or a professional in our own right, we will be the user of the information system and will want to make sure that it is designed to meet *our* needs. As top management, we will wish to ensure that our strategic needs are catered for in the system. At senior to middle grades we will probably be more interested in tactical issues and unless the information system actually makes our job easier we will be unlikely to 'buy in' to it. At the operational level people have become adept at getting round or ignoring systems that they think get in the way of actually doing the job!

Consultation with all the stakeholders is essential but requires hard work and co-operation throughout all the stages of the basic project model, from the requirements analysis – the analysis of the business processes and the associated information needs – to handover and review. There is a variety of proven methods that can help us with these activities however, always remember that they need the active involvement of the final users of the system. The users' needs are paramount in designing, developing and maintaining our information systems. In this chapter we will discuss each of the stages of the basic project model in turn.

Finally, we need to give thought at the design stage to the

security issues, how we are to protect the system and its data from misuse and abuse and how to recover the system and the data from any disaster that may befall it.

BASIC PROJECT MODEL

We advocate a systematic approach to the design of the information system. This is so that there is a decent chance of ending up with a system that actually makes life easier rather than more difficult! This is not to say that local circumstances will not dictate some variation on this process but being systematic actually improves the odds in favour of our success. With this in mind we have set out below the typical project stages (sometimes known as *the deliverables*) that need to be followed in the development of any information system:

- project initiation
- requirements analysis
- system design
- programming and program testing
- system integration and testing
- user acceptance testing
- system handover and implementation
- review, amend and maintain the system
- evaluate the project.

Based on Lambert in Peppard (1993).

Figure 6 sets out these project stages and the level of involvement of both users and IT specialists at each stage.

PROJECT INITIATION

The deliverable from the project initiation stage is the feasibility report. There needs to be extensive discussion between prospective users and technical staff on the need for this particular information system. In order to decide its objectives we need answers to the questions:

• What businesses are we in and will be in, in the future?

Figure 6 Basic project model – balance of effort between IT staff and end users. Based on Lambert in Peppard 1993, p262.

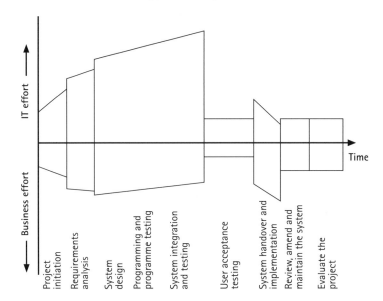

- What are the information requirements of the business?

- What are the required outcomes from the system?

- What will the system do for the business?

We should recognise that the information system is a part of the wider management system and that it will help managers and specialists plan, control and review, and replan their operational functions against corporate business standards.

The feasibility study will also consider:

- the scope of the new information system, its boundaries, etc

- the timing of the project

- the anticipated risks

- data and system security issues (including disaster recovery measures)

- costs and benefits in designing the new system when

compared with the existing system and other possibilities for managing the business information.

It is at this stage that the balance of involvement between potential users and information/computing specialists will be thrashed out. In particular, Harry suggests establishing the:

- client *identity*. Who is the client?
- client *perception*. What does the client consider the problem to be?
- client *motivation*. What does the client want from the solution of the problem?

(Harry, 1997, p286)

This concentration on the clients' needs is so important. It is from the clients' needs that the hierarchy of objectives for the project overall will be established and give us the opportunity to identify the critical success factors – 'those things we must get right in order to achieve the objective'. (Ward, 1995, p73) – that will help us keep the project on course and help us to evaluate the project.

REQUIREMENTS ANALYSIS

The next stage is to carry out the detailed analysis of requirements, recording all the data systematically and comprehensively – processes, volumes, information flow, etc now and what is required in the future. It is very tempting for the experts on the project team to decide that they know best and that the simplest approach is to produce an outline system and then ask the managers or the other professionals, the users, to comment on them. This approach is fraught with dangers! Apart from probably not winning the commitment of the other managers to using and supporting the system, it is approaching the problem from the wrong direction. The right approach is for the IT specialist to spend as much time as it takes with the potential users, finding out about their information needs. The interviewing skills of the system designers will have to be of the highest order and they may use tailored questionnaires to assist them in this process. They will typically cover the key areas of:

- what the manager/specialist does and/or what his or her responsibilities are

- what decisions the manager/specialist takes, that is, for what purposes the manager requires the information

- what the most useful form is for the information to be presented to the manager/specialist

- how often, and when, the manager/specialist needs the information.

The main deliverables from this stage are a clear and very specific statement of the requirements to be met by the information system, and the standards for acceptance and evaluation. The close involvement and commitment of the users is crucial to the success of this stage. It can be hard work and sometimes very frustrating. Many managers and specialists will initially be unclear on what information they need, even supposing they are perfectly clear as to what are their exact responsibilities! Some potential users will have difficulty in seeing the usefulness and/or the relevance of the information system and, in any case, will probably change their minds on their requirements as the systems review proceeds and they develop their knowledge about what the system can do for them. Our experience is that this is par for the course and, again, it is vital that sufficient time and other resources are devoted to getting this stage right. Because of the importance and complexity of this stage we discuss some of the methods and techniques available in detail later in this chapter.

SYSTEM DESIGN

At the system design stage the deliverable is a detailed specification of output, input and processes needed to satisfy the user requirements clarified in the requirements analysis. This stage has been described as creating 'the bridge between the user's need and the hardware and software capability'. (Edwards *et al*, 1995, p144). The task of the project team is to take the results of the earlier research and consultations and turn them into the information system. Often the process will require frequent returns to the users to clarify points and to test out ideas and output reports. It is at this stage that collaboration between users and IT specialists can be strained as the users struggle to understand the technicalities involved. While the computing side is clearly the province of the IT specialist the users have an obligation to achieve at least a working level of technical knowledge. Achievement of the project objectives will depend on both sets of colleagues ensuring that effective communication is maintained through the project.

As well as providing the detailed technical specification for the programming stage, the system design stage may finalise the format in which the documentation will be set out, both for users and for technical staff, and define the system test plan, described later.

PROGRAMMING AND PROGRAM-TESTING

This stage is rarely the province of the user due to the technical nature of producing the working computer systems. There will be a number of software options to be considered, to:

• use a standard, predesigned package if one is available

• use a standard, predesigned package with adaptations to cope with the particular needs of our information system

• design the software from scratch, specifically tailored to our needs.

It is rare that a standard package will meet completely an individual organisation's needs and considerable problems can occur if you try to shoehorn your information requirements to fit the package. This route is often chosen because it is perceived as a low-cost option. However, it can be a false economy if the system does not meet user needs! The third option is usually very expensive although, done properly, it can ensure that the system design actually does match the information needs. In practice, the second option is the one most often adopted and, although a compromise, can work well. However, the choice of the package is still very important as too many alterations and adaptations to the original can be expensive and may well prejudice the overall robustness of the system.

If the organisation does not have its own computer(s) or agency agreement, this is the stage at which the hardware is chosen. The overall size of the proposed system and the choice of software will usually dictate the type of hardware chosen.

The main deliverable at this stage is the production of the individual program modules and their documentation. This is also time for some initial thoughts to be given to the training that will be required for both IT staff and end-users.

SYSTEM INTEGRATION AND TESTING

While the individual modules might work by themselves, there is a need to test them when the system is running as a whole. Tests will be used to ensure that the system meets its technical specification correctly and at the right speed. It is important that the system can deliver information in an appropriate timescale – there is nothing more frustrating than a system that appears slow to the user. Customer expectations here are increasing all the time. In the early days of mainframe computing it was acceptable for users to wait overnight for their reports. Nowadays, users often *expect* information to be delivered within seconds. A range of data will be fed in to reflect the range of expected conditions, to test that the system can cope with any demands put upon it in operation. It needs to be understood by all concerned that these tests are designed to assess how the system works and not whether it meets the business needs; that comes later in user-acceptance testing.

However, there are some non-technical activities that can be planned and scheduled at this stage, for example:

• training

• communication with all concerned

• any parallel running of old and new systems

- housekeeping issues of file conversion

- production of documentation.

USER-ACCEPTANCE TESTING

This stage in the design process brings together all the disparate requirements of the users into a total system and ensures that it has the following principal attributes:

- it will provide all managers and specialists with the information they require, in the right form and at the right time

- the system should be sufficiently robust to allow modification to meet changing needs

- the system should be user friendly to allow the manager and/or specialist to make efficient and effective use of it.

It is a key stage in the development of the application and users will be closely involved with the IT specialists in ensuring that the system does what is intended. All the stakeholders will need to give an appropriate amount of time and such time is usually well spent. It is the time when all users receive their training, where the documentation is issued and arrangements made for the 'help desk' queries that will inevitably arise. It is also a key stage in ensuring a smooth handover to the users.

We cannot over emphasise the need:

- for really good communications between the parties to keep all the stakeholders – the main users, any support staff, technical staff – informed about progress and the resolution of any problems

- to ensure the training is meeting the needs of the users and is delivered at an appropriate time. There is a multitude of sad stories of training being delivered too soon, before there is any opportunity to practice on the system; or too late, when users have struggled to operate the system but have become frustrated and disillusioned

- for the documentation to be really good, comprehensive, easy to understand and with good indexing to help the users find their way around the manuals, etc. Also, as users become more sophisticated, many of them may prefer to have good *on-screen* help at their fingertips

- for good support through having good technical staff on hand, good help-desk facilities, etc.

SYSTEM HANDOVER AND IMPLEMENTATION

The big day has arrived; the system is live! This is where the results of all the hard work and skilled project management show themselves. The information system is up and running and paying its way – or so you hope! While it may be a time for celebration or mourning the break-up of the project team it is also a time for close control to review whether or not there are any small amendments to make to the system and to initiate the maintenance programme that all systems need.

REVIEW, AMEND AND MAINTAIN THE SYSTEM

In the initiation stage of the design project we stressed the need for clear business objectives that the information system should help achieve, and for critical success factors to be defined by the managers and specialists who will use the system. We can now close the circle on these objectives and assess the extent to which they are being met. Amendments may be needed where the business needs have changed during the time taken to develop the information system or perhaps where estimates of volumes of transactions or timings have proved to be inadequate. Great care needs to be taken with making any amendments and those that are made should be subject to the same rigour as in the original project. Where errors, breakdowns and/or other glitches occur they should be carefully logged, analysed and brought to the attention of management at an appropriate level. This is also the stage when any maintenance agreements come into play to ensure that the system continues to meet the identified (and modified) business requirements.

EVALUATE THE PROJECT

When we carried out our research for our earlier book *Project Management – The people challenge* (Bee and Bee, 1997) one of our findings was that there was a tendency for project teams, at the conclusion of a project, to move quickly onto their next project. We could understand why this was – the previous project was history, while the next project was the brave new exciting world of tomorrow! However, we found that a lot of potential organisational and individual learning was lost as a result of this failure systematically to review what had hindered the project along the way and what had contributed to project success. In the book we suggested that members of project teams should maximise their individual learning from involvement on projects by maintaining *learning logs* and that there should be a short evaluation or audit of the project itself, to maximise organisational learning.

TECHNIQUES FOR REQUIREMENTS ANALYSIS

In our earlier section on Requirements Analysis we said that we would return to the analysis techniques. Many of the techniques are highly sophisticated and can be the subjects of books in themselves. Most of them need formal training to use. Here we will cover them only in summary form and point the reader to sources of further reading where more detail is available. In very general terms the techniques for analysing our system requirements fall into two categories, namely process analysis techniques and information analysis techniques.

Most proprietary analysis systems available are based on these two approaches. Process analysis techniques show in diagrammatic form what people are doing, what is actually happening with items or documents. Information analysis techniques, on the other hand, concentrate on the information flows that support those activities. The techniques we will look at are:

• procedure narrative

- decomposition diagram

- structured systems analysis and design methodology (SSADM)

- data flow diagram (DFD)

- soft systems methodology (SSM).

Procedure narrative

Traditionally, a very basic technique for analysis has been what is known as the *procedure narrative*. This sets out in text form exactly what happens in the process, ie:

> A customer orders an item from a supplier.
> Supplier checks the stocks and, if sufficient, picks the order and delivers it to the customer.
> The supplier adjusts stock record.
> The supplier raises an invoice and sends it to the customer.
> The customer pays the invoice.
> If not in stock, the supplier notifies the customer and places the order in 'pending'.
> Supplier obtains more stock.
> Supplier picks the order and delivers it to the customer.
> The supplier adjusts stock record.
> The supplier raises an invoice and sends to the customer.
> The customer pays the invoice.

In a complex system the procedure narrative can go on for pages and while it provides a comprehensive record of what has transpired it does not show the dynamic nature and interdependence of the activities.

Decomposition diagram

In the sense that 'every picture paints a thousand words', procedure diagrams have been developed to translate the narrative into a diagrammatic format. An example of one such diagram is the *decomposition diagram*. This diagram deals with complexity by dividing the process into parts and then showing each level one at a time – rather like the organisation chart which shows how an organisation is divided into departments, then into sections and then into individuals. An example of a decomposition diagram is shown in Figure 7.

Figure 7   Decomposition diagram of an organisation

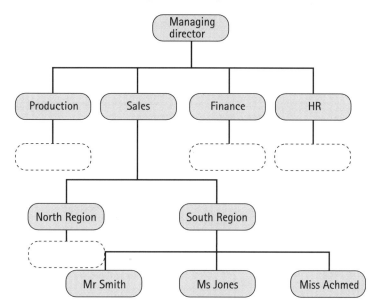

Structured systems analysis and design methodology (SSADM)

Once again, although helping to reduce the complexity of setting out the process, the decomposition diagram still does not show all the relationships and the information flows, and various techniques have been developed to do just this. One example that is used in all but the smallest government IT projects is known as *Structured Systems Analysis and Design Methodology*. Briefly, SSADM sets out to describe in detail the new system that is required without taking into account any specific software or hardware. SSADM sets out the logical system of what is required so that the systems designer can go on to set out how it will be achieved. It puts the emphasis on information analysis and includes techniques such as data flow diagrams (described in the next paragraph). SSADM works best on projects where it is possible to set out clearly defined objectives.

One of the charting methods used in SSADM for showing information flows is the *Data Flow Diagram* (DFD), which represents the information flows in a system and between

Table 2 National Computing Centre (NCC) data–flow diagram symbols

SYMBOL	MEANING
☐	*Process* ie processing actions that transform flows of data
→	*Flow of Data* ie movement or transfer of data from one point to another; it may be a document transfer, a telephone message, a screen display etc
☐	*Data Store* ie a point that holds data and receives data flow; it may be a card index, a magnetic tape or disk, a document, a clerical file etc
⬭	*Entity* ie a data source or destination; it may be an individual, group, department or organisation; sometimes known as 'sources' or 'sinks'

the system and its environment, together with the functions that are performed. They are very effective in defining data needs and clarifying any inconsistencies in the process and in the flow of data. There is no universally agreed terminology or symbols in this area so for clarification in this book we will use those of the National Computing Centre (NCC) and set them out in Table 2.

DFDs start with a high-level diagram followed by progressively more detailed diagrams showing linkages to the higher diagram. They can be separated into what are known as the *physical* and the *logical* diagrams. The former is a picture of how the system operates at present, showing physical details such as names of people operating the process, titles of document or forms used, etc to clarify information flows and any logical inconsistencies. In the latter, the names and titles are removed allowing concentration on the logical flow of information. An example of how DFDs work is given in Figure 8 using the details from our earlier procedure narrative.

Figure 8 Purchase/sale of item data–flow diagram (DFD). Based on Lucey 1997, p211

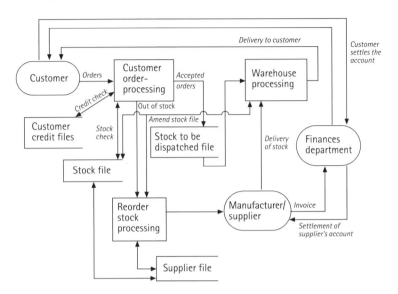

Soft systems methodology (SSM)

We mentioned earlier that SSADM works best on problems where the outcome objectives can be clearly defined and it would be splendid if all situations had such structure and clarity. Clearly this is not the case and *soft systems methodology* was developed to cope with the analysis of unstructured and poorly defined problems. SSM starts from the premise that there is no such thing as *reality*, individuals' real worlds being a composite of their previous experience. This reality changes as people gain further experiences. SSM has two strands – *cultural enquiry* (such as relationships, social systems, power and political influence) and *logic-based enquiry* ('hard' factors such as the systems themselves, models, etc). The SSM methodology helps in analyses where there is conflict, for example, as to what tasks should be carried out, and where there are differences between individual views. The main stages in SSM are set out in Figure 9.

Establishing the *root definition*, which is helpful in exposing the differing views of the people who are affected by the system, is a key stage in the process.

Figure 9 The stages in soft systems methodology. Based on Lucey 1997, p212

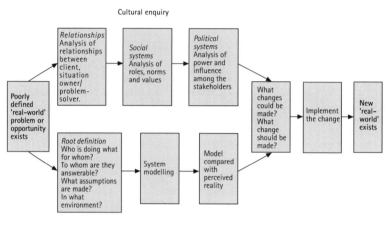

The root definition is a concise, verbal description of a system that captures its essential nature and core purpose. In forming root definitions it is necessary to ensure that six characteristics are present ie *who* is doing *what* for *whom*, to whom they are *answerable*, what *assumptions* are being made and in what *environment* is this happening.

(Lucey, 1997, p213)

A model of the system is then created and compared with the real world. This is not only to check its validities but also to encourage further debate. An example could be the school system viewed through the eyes of students, parents, teachers, school governors and community representatives.

DATA SECURITY

Organisations and individuals are becoming more and more dependent on computer systems, and the associated information systems, day by day. Systems are becoming increasingly global and more dependent on networks. Even in the smallest organisation we have become dependent on using our computers for:

• simple things like producing a letter, an invoice or a cash flow forecast

- providing access to key data

- our ability to manipulate these data into manageable information

- electronic data interchange (EDI), eg to network our purchaser/supplier activities

- providing information to give us competitive advantage.

The scene is set, therefore for something to go wrong either accidentally and/or maliciously to the mechanical and/or electronic components of the computer system, or to the software that runs the computers and to the data stored on them. Many of us are familiar with the horror of finding that our computer systems are 'down', even temporarily. If this happens organisation-wide, it can be disastrous – on our customers, our stocks, our finances, etc. Facing all these perils, it is imperative that we have in place systems and procedures to minimise such occurrences and if they should happen despite our precautions, provide us with the means by which we can recover from these disasters.

Disaster recovery should be a matter of concern at the outset of the project. The main issues should be set out in the feasibility study and then progressed so that the recovery processes are in place even before the system goes live. Such measures might include:

- setting up alternative premises with compatible equipment

- making contingency arrangements with a commercial disaster recovery agency for support to be available if needed

- having temporary reciprocal arrangements with another organisation in your vicinity

- having comprehensive documentation of systems for back-up and recovery, and practise their use from time to time as we would practise escaping from a building in the event of a fire

- ensuring all data, files, applications and operating systems are regularly copied and the copies placed in a secure, remote location

- allocating responsibility for security and back-up clearly in the organisation to a specified individual in the same way as we would allocate responsibility for the management of health and safety.

Let us look next at the legal framework for data protection. The *Data Protection Act 1984* (DPA) places a legal obligation upon computer users to ensure that the data they hold on living individuals is accurate and secure. The individual can seek damages through the courts for any damage or distresses caused by any inaccuracies and apply to the courts for rectification or erasure of the inaccurate data. We are required to notify the Data Protection Registrar of, among other things, what data we hold on whom and for what purpose and in particular that 'appropriate security measures shall be taken to prevent unauthorised access to personal data and against accidental loss or destruction of such data'. (Lucey, 1997, p252).

The Computer Misuse Act 1990 (CMA) provides powers to prosecute people who, deliberately and without authority, misuse computer systems. The CMA defines three offences:

- unauthorised access – commonly known as 'hacking' but also includes users who deliberately exceed their authority

- ulterior intent – unauthorised access with the intention of carrying out some serious crime, ie fraud or obtaining information for the purposes of blackmailing someone to whom the data relates

- unauthorised modifications – in any form, including computer viruses that are intended to impair the use of the computer system.

So the law is comprehensive and all embracing. Ulterior intent and unauthorised modification can lead to unlimited fines and, for individuals, up to five years' imprisonment.

The business 'owner' of the data is responsible for defining the security parameters for that item of data based on the business uses to which the item might be put. Ward sets out three aspects to security:

• Protection – how confidential is the information, and therefore to what extent should access be allowed by others, or how carefully protected must it be?

• Recoverability – how quickly in the event of a system or computer failure does the data have to be available to avoid major business problems?

• Back-up – how frequently should the data be copied and how long do the copies need to be kept?

(Ward, 1995, p191)

Firstly, we can deny unauthorised people physical access. We can lock our doors and keep such people out of our buildings. Secondly, we can put a physical lock on the computer which either prevents the keyboard or the disk drives from working. However, in these days of modems and remote access these two measures are not enough and we need to have some software barriers to the outside world (commonly known as 'fire walls'). With regard to the confidentiality and integrity of the stored information we can:

• assign a password necessary to get into the system or document thus denying unauthorised users access

• assign a password to modify the document, which allows access to the document or information but without the ability to change the data

• assign a password which logs or tracks any changes made

• install virus protection software that automatically scans the system on start-up and provides background protection while the computer is working.

CONCLUSION

With all these possible pitfalls and problems it is all too easy to take a mechanistic approach to the introduction of the information system, that is, to treat the exercise as simply reading items off a checklist. However, we cannot stress too strongly the need to be aware of all the technical and human implications and of the possible range of responses and reactions of people to the new system. The success of an information system will depend entirely on the use to which all users put it. It can be technically the best system in the world, but if the users do not perceive it as such or understand how to get the best from it, it will be a failure. In particular, if we fail to secure the data and the system so that if misused accidentally or maliciously there will be business or organisational opportunities missed as a result, then it could be a very expensive failure indeed. It is up to us, all of us, to play our part as appropriate in the design, development and maintenance of the information system.

7 Information systems for human resource applications

INTRODUCTION

We find it interesting, as we write this book on information systems (which are inevitably computerised these days) to look at some of the similarities between the two aids to strategic and tactical business success – information technology and human resource management (HRM). Both have struggled to be seen and used as a strategic and in some cases even as a tactical resource but, as we turn the corner of the millennium, both appear to have achieved this recognition at last – at least in the more go-ahead organisations! In the early days of computers the majority of the information systems to be computerised were the financial systems. Until recently in many organisations, HRM was seen as primarily an administrative function, keeping the personnel files and perhaps in some cases administering the wages, company cars, etc. A salutary example of this was supplied to us by Tony Reid during our research for *Project Management: The people challenge* (Bee and Bee, London, IPD, 1997). Reid was at that time chairman of one of the major committees of the Association of Project Management. He quoted from his wide experience that HR staff were not usually involved in major activities on forming project teams, such as the selection of the project leader, saying that HR staff's traditional involvement on project teams was:

> in determining salary bands, pay and conditions and especially, where there is an overseas element to the project, the expatriate arrangements. Otherwise their involvement is usually around the administrative aspects of recruitment – processing the appointment forms after the decisions have been taken.
>
> (Bee and Bee, 1997, p48)

It was not surprising that many personnel departments,

trying valiantly to cope with all the downsizing, resizing, right-sizing, etc were overwhelmed with their paperwork and always so far behind the strategic issues facing the business. The emphasis has been, and still is to some extent, on coping with the present rather than focusing on the future.

For many organisations, introducing computers into HR departments was a low priority on the list of their IT managers. We are aware of one HR manager who, in desperation, bought and installed his own computer. Then, even when they did arrive, computerised HR systems were largely an electronic version of what had gone before.

Things have clearly moved on, relational databases are now the norm. We cannot imagine a system being installed without the opportunity for the users, through SQL or an equivalent, to be able easily to pull off their own customised reports. Local and wide area networks and security systems, such as those discussed in Chapter 6, have made it possible for the systems and their data to be distributed throughout the organisation. This allows other users, where authorised, to input, change and amend the data, and *drill down* to the level of detail they require to produce their own information and reports. As we will show shortly these systems, when used in multinational organisations even allow the users to produce their reports in the language of their choice.

This chapter is about using information systems to support HR professionals in their roles. We start by looking at the core features of HR information systems and then at specific modules aimed at particular activities, for example, recruitment, training and development. We use two case studies to illustrate some of the points made. It is not our intention to present you with a complete review of what is available. Nor does the fact that we mention products by name mean that we are endorsing those products. We are simply using them as examples to demonstrate how some HR information systems have been developed.

CORE FEATURES OF HR INFORMATION SYSTEMS

Whatever features are included, in overall terms the system should be simple to use, have good help facilities (including printed user manuals) and be sufficiently flexible for non-computer specialists to 'do it themselves'. In these days of multi-site/multinational operations the system needs to have an *Intranet* (a communication system, internal to the organisation) and possibly even an *Internet* (a global communication system, external to the organisation) capability. With this distributed IT facility, it will need to have a security system capable of restricting access to groups of records for authorised users, for example, line managers having access to the records of those reporting to them. The security system will also monitor and show an audit trail for all changes made. Finally, considering what we said in Chapter 5 the databases should be 'relational'. We will consider in the following paragraphs some of the individual features that would normally be included:

- To help all HR people with their time management, the system should have a diary management function, so that important dates, for example, end of probation period, long service and/or retirement dates, can be brought forward automatically. It is also helpful to have the facility to enter diary dates manually. Many systems include electronic personal diaries for recording and sharing diary information between members of the HR team.

- The system will need to interface with other HR systems such as Time and Attendance and payroll.

- It will allow easy import and export with other packages, for example, word processing, spreadsheets and databases. To make the statistics produced more informative it is useful if the output is linked to a graphics package.

- Being 'relational', the system will be capable of accepting global updates, for example, when salary scales are changed or when parts of the organisation change their names.

- There will be standard reports and self-generated reports, plus the capability to produce cross-tabulated reports and perform 'what if' calculations.

• It is very useful for the system to be capable of storing images such as photographs, application forms and, where there are standard letters, to scan in the signatures of the originators. A useful by-product of this function is the ability to produce permanent labels such as staff identity labels and temporary labels such as conference and training course labels.

• Most proprietary systems today have at their core a personnel records system. The system should be capable of providing selected information on an individual or group of individuals for, say, training course profiles, performance review meetings, etc.

• The system should also make it possible to extract all the data held on the individual to satisfy the employer requirements under the Data Protection Act where the employee requests that information.

• Where the organisation has a multinational workforce there should be the facility to pick off reports in the language of the end-user.

What follows now is a case-study describing the introduction of a comprehensive HR information system into an international law firm.

Case study: Allen & Overy Personnel Project

Allen & Overy
Allen & Overy is a leading international law firm with offices in London and 18 other cities across the globe. The firm employs in excess of 2300 staff, including 200+ partners and 700+ associates.

Background
The personnel department, numbering nearly 40, used a computerised system for maintaining personnel records and running the payroll. This system was considered to be cumbersome to use, lacked a lot of required functionality, for example, there was no absence management or recruitment facility and offered poor performance on payroll because the payroll run took around nine

hours to complete. The main problem with the original system was that being so 'user unfriendly', people avoided using it and it began to fall into disrepute as the quality of the information provided could not be relied on.

When the supplier announced that they were to withdraw support on the version of software running at Allen & Overy, the firm had to decide between taking the proposed upgrade or looking elsewhere. The decision was to conduct a full review of the personnel function and identify exactly what was required. Two projects were set up, one a business process re-engineering exercise, the other to establish what data was held on individuals in the 20 or so unsynchronised, different applications. The outputs from these projects were used to assess the upgrade on offer; however, this fell a long way short of what was required.

A business case was made for replacing the existing system and a fall-back strategy put into place for the temporary outsourcing of payroll pending the decision and implementation of a new system(s).

Evaluation and Selection
A requirements specification was produced from the review exercise together with a technical element based on the planned migration within the firm to a Windows NT/SQL Server platform.

A number of products were reviewed but were soon reduced to a short list of three. Those were reviewed in detail and scored against a weighted version of the requirements specification. The three products all scored very much the same and so other factors came into play. The firm considered such factors as reference sites where the products were already in use, reputations – market position, direction the supplier's business was going. They also had numerous meetings with the vendors aimed at building relationships as Allen & Overy had decided that they wanted more than just the purchase of a product. They wanted a vendor with company growth and direction in line with their own business aspirations.

Allen & Overy decided to go with Peterborough Software. The decision was based both on their current offerings plus their future plans, especially in the international arena.

PS enterprise is a very user-friendly product that is simple to install and configure. Like most projects, the difficult part is managing the transition from your existing systems. Because of the functional inadequacies associated with the previous system, a plethora of personnel-related subsystems had evolved. The implementation plan was constructed to facilitate the systematic migration from each of these subsystems onto *PS enterprise* together with a roll-out starting in London and then moving to the larger international offices.

To date some seven months after signing contracts, Allen & Overy have implemented the core personnel module, payroll is being run in parallel, a start is about to be made on the recruitment module and the firm expects to get to the Intranet in around three months time. This will allow managers and individuals to access authorised levels of data from any place in the world at any time of the day or night. In addition, the open architecture of *PS enterprise* allows easy integration with the existing desktop environment. Eventual use of the recruitment module and the Internet will allow prospective applicants to complete an on-line application form. The sophisticated security system and audit trail incorporated into the system will be used to protect personal and confidential data from unauthorised use.

Costs and Benefits

A case can be made for calculating the financial cost of the new system against cash benefits such as increases in efficiency and there will clearly be financial benefits as administrative processes are automated. However, the real business benefits are derived from having an accessible, cohesive and up-to-date database providing personnel information in a form that is required, when it is required and without the need for cumbersome reprogramming. The business need of Allen & Overy is to recruit and retain the best legal minds for the partnership and they are using information systems and information technology to give them their competitive advantage and this benefit will only be seen in the longer term.

PS enterprise is not so much the solution but the vehicle with which Allen & Overy can achieve their business requirements. The basic premise being that data should exist only once, they should, where possible, be captured at source, validated and then stored in a central repository. That repository should facilitate multiple types of access and retrieval of the data in conjunction with a security mechanism which itself must be easy to administer.

Functionality is important and clearly one of the reasons for selecting a package over a bespoke development is that a whole host of functions are available from day one. Said Martin Onley, the Programme Manager at Allen & Overy 'Wherever possible, we are looking to "flex" our business processes to suit the package but where this is not possible, we need to be able to "bend" the package or develop a "bolt on".'

'The system also needs to be responsive to change, which could be business, technology or legislation led. As an international player, Allen & Overy needs to be able to manage their people data collectively and at the same time be aware of and understand local variations in requirements.'

The success of this project should be judged by the responsiveness of the implemented package in supporting the evolving business requirements of the firm.

Source: Martin Onley, programme manager, Allen & Overy

All the features described on pages 87–88 are of a general nature and it is important that there is the capability of adding specific modules to the core system. Two of the most frequently requested modules are the recruitment module and the training and development module. We will discuss these modules in more detail below.

RECRUITMENT MODULES

The bane of many HR professionals' lives is the mass of paperwork associated with recruitment. It is not unusual to have scores of applicants, even with the most tightly drawn personnel specification. All these applications need to be acknowledged and tracked through the process. At each stage there is the requirement for an appropriate letter to be generated and sent off to advise of the good news or the not so good. Most recruitment modules will do these chores automatically thus saving an enormous amount of repetitive effort. What they do not do is make our selection decisions for us, although even here we are beginning to see this happening in part with the introduction of some mechanistic sifting through of candidate details which have been input to the computer. This feature can be further developed where the organisation is using clearly defined competencies and/or behaviourally anchored ratings to differentiate between the candidates and may go yet further in some recruitment applications with the development of expert systems.

The systems allow for the automatic collection of data and, for example, the automation of the recruitment process as described above also makes the systematic monitoring of equal opportunities in recruitment a reality.

Most of the modules available provide for automatic media analysis (ie which publication produced the best recruitment response) and vacancy cost analysis (ie which media were the most cost effective) as a standard feature. They will also provide for the successful applicants' details to be automatically input into the personnel records system.

TRAINING AND DEVELOPMENT MODULES

Like his or her recruitment colleagues, the trainer will from time to time disappear into the paper quagmire. Training records get out of date and the administration associated with a single training course can overwhelm even the most efficient trainer, not to mention the perennial problems surrounding the allocation of training rooms. Also many organisations use outside training facilities and contract with independent, freelance trainers to run the courses. The efficient training professional will want to have the facts about these external resources immediately accessible. The training and development modules can automate and therefore simplify all of these administrative training functions. The case-study on pages 93–95 describes the use of such a training and development information system.

The identification and analysis of training needs is another area where the power of the computer can be harnessed to the advantage of the training professional. It is particularly helpful where there are clearly defined competency levels specified for different jobs and individuals can be assessed against these competency levels so that training and development needs can be allocated. Some systems also include specific training interventions with the competencies they address so that once a need has been identified an appropriate intervention can be identified. The data on needs can be collected directly and relatively easily from potential participants and/or their managers using the Intranet facility where this exists. The ability to model future organisational structures can make it possible to assess the volumes of training (different subject areas and levels) required in the future. In these ways, and probably others in the future, the computer gives some opportunity for the training professionals to be liberated from the present and to be able to cast their eyes into the future – to become more strategic!

Another area, which has received little attention from the computing specialist, is that of training evaluation. There are some packages available that offer this capability. However, most are fairly limited and operate only at reaction level, the very basic *happy sheet*, testing participant satisfaction with the training as delivered by the use of simple questionnaires and analysis features. With the computer's ability to track peoples' progress in the organisation after training there is the possibility of using the computer further in the evaluation process. This is to identify the success of certain kinds of training such as supervisory and management skills back in the workplace – at the intermediate level of evaluation. Use of the Intranet capability would allow data for intermediate evaluation to be collected easily from participants and other interested parties say, three months and six months after the training.

Case-Study: Eastern Electricity Training

In late 1996 staff in the HR function in Eastern Electricity decided that they wanted to install a computerised information system to cope with the throughput of delegates on their large range of training programmes. This vast amount of training activity generated masses of paper and did not always work as efficiently as they wished. They were looking for a system that was efficient, less labour intensive, involved less duplication of effort, was very customer focused and was in line with Eastern's paper reduction policy. The targets for the system were all the people in the training chain – the nominees, the training providers, the staff at the residential training centre and the print unit, who deal with the handouts, exercises, etc.

They decided on a system built by Logsys Ltd, a bespoke software company based in Wokingham, which went 'live' in 1997. Gareth Scragg, the Marketing Manager of Logsys described the system as 'a work-flow automation based system that proactively manages the training administration process from delegate nomination to delivery, by the application of business rules and deadlines which ensure that the training function provides an effective, high quality service to the rest of the organisation'. The system cost around £40,000 to install and it is estimated that, while around one person's time will be saved as a result of the information system there will be additional benefits, both financial and otherwise, that are difficult to quantify at this stage. Examples of such benefits are:

- The better management of business processes enables better communication.

- By making the current business processes more efficient it is possible to optimise the use of resources, eg number of delegates per course, and enable training needs to be met more quickly.

- Better productivity allows greater volumes of work to be achieved, faster and to higher levels of quality by existing resources.

- By making the process more accessible to potential delegates it will encourage the use of training and development internally.

- There is complete auditability and reporting on all processes.

The system is, as yet, only semi-automated and the training staff initiate many of the activities; however, further developments are being considered in this direction. Another major development is to use Eastern's Intranet facility to allow direct customer access into the database.

Sue Burstall is Eastern's training co-ordinator and joined the project team in the early design stage. Burstall highlighted the main aspects of the system as:

1. Once a person has registered an interest in a particular course (by telephone, fax or e-mail), their application is currently keyed into a screen-based form that assigns them to the relevant waiting list.

2. As soon as there are enough people on the waiting list to make a course viable, one is set up on the system.

3. People from the waiting list are then invited by a system-generated e-mail to confirm their commitment to attending the new course.

4. If their reply is 'yes', their status (keyed in by Burstall) is changed from applicant to delegate.

5. Once all the replies are in, a standard e-mail confirmation message is sent to Eastern's Essendon Training College advising that the course will go ahead and automatically attaches the names of the delegates.

6. Two weeks before the start of the course the delegates are e-mailed their joining instructions, together with any pre-course work. An e-mail is sent to the print unit requesting that 'the attached inserts for the workbooks are copied' and actually specifies how many copies of the handouts and exercises are needed. The system takes the number of copies required from the delegate list.

7. After the course has taken place any non-attendees are placed back on the waiting list by Burstall in order to give them a further opportunity to attend.

Overall, the system is a relational database with standard reports, for example, on volumes of training taken up whether classroom based, distance learning or by outside providers. There is the opportunity for the system operators to produce their own, *ad hoc* reports using a type of SQL enquiry system and the information is passed to the personnel system to update their records. This function is not yet fully automated but is one of the planned developments. The system is password protected and has a built in audit trail. Burstall confirmed that at some stage it is their hope that employees will have the opportunity to key in their own data at source.

In summary, Burstall had this to say about the problems and other issues the section had faced along the way: 'We didn't actually encounter many problems. It was helpful that I was involved right from the start in the specification and having regular input into the look and feel of the system. What few problems we had were quickly resolved with Logsys and the system has worked really well.'

Source: Sue Burstall, training co-ordinator, Eastern Electricity

OTHER MODULES

The range of add-ons to core HR systems is growing all the time. Health and safety modules, absence and leave management (often integrated with time and attendance systems), payroll, pension and sophisticated salary modelling packages are all available. Also, IT companies have not been slow to appreciate the commercial opportunities presented to them by the Inland Revenue's demanding self-assessment/P11D computations and such modules are already available.

In our experience the development of modules to help with

strategic HR planning has not kept pace with the more 'administrative' HR systems. While there are modules that will help with career planning and succession planning we have yet to come across strategic modules that are used in HR planning. HR planning systems probably do exist in some organisations but are designed specifically for those organisations. The reason for this is that there are so many variables that affect a single organisation that it is impracticable to design a single system for general needs. Where it happens at all, strategic HR planning is likely to be the province of the specialist and the specialist system. Due to the use of work measurement techniques, such as clerical work measurement and methods time measurement (MTM™), masses of data are available on the standard times allowed for an experienced and motivated worker to complete a unit of production. Thus HR planning in the production area tends to lead other areas. It seems to us that there is still some way to go in HR information systems in the HR planning field.

CONCLUSION

We have seen in this chapter that the development of relational databases and the ease of producing custom made reports has given the HR professional, whatever his or her specialism, the opportunity to get to grips with all the data on people that is available within the organisation. The technology has also given the HR professional the opportunity to automate many of the administrative processes that have previously absorbed their energies in the day-to-day running of the function. This has enabled HR staff to tackle their operational and tactical roles efficiently and effectively. The future lies in the extent to which HR professionals can harness the power of information systems to develop their strategic role.

8 Looking ahead

INTRODUCTION

And so we arrive at the final chapter in this part of the book. Our purpose so far has been to introduce you to the concepts and applications of information systems. We have talked about the way in which technology now liberates us from the IT specialist. We mean no offence to the IT specialist – handing over the reins to the user can leave the IT specialist free to use his or her abilities for creative and innovative developments. We have distributed hardware, and dedicated professional software that is compatible with all our other business software. We have corporate databases where all the files have a relationship with other files, making it possible for us to access and update the data wherever it is filed. We can drill down and access the information at whatever level of detail we need. We have standard reports that we can draw off on a routine basis and also the availability of SQL, making it possible for us to interrogate the database and produce the tailored reports we need. Finally, we have integrated our information systems and our administrative systems to take much of the drudgery out of them and free us up to use our creativity to the benefit of the organisation.

So, how will this affect the average manager/specialist? We would argue that through the combination of the two parts of this book – information systems and statistics – we have access to comprehensive, up-to-date data converted into the information we need to do our jobs effectively. We already have the computing and communication technology to dramatically change our lives. Technology that allows us via our hand-held 'gizmos' to ensure the curtains are drawn in our house or flat, and that the oven is already turned on cooking our meal as we fight our way home with all the other commuters. The Internet has opened up unparalleled opportunities for global communication and access to information on a vast scale. It is almost impossible to forecast where the technology might take us, even in the next few years. We have set out a few of our thoughts below such as the use of virtual reality, the impact on organisational structures, the development of decision support systems, the use of robotics, application of competency profiling allied to expert systems and growth in the use of the Internet.

VIRTUAL REALITY

Virtual reality is with us today – although its full potential is still being realised. For example, when choosing a car from a catalogue, how nice it would be to be able to walk around the car and see it from all angles – to sit in the car and see how good is the visibility, how easy it is to reverse park – all without leaving our desks. Translating this to a business example, when deciding on the layout for our new offices, to be able to walk around the inside and see the virtual image as it is in reality, and so produce the ideal office layout. Perhaps it is only one small step forward to add the sounds of the traffic outside the window, experience the solar gain at midday and the smells from the restaurant across the road. The technology is there for us now and already beginning to be used.

Why travel miles to a meeting when yesterday's technology of the 'video conference' will be replaced by the 'virtual reality conference'? It will be as if you had actually made the journey although you had not stirred from your office or home workstation. In these days of global organisations and global markets, think of the time and energy saved, and for those people who have not had the time or inclination to learn all the languages of the world our virtual conference could supply instant translations into the language of our choice.

ORGANISATIONAL STRUCTURES

There will be changes in the way organisations are structured. In the dim and distant past, we clustered all the people of the same profession together on the same floor of the office block or in the same group of offices because of the

Figure 10 Future organisation structure. Based on Redmond, in Peppard 1993, p236

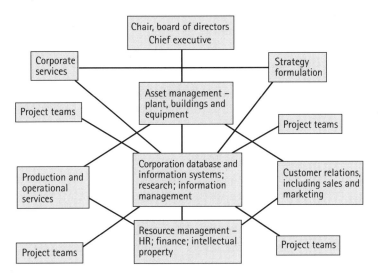

need for their people to be physically close to their (paper) files. Even a casual observation of the layouts of our office blocks today will show that we still tend to have our finance staff, HR staff, production team, etc, all located in their specific piece of floorspace. This will no longer be necessary due to our distributed IT systems – people will be located closer to their internal customers and suppliers. It may be that, on occasions, members of a specific profession will need to be physically together to solve particular professional problems, however, the majority of their time they will actually be solving problems with their customer and supplier colleagues. Does this suggest the possibility of distributed professional staff as well as distributed information systems? When thinking about this philosophy there are no boundaries to this 'distribution' and the future may see much more of the physical integration of staff throughout the supply chain; staff from purchasers and suppliers working together to mutual competitive advantage. We are already beginning to see this as organisations move towards project team working. Multidisciplinary project teams, or 'task teams' as they are sometimes known, have taken over from single function teams in tackling complex business problems in many organisations. Our research has already identified such organisations as ICL, Rank Xerox and Eastern Electricity as being well down this road. Distributed information systems will accelerate this tendency, as exemplified in Figure 10.

DECISION SUPPORT SYSTEMS (DSSS)

Perhaps some of the greatest changes in the future will come about as a result of developments in decision support systems. We briefly introduced the concept of DSSs in Chapter 5 (see page 62). One of the problems with DSSs has been that, due to their complexity, they have tended to take a long time to deliver and have attracted the criticism that at best they give results that approximate to the real world at sometime in the past. There is the criticism that the need constantly to feed them with copious amounts of day-to-day data renders them incapable of reaching the levels of responsiveness required by organisations operating at the forefront of competitiveness. The manager/specialist takes the decisions based on the 'support' given by the DSS and there is no arrangement for the DSS automatically to receive feedback on why option 'A' was selected over option 'B'. Therefore the DSS does not 'learn'. Also there was rarely any evaluation of the effectiveness of the 'support' in the fullness of time, presumably because DSSs tend to be used towards the strategic end of the decision-making chain and by the time the strategy is assessed the organisation has moved on a long way.

We can perhaps use the analogy of warfare and the preparation of facilities to support the land battle. There needs to be clear information (or in military terms, intelligence) as to where the battle is going to be fought and therefore where, say, *Jump Jet* airbases are needed during the period when the battle is to be fought. Now, even the simplest of airbases has a significant lead time for its preparation and the fighting 'front' can sometimes move very quickly. Taking the two together, by the time we have prepared our forward airbase the fighting may have moved on and rendered it useless. It is for all these reasons that the military in particular have been keen to sponsor the development of *neural networks*. Neural networks have sought to model the way in which a neuron in the human brain holds and passes information. They are not programmed to do something by a series of software instructions but are taught to 'learn' to do things – only in real time, rather than according to yesterday's programmed rules. For example, if properly trained, they can mimic some things that the brain is very good at, such as detecting identifiable patterns of communication from background noise, so recognising friendly from hostile 'fingerprints' on a battlefield.

When this almost human, or even superhuman, intelligence is applied to our corporate database and information system it can become the dynamic centre of the decision-making process. It does not have to be told what to do, it 'learns' by experience so that it will remember what has gone before and modify its 'support' in the light of current circumstances. It will contain the sum total experience of its organisation and it will truly support all decision-making aspects of the business it serves. It is the very stuff of science fiction stories that take survivors from earth at Armageddon in their life protecting cocoons, taking the decision to awaken them only when they have reached their brave new world.

USE OF ROBOTICS

We have become accustomed to reading about the use of robotics in spacecraft, whether manned or unmanned and many of us will have benefited from the use of terrestrial robots in manufacturing processes that involve an environment that is unfriendly to humans. We have yet to see them move into the everyday life of the family home, although this might be just around the corner. It is possible that developments in neural networks could revolutionise the science of robotics as we know it – the design and development of robots that require little conventional programming but which learn experientially as they go along, like humans.

SOME FUTURE DIRECTIONS FOR HR

Access to better information and the use of more sophisticated techniques for modelling an uncertain future may at last allow HR staff to get ahead of the game – by getting to grips with, say, HR planning. We foresee a far greater emphasis on HR planning in the future, both as part of organisational planning and planning on the wider social, political and economic front.

Developments in competency profiling, matching people to vacancies, now and for the future, and harnessing the power of expert systems, could see dramatic improvements in our ability systematically and without prejudice to produce shortlists for interview, leading to better selection decisions. Similar sorts of approaches could revolutionise the way we identify and analyse our training needs.

INTERNET

Last but by no means least, is the potential of the Internet. Already it has given anyone with a PC and modem, and on payment of a relatively modest fee to connect, access to an enormous amount of information. This ranges from basic, everyday information such as train times, to really sophisticated research information. It already provides the opportunity to view products and buy them at the press of a button. Only recently we located and purchased a specialist book from an American bookseller – it took us a matter of minutes.

The potential for the Internet to change our personal and our business life is almost beyond comprehension. Already e-mail and video conferencing is allowing more and more people to work from home. Similarly we are already seeing education, certainly higher education, being delivered by telephone line and satellite directly into our computers. How long will it be before the majority of shopping for our goods and services will be done from our armchairs – making virtual visits to the supermarket and the department store.

At Newsons Farm, we live in a very rural area and there has been much concern about the closure of livestock markets and the associated need for farmers and their animals to travel further. However, almost certainly, the future lies in the virtual buying and selling of livestock through the

Internet, making livestock markets a relic of the past rather like the horse and cart.

Access to almost limitless amounts of information allows the possibility for all of us to become experts – it also poses horrendous challenges on how to search for and identify that piece or those pieces of information that are particularly relevant to our needs.

CONCLUSION

Information Technology has moved so far and so fast in the last few years that the future can be bounded only by the limits of our imagination. What is certain is that effective information management and IT have the power to free us from the drudgery of many of our mundane activities, for example, through the use of electronic data interchange. Our ability to manage information effectively is tomorrow's competitive advantage if only we are able to harness it and make the conversion. We cannot afford to ignore the technology – we would be abdicating our business responsibilities to the mercies of our competitors.

It is with a certain humility that we write this chapter. Almost as the proverbial ink dries on the paper it is likely that a technological breakthrough has occurred. Our future will be both dominated and liberated by our abilities to handle the power of the information and technology on offer.

Part 2

INTRODUCTION TO STATISTICS

'NUMBERS INTO INFORMATION'

Part 1 of this book is all about how we can use a systems approach to ensure that we have the right information, in the right form at the right time, to enable us to make the most effective decisions. Using statistics, which is essentially a collection of quantitative techniques, is an important part of this process – they can help us interpret and transform a mass of data into information for our decision-making. They play a crucial role in enabling managers and specialists to actually *manage* their information. We have chosen those techniques that we feel will be most useful to the practitioner and tried to present them in a straightforward and understandable form.

In introducing you to the techniques we have tried to keep the theory to the minimum and concentrate on how they can be used. However, in order to use the techniques in the most effective way it is important to understand a little about the rationale and thinking behind them. We have used examples from across the organisation – from the world of marketing, production management, etc – as well as focusing on personnel and training examples. It is becoming increasingly important that we develop a wide understanding of all aspects of our organisations' work and do not become too insular within our own functions. Also, in this edition we include exercises for you to try yourselves (at the end of the Chapters), but with answers provided as well (in Appendix C)!

The first chapters in this part of the book, Chapters 9, 10 and 11, cover what we call descriptive statistics. These are techniques that can be used to help us present information to our bosses, staff, colleagues, shareholders, etc, in ways which they will find most easy to understand. Chapter 12 contains some essential stepping stones to the next chapter. They may seem a little theoretical and, dare we say, heavy going! Please persevere because they are the gateway into the fascinating and very useful techniques of sampling and hypothesis testing which are covered in Chapters 13 and 14 respectively. Chapter 15 addresses the subjects of regression and correlation. Do not be put off by these technical terms – this chapter simply helps us to identify and understand relationships in our data. The following chapter, Chapter 16, as its title – Forecasting and Time Series – suggests is all about helping the manager to look into the future (the modern equivalent of the crystal ball!). Chapter 17 opens up the world of those peculiar numbers – indices – and Chapter 18 introduces the fascinating world of decision-making. Finally, Chapter 19 harnesses the power of the computer to show us how to carry out all these useful statistical techniques without getting bogged down by the algebra and arithmetic.

We hope that these chapters present the techniques in a way you find easy to understand and absorb. However, if a particular section seems a little more difficult, please persevere. We promise you that none of it is too bad and we hope some of it you will find fun!

9 Tabulations

INTRODUCTION

Data, in its **raw** form, often does not readily convey much information and, as managers/specialists, information is what we need to make decisions that are appropriate to the circumstances and produce the outcomes we require from our interventions. You will recall in Chapter 1 that we used the example of absence figures. In their raw form they did not convey much information, however once you started to manipulate them, by showing them as a percentage of working days, they started to provide useful information. In this chapter we will look at a range of techniques, which have as their basis organising the data into tabular format.

To illustrate what we mean, let us take a typical set of data (potential information) that you might come across. For ease of demonstration we have chosen a simple example:

Table 3 Salaries of semi-skilled employees in a small firm

(Number of employees = 20)

Employee	Salary (£)
A	11,000
B	11,500
C	10,500
D	12,500
E	11,500
F	11,000
G	12,500
H	10,000
I	11,000
J	9,500
K	9,000
L	10,500
M	11,000
N	13,500
O	11,500
P	13,000
Q	12,000
R	12,000
S	9,500
T	10,000

What can we infer from this table? Not a lot, other than if we look hard, we see that the lowest salary is £9,000 and the highest is £13,500, and the other salaries are spread out randomly between the lowest and the highest in steps of £500. Indeed, we may ask why we have bothered to set out data in this way anyway? Let us suppose for the moment that the reason is that we wish to establish whether or not the company is paying market rates to its employees. If this was the case we might start by setting out the facts in some sort of table, probably in the order in which it has come from the salaries records. The table used on page 107 has set out the salaries in alphabetical order of employee surname.

ARRAYS

One way in which we can start to get a feel for the information that is locked inside the data is to see how it is distributed or spread between the highest and lowest salaries. To do this we set out the salaries in ascending order of value – forming an **array** in ascending order. (See Table 4.)

(We could have set out the data in an array of descending order, by putting the highest salary first and the lowest

Table 4 Salaries in an array of ascending order

Employee	Salary (£)
K	9,000
J	9,500
S	9,500
H	10,000
T	10,000
C	10,500
L	10,500
A	11,000
F	11,000
I	11,000
M	11,000
B	11,500
E	11,500
O	11,500
Q	12,000
R	12,000
D	12,500
G	12,500
P	13,000
N	13,500

salary last.) Does this start to tell us anything more? Again, not a lot except, perhaps, that more people are paid at the £11,000 salary level than at any other. So, how can we summarise the data to give us more information?

FREQUENCY DISTRIBUTION

One such way is to prepare it as a **frequency distribution**, that is, by showing the number of employees at each salary level: see Table 5.

This way of setting out the data is beginning to tell us, for example, how the most frequently occurring salaries 'bunch' around £11,000–£11,500 and tail off towards the lower and higher salary levels. More people are paid £11,000 than any other salary and we could, if we wished, use this as a crude comparison with another employer to test the competitiveness of our pay rates. It would not be a very efficient comparison because it would show the same result against an organisation, for example, who paid no salary over £11,000 provided that their most 'popular' salary was £11,000.

Now, if there was a large number of salary points it might be helpful to *group* the salaries into salary bands, as shown in Table 6. It is important that there are no gaps between the bands or classes and that they do not overlap. The bands should always be the same size, unless this proves difficult as it sometimes will at the extreme ends of a widely spread distribution.

Table 5 Frequency distribution of salaries

Salary (£)	Frequency
9,000	1
9,500	2
10,000	2
10,500	2
11,000	4
11,500	3
12,000	2
12,500	2
13,000	1
13,500	1
Total	20

Table 6   Grouped salaries

Salary band (£)	Frequency
9,000– 9,999	3
10,000–10,999	4
11,000–11,999	7
12,000–12,999	4
13,000–13,999	2
Total	20

Relative frequency distribution

Are we now at the stage where we can start to compare our salary levels with those of another organisation? We could lay out, or group, their salaries as we have our own. However, what happens if the other organisation, as is quite likely, has a different number of employees? The way to tackle this situation is to look at the *percentages* of the total number of employees in each organisation at certain salary points or in particular salary bands. In this way we would produce a **relative frequency distribution**. Taking our two previous tables (ie Tables 5 and 6), we can produce relative frequency distributions as shown in Table 7.

If we look at the grouped data, that is in the salary bands, we can easily see that about one third of the employees (15% + 20% = 35%) are paid in the range £9,000–£10,999, about one third (35%) are paid in the range £11,000–£11,999 and about one third (20% + 10% = 30%) are paid in the range £12,000–£13,999. We can

Table 7   Relative frequency distribution of salaries

Salary (£)	Frequency	%	Salary band (£)	Frequency	%
9,000	1	5	9,000– 9,999	3	15
9,500	2	10	10,000–10,999	4	20
10,000	2	10	11,000–11,999	7	35
10,500	2	10	12,000–12,999	4	20
11,000	4	20	13,000–13,999	2	10
11,500	3	15	Total	20	100
12,000	2	10			
12,500	2	10			
13,000	1	5			
13,500	1	5			
Total	20	100			

now quite readily make the comparison between our organisation and our competitor(s) in terms of what percentages of their employees fall into the various bands. The answer will give us information on the competitiveness of our salaries.

Cumulative Frequency Distribution

Sometimes it may be helpful to know how many employees earn more than or less than a certain amount. In order to do this we would produce a **cumulative frequency distribution**, as shown in Table 8, for the grouped salaries used in our previous example.

Table 8 Cumulative frequency distribution of salaries

Salary band	Cumulative frequency	Cumulative %
Less than or equal to £ 9,999	3	15
Less than or equal to £10,999	7	35
Less than or equal to £11,999	14	70
Less than or equal to £12,999	18	90
Less than or equal to £13,999	20	100

Looking at our cumulative frequency distribution, we see that 15 per cent of the employees earn less than £10,000, or alternately, 85 per cent (100% − 15%) earn £10,000 or more. 35 per cent earn less than £11,000, 70 per cent earn less than £12,000 and so on. Now we have another good basis on which to make some sort of a comparison of this organisation's salary structure with that of other organisations. Useful information, and for very little effort on our part – certainly no massive amount of number crunching, no complicated formulae around and not a single Greek letter in sight!

Before moving on let us try the following example.

EXAMPLE

Set out below is some data on the ages of employees in a small organisation:

Ages of employees:

25	56	22	53	21	30	30	18	39	43
32	42	35	41	29	35	39	32	37	47
29	38	46	36	17	22	24	16	27	37
35	29	62	34						

What information can be drawn from this data? Where do we start? We could work out the average but, as yet, we do not know what the average is (we will cover averages later, in Chapter 11). For now we will stay with the methods we have discussed already.

Our first approach, again, is to set out a table showing the ages in an array of ascending order of magnitude:

16	17	18	21	22	22	24	25	27	29
29	29	30	30	32	32	34	35	35	35
36	37	37	38	39	39	41	42	43	46
47	53	56	62						

We can then go on to group the data in age ranges, say, with five-year intervals, and show the grouped frequency distribution, the relative frequency distribution and the cumulative frequency distribution – see Table 9.

Now we can begin to understand what the data might actually mean to the organisation. For example, from the table below, we can see that only three of our staff are going

Table 9 Employee ages – relative and cumulative frequency

Ages (years)	No. of employees in age group	Relative frequency %	Cumulative frequency %
Under 20	3	8.8	8.8
20 – 24	4	11.8	20.6
25 – 29	5	14.7	35.3
30 – 34	5	14.7	50.0
35 – 39	9	26.5	76.5
40 – 44	3	8.8	85.3
45 – 49	2	5.9	91.2
50 – 54	1	2.9	94.1
55 – 59	1	2.9	97.0
60 – 64	1	2.9	99.9*
Total	34	99.9*	

*varies from 100% due to rounding

to retire during the next 15 years. If these are managers, what are the implications for the organisation's succession plan? We do not have the problem of a concentration of retirements, possibly leaving the organisation short of experienced people. Instead, we might have the problem, if the future management team is currently in the 30–34 and 35–39 age groups (some 40 per cent of the employees fall in these groups), of employees finding their career advancement is restricted by this bottleneck.

Unless something is done to prevent frustration driving these up-and-coming middle managers to seek advancement by moving to other organisations, we could experience high levels of staff turnover within these middle grades in the not-too-distant future. The intelligent analysis of the age profile may be the first early warning signals that this might be about to occur. Here is an example of an opportunity for the personnel professional to get in early to influence what is happening, rather than being left only to react to the crisis after the event.

Another interesting piece of information to come from the cumulative frequency table is that 35 per cent of the staff are under 30 years of age, 50 per cent under 35 and 76 per cent under 40 – quite a young age profile. What implications might this have for, say, the development of a new benefits package? For example, the staff might be more interested in bonus payments than in pension provision. These issues would not have emerged from looking at the raw age data. We set off with a jumble of numbers and transformed them into useful management information.

CONCLUSION

In this chapter we have looked at ways in which raw data can be converted into meaningful information by setting it out in tabular form of arrays and frequency distributions. By using the relative and the cumulative forms of the distributions we continue this process of further refining our data. It is only when we have carried out this analysis that useful information is brought to light. In the next chapter we go on to look at other ways in which we can present our data so that it contributes to our decision-making process.

EXERCISES

9.1 The following table sets out productivity figures for operatives in a department manufacturing parts for a lighting system. The target levels for performance are 2,501 to 3,000 parts per day.

Parts/day	No. of operatives
2,001–2,250	8
2,251–2,500	2
2,501–2,750	20
2,751–3,000	25
3,001–3,250	3
3,251–3,500	2
	60

Calculate the relative and cumulative frequency distributions and comment on the results.

9.2 A charity offers an advisory service with booked appointments. There have been complaints about waiting time at one of their two offices. The organisation has analysed the time that clients have to wait over a one-week period in both offices:

Time (mins)	Frequency Office 1	Frequency Office 2
<5	1	7
6–10	6	40
11–15	30	35
16–20	26	5
21–25	10	0
26–30	9	0
Total	82	87

Comment on the results.

10 Diagrammatic methods

INTRODUCTION

So far, we have discussed organising the data into tabular form and seen the benefits of this type of presentation in helping us draw out some of the key information messages. However, some people find it easier to understand information displayed in diagrammatic form. This can be a particularly useful approach if the information is being presented to people who are not use to dealing with and understanding figures, eg in a report aimed at general employees or shareholders. Also information presented diagrammatically can make a big impact and is often used when making presentations to groups of people. The saying 'a picture paints a thousand words' is particularly apt as a well chosen and presented diagram will often convey a complex message more simply and succinctly than a mass of figures. This chapter looks at a range of diagrammatic techniques.

BAR DIAGRAM

The simplest technique is the **bar diagram**. Let's look at an example of the use of a bar diagram in a sales situation. Suppose that there are three sales staff and the sales manager wants to keep a check on their progress. The sales manager can compile the monthly sales figures on a tabular basis, as shown in Table 10, setting out the actual sales per month and the relative sales per sales staff as a percentage of the monthly total.

What does this tell the sales manager? Sales are obviously rising sharply month by month but who is actually scoring with the customers. Let's see what happens when we set out these figures in the form of a bar diagram – see Figure 11.

Table 10 Sales performance

	January sales £	%	February sales £	%	March sales £	%	Quarterly total £
Brown	10,000	32	12,000	24	18,000	17	40,000
Jones	9,000	29	18,000	36	50,000	46	77,000
Smith	12,000	39	20,000	40	40,000	37	72,000
Month total	31,000	100	50,000	100	108,000	100	189,000

Figure 11 Bar diagram showing sales performance

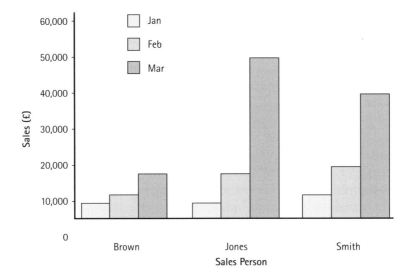

From this *picture* we can see easily that Brown's progress is modest, Smith's results are very good while Jones's results are quite spectacular, starting from the lowest base of £9,000 in January to achieving the highest sales total of £50,000 in March. Well done, Jones!

In a development of the bar diagram principle we could show the monthly sales total by way of a **stacked bar diagram**. In our example we have stacked the sales for each of the sales staff by month, that is the monthly sales of Brown, Smith and Jones are added together and distinguished by colour or different shading, as shown in Figure 12. This has the advantage that it shows the growth in total sales very clearly. We have also shown a quarterly 'stack' as well.

Figure 12 Stacked bar diagram showing sales performance

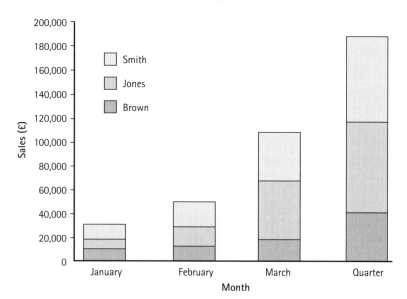

PIE CHARTS

Another useful way of depicting the above information in a relative sense, that is, to show pictorially the relative merits of the sales figures of Brown, Smith and Jones is by use of a **pie chart**. As the name suggests, the total sales are shown as a circle with the sizes of the slices depicting the values of sales for the three staff, as shown in Figure 13.

Figure 13 Pie charts showing monthly sales

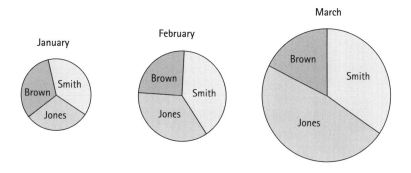

Note how the area of the *pie* reflects the size of the total sales for the month, whereas the area/size of the slice equates to the proportion of total sales achieved by each sales person. In this way, we see at a glance that Jones is actually achieving a rising proportion of a growing monthly sales total.

PICTOGRAMS

One of the really eye-catching ways of presenting statistics is by using pictures instead of bars in our bar diagrams. This is called a **pictogram**. Let's look at some examples:

- Suppose we were a charity and wanted to show fund-raising in different regions of the country. A picture we might use is a symbol depicting a pile of coins, or perhaps the '£' sign or, perhaps, if we were a charity concerned with looking after cats, we might use cats! (Using a cat as a symbol would be a particularly good way of showing the number of cats rehomed, etc.)

- Suppose we want to demonstrate the change in numbers of employees over a period of time. Here a picture we might use is the stickperson.

- Suppose we are a local authority and we want to show how the money we allocated was spent on council services. Here we might use bags of money as our pictorial representation.

Figure 14 Pictogram of funds raised

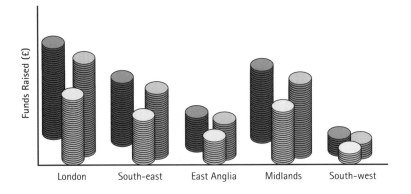

Figure 15 Pictogram showing changes in staffing

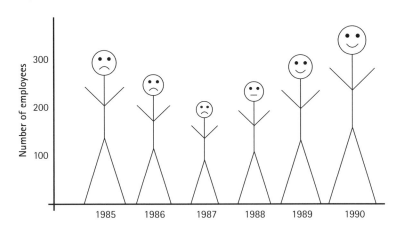

Figure 16 Pictogram showing allocation of income to services

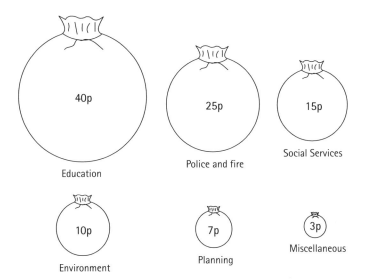

As you will see from Figures 14 and 15, the heights of the pictures represent the numbers involved and are equivalent to the heights of the bars in a bar diagram. In Figure 16 it is the area of the bag (rather like the area of a pie chart) which provides the scale for comparison. It is most important to ensue that the dimensions we have used for comparison are made clear to the reader. With pictograms, there is endless scope for us to use our imagination to provide good *visuals* to help get our message across to our audience – be they specialist and management colleagues or customers or members of the public, etc. Pictograms are of particular use when we are trying to communicate with a wider audience, some of whom may not have a good understanding of the more sophisticated graphical and diagrammatic methods. A good example of the latter is the summary version of Company Annual Report and Accounts produced by large companies for the benefit of their shareholders. However, when producing our pictograms we do not need to take care in judging what the audience would find appropriate to their needs.

HISTOGRAM

One of the best ways of representing a frequency distribution is by means of a **histogram**. Take the following set of data about calls to a switchboard – a sample of the number of calls per hour has been made as a result of concerns about staffing levels.

Table 11 Calls per hour

69	70	73	70	71	71
67	72	71	71	68	73
67	70	74	68	70	70
66	68	67	70	69	69
68	70	72	73	72	71
70	69	69	72	70	73
66	70	72	73	74	68
70	70	73	68	66	67
71	65	68	70	72	70
70	70	68	74	72	71

Once again the raw data does not give us very much useful management information, in fact it is a quite meaningless jumble of figures in its present form. However, we can start to make sense of the data by going through the process described in Chapter 9 of setting out the data in an array of ascending order. From this we can produce a frequency distribution listing the number of hours when '65' calls occurred (that is, 1), then the number of hours when '66' calls occurred (3), then the number of hours when '67' calls occurred (4), and so on to all the hours when '74' calls occurred (3), as shown in Table 12.

Table 12 Frequency distribution of calls per hour

Calls/hour	Frequency of occurrence
65	1
66	3
67	4
68	8
69	5
70	16
71	7
72	7
73	6
74	3
Total	60

By setting out Table 12 in the form of a bar diagram of frequency against calls per hour we get our histogram. The difference between a bar diagram and a histogram is that the data about which we have frequencies is in a quantitative form and must be laid out in the order shown, ie 65 followed by 66, etc. With bar diagrams, the order does not matter – in our earliest example of sales staff's performance it did not matter which order we displayed the sales, we could have

Figure 17 Histogram showing calls per hour

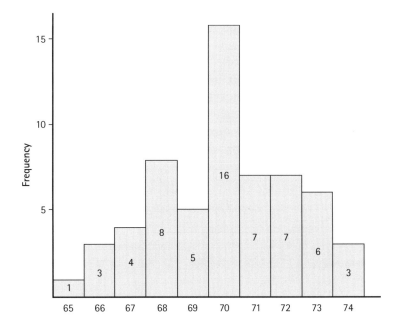

shown Jones first and Brown last (although clearly with time data, it is more helpful to show them in time order). Similarly, with our pictogram of fund-raising the order in which we show the region does not matter, although the organisation may have an order they commonly use.

Our histogram shows the frequency of occurrence of different levels of calls per hour and we can see that the tops of the columns form a sort of graph, rising in the middle and tailing off at both ends. Even now the information is still not leaping out of the page at us, although by inspection you can see that '70' calls per hour occur more often than the other levels, and the level of calls per hour seem to be fairly evenly spread above and below the '70' figure.

How can we take the presentation a step further? Statisticians use the technique previously mentioned of grouping the data. Let us see what happens to our histogram when we group '65' calls per hour with '66' calls per hour, '67' calls per hour with '68' calls per hour, etc, and in addition present our information as relative frequencies, that is, percentages of the total. The information in tabular form is set out below in Table 13. We have to think a little at this stage about the group or class boundaries. Sometimes the real boundaries are the mid-point between the top of the previous class and the bottom of the next class. In our table below, the real boundaries are 64, 66, 68, 70, 72 and 74. When we come to draw our histogram it is sometimes easier just to show classes and other times to show the real boundaries. In the histogram in Figure 18 we have shown both to emphasis this point.

Table 13 Relative frequency distribution of grouped calls per hour

Grouped calls/hour	Frequency	Relative frequency (%)
65–66	4	7
67–68	12	20
69–70	21	35
71–72	14	23
73–74	9	15
Total	60	100

Figure 18   Histogram showing grouped calls per hour

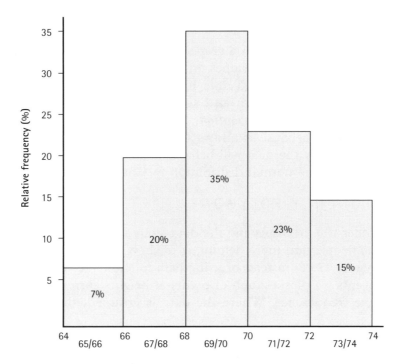

You may be forgiven at this stage for asking what practical significance all the above might have. Well, imagine you are the manager of the switchboard which is receiving the calls data that we have been working on. Assuming that your requirements for staff are in some relationship to the volumes of calls, you could get an indication of the 'right' level of staffing from this exercise. From our grouped data histogram we can see that '65' to '68' levels of calls occurred on 27 per cent of the hours; '69' to '70' calls occurred on 35 per cent of the hours; and '71' to '74' calls occurred on 38 per cent of the hours. As it is often unpredictable as to which are the busy periods and which are the quiet ones and also unlikely that the manager will be able to deploy additional staff at short notice at the busy times, then the grouped data histogram would be of some help. By staffing up to the '69' to '70' sales days the staffing levels would be correct for 35 per cent of the time. For 27 per cent of the time the switchboard would be overstaffed and 38 per cent of the time it would be understaffed – very approximately one third of the hours falling into each category.

Incidentally, the data in a graph or histogram which rises to about the middle then slopes off at about the same rate as it rose, as in our grouped data histogram, is said to have a symmetric distribution and something approaching the celebrated *normal distribution*. Statisticians love a normal distribution because it allows them to make assumptions about the way the data will behave in their calculations. We will look at the normal distribution in Chapter 12.

FREQUENCY POLYGON

Another way of displaying the data from a histogram, which some people find more helpful, is to show it as a **frequency polygon**. Here, instead of using bars to show the frequency of events we plot a graph of points at heights corresponding to the frequencies. Where the data is grouped, the points

Figure 19 Frequency polygon showing grouped calls per hour

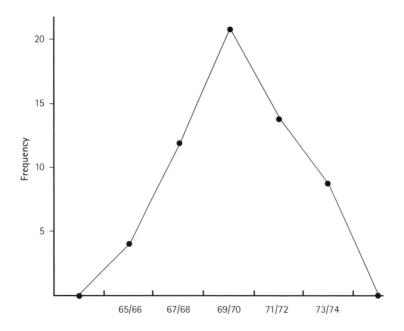

plotted are the group frequencies and are shown above the mid-point of the group intervals, as in Figure 19. In order for our frequency polygon to touch the horizontal (x-axis) we have added groups of zero frequency at both ends of the graph.

OGIVE

Sometimes it is helpful to plot a graph of the cumulative frequency distribution. This is called an **ogive** and here the cumulative frequencies (of occurrences of calls per hour in our example) are plotted on the vertical axis (that is, the y-axis) and the levels of calls per hour along the x-axis. The ogive can be particularly helpful to us in a situation where it is useful to know, for example in the switchboard situation above, the number of hours when the number of calls is equal to or less than a particular figure. We are easily able to draw up a table showing the cumulative frequencies from Table 13 – see Table 14.

To plot an ogive, the cumulative frequency is drawn against the upper boundary of each class, for example, 4 is plotted against 66 on the x-axis, 16 is plotted against 68 on the x-axis, etc. The zero point of our ogive is shown at the lowest boundary, that is, 64. Our ogive is shown as Figure 20.

Coming back to our staffing example in the switchboard, if our manager knew that the staff could cope with up to 70 calls per hour she or he could tell from the cumulative frequency table or the ogive that they would cope on 37 out of the sixty hourly periods. The usefulness of the ogive is that it allows readings from intermediate points, for example, if the manager wanted to staff up to be able to cope with calls

Table 14 Cumulative frequency distribution of grouped calls per hour

Calls/hour	Cumulative frequency
Less than or equal to 66 units	4
Less than or equal to 68 units	16
Less than or equal to 70 units	37
Less than or equal to 72 units	51
Less than or equal to 74 units	60

Figure 20 Ogive showing cumulative frequency of calls per hour

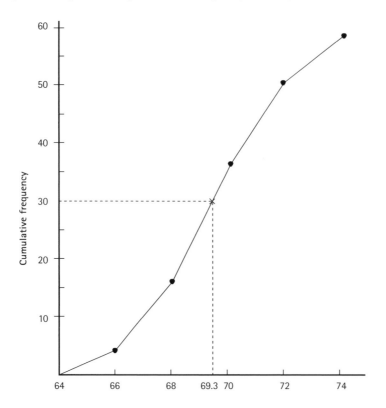

on half of the hourly periods, she or he could read across the ogive curve from the cumulative frequency of 30 to give a result of 69.3. Therefore if she or he staffed up to deal with 69 calls per hour, then for about half of the time the switchboard would cope. This is a particularly useful facility if the groupings are larger than those used in our example. Of course, the intermediate points could have been worked out from the table, but it is a lot easier to read off from a graph and certainly easier to communicate from this particular picture in, say, a presentation to colleagues.

GRAPHS

Last but not least is the diagrammatic method that is probably most familiar to us – the **line graph**. These are most frequently used to show changes in data over time.

Figure 21 Graph of training expenditure per employee over time

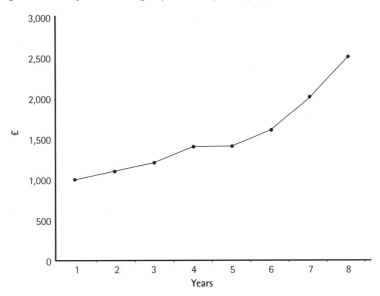

Figure 21 shows the change in training expenditure per employee. It shows very clearly that there was a steady growth in the early years, expenditure plateaued in Year 4 and then rose rapidly thereafter.

Figure 22 Scatter diagram and regression line of training score versus on-the-job scores

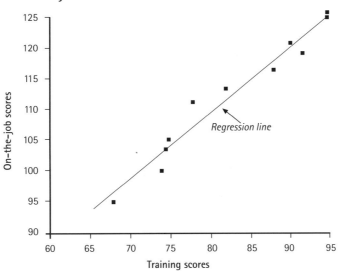

Line graphs can also be used to show relationships between variables. Continuing with the training theme Figure 22 shows a **scatter diagram** plotting the scores of delegates in tests carried out in the training session against the results in on-the-job performance tests. Each point represents a delegate. We are looking to see if there is a relationship between the two types of test – whether training test results are a good predictor of on-the-job performance. It is possible to fit a straight line through the scatter of points – called a regression line, which will give us information on the relationship. We will discuss this approach in depth in Chapter 15.

CONCLUSION

We have demonstrated how the picture, by way of diagrammatic and graphical methods, can paint a thousand words. We have covered the bar diagram, pie chart, pictogram, histogram, frequency polygon, ogive and line graphs for this purpose, hopefully showing how easy it is to present the data in these ways. In the next chapter we go on to look at the ways in which numerical methods can help provide management information for the decision-makers.

EXERCISES

10.1 A training programme has been carried out and the delegates were asked to comment on the quality of the tutor, with the following results.

	Very Good	Good	Fair	Poor	Total
Knowledgeable	15	5	0	0	20
Appropriate pace	0	4	12	4	20
Creates interest	10	5	4	1	20
Involves the group	1	8	7	4	20

Present the results diagrammatically and comment on them.

10.2 You have been asked to prepare an eye-catching presentation to staff. You have to convey the following information over a five-year period.

- no. of days lost through accidents

- consumption of water

- administration costs

- staff turnover.

Explain briefly your choices for the presentation.

10.3 Currently all staff have their own desk in the sales department. The department is a mix of staff who spend much of their time out selling and administration staff who are largely desk bound. As pressure on space increases, the organisation decides to investigate the concept of 'hot desking', ie staff sharing desk space in the department, and has conducted an initial survey of the time spent by staff at their desks during a day:

The following data was collected:

Hours spent at their desks

1.3	4.6	2.0	0.8	7.5	2.6	6.2	7.8	2.8	5.3
8.4	1.5	3.5	7.0	2.6	9.3	1.9	3.9	6.3	1.1
7.2	0.9	2.8	6.6	3.3					

Summarise this data by producing:

- a frequency distribution

- a relative frequency distribution

- a cumulative frequency distribution

- a histogram.

Comment on the results.

11 Numerical methods

INTRODUCTION

So far, so good, but what about all the figure work that statistics is supposed to be about? Where are all those calculations and formulae with all those funny Greek letters that are so confusing to the non-statistician? Well, in Chapters 9 and 10 we covered ways of presenting and summarising data using tables and then diagrams and graphs. Both these methods are very useful in illustrating points you may wish to make in a report or as visual aids in a presentation. However, numerical methods are sometimes very effective in summarising data and become particularly valuable when the data is a sample from which you wish to draw inferences about the overall population. We will come onto this very exciting subject of sampling in Chapter 13, but for the moment let's get back to our numerical methods.

There are usually two aspects of a *data set* which will interest us. The most common are indications of the *middle* or *average* value of the data set – referred to as **measures of location**. The second type are concerned with the spread or variability of the data – referred to as **measures of dispersion**.

MEASURES OF LOCATION

There are three main measures of location with which you will need to become familiar – the mean (sometimes called the arithmetic mean or average), the median and the mode. The first is probably the most widely used. These are all measures of the *middle* part of the data.

Mean
The **mean (or average)** is obtained by adding together all the individual items of data and then dividing by the number of items in the data set. Let us look at a simple extract from

one of our earlier examples. Do you remember the monthly sales figures of Brown, Jones and Smith? Here are their January sales figures again to remind you:

Table 15 Sales performance for January

Sales staff	Sales (£)
Brown	10,000
Jones	9,000
Smith	12,000
Total	31,000

Some organisations measure the performance of their sales people by comparing individual monthly sales figures with the mean for all the sales staff. The mean of the January sales figures is obtained by adding up the totals for each sales person and dividing by the number of data items, in this case three, to get a mean of £10,333. The statisticians have a beautiful way of complicating this simple principle. They say, let x_1, x_2 ... x_n be the individual values of a data set with 'n' points in it, then the mean is calculated by the following formula:

$$\text{Mean} = \frac{x_1 + x_2 \ldots + x_n}{n}$$

A mathematical notation which is commonly used by the statisticians to indicate 'the sum of individual data items' is the Greek letter Σ (capital sigma), so, for example:

$$\sum_{i=1}^{5} x_i = x_1 + x_2 + x_3 + x_4 + x_5$$

x_i is a typical data item and the terms 'i = 1' and '5' below and above the sigma indicate the range of data items to be summed, ie from one to five. This formula can be generalised to any range of values, eg 'n':

$$\sum_{i=1}^{n} x_i = x_1 + x_2 \ldots + x_n$$

and the mean, therefore $= \sum\limits_{i=1}^{n} \dfrac{x_i}{n}$

We now have a formula which we can use with any data set.

Here we must pause for a moment and introduce the concept of a population and a sample. A **population** is defined as being a collection of all items in which we are interested. For example, if we are marketing managers interested in promoting the sales of cosmetics in the UK – our population of interest could be all women in the UK over the age of 14. Alternatively, the production manager in a factory making radios could be interested in quality control. His or her population here would be the total production of radios. A **sample** is a portion of the population selected to represent the whole. Going back to our examples, we might choose a sample of, say, 500 women aged over 14 and find out what cosmetics they use. Our Production Manager might choose a sample of, say, 100 radios and test to see how many were defective. We would then use the results from our sample to tell us about the population as a whole.

We will return to this fascinating subject of sampling in Chapter 13. However, it is useful to come to grips with some conventions at this stage. The mean of a population (with N values) is usually referred to by the Greek letter 'mu', written μ. The mean of a sample (with n values) is represented by the symbol $\bar{x}$ (called x bar). The means for a population and sample are calculated using the same formula – as shown earlier.

Let us take another example to reinforce the message. Table 16 sets out the sales figures for a company over a period of twelve years. What is the mean (average) sales for the period?

Table 16 **Company sales**

Year	Sales (£000)	Year	Sales (£000)
1	100	7	250
2	200	8	200
3	250	9	100
4	300	10	250
5	250	11	300
6	150	12	150

Substituting this data into our formula we have:

$$\text{Mean} = \sum_{i=1}^{n} \frac{x_i}{n}$$

$$= \frac{x_1 + x_2 + x_3 + x_4 + x_5 + x_6 + x_7 + x_8 + x_9 + x_{10} + x_{11} + x_{12}}{12 \text{ (the number of years)}}$$

$$= \frac{2{,}500}{12}$$

$$= 208.333$$

Therefore the average sales per year is £208,333.

What happens if our data is presented in the form of a frequency distribution, for example, the visitors to a hotel were asked to rate the hotel on quality of service on a scale of 1 (poor quality) to 6 (excellent quality):

Table 17 **Ratings for hotel**

Rating	Number of delegates
1	0
2	2
3	3
4	10
5	12
6	3
Total	30

Using our previous formula:

$$\text{Mean} = \sum_{i=1}^{n} \frac{x_i}{n}$$

$$= \frac{2 + 2 + 3 + 3 + 3 + 4 + 4 + 4 + 4 + 4 + 4 + 4 + 4 + 4 + 4}{30} \text{ and so on}$$

Clearly the quick way to calculate this is:

$$= \frac{0 \times 1 + 2 \times 2 + 3 \times 3 + 10 \times 4 + 12 \times 5 + 3 \times 6}{30}$$

$$= \frac{131}{30}$$

$$= 4.4$$

The formula we are using is mean

$$= \frac{n_1 \times x_1 + n_2 \times x_2 + n_3 \times x_3 + n_4 \times x_4 + n_5 \times x_5 + n_6 \times x_6}{6}$$

where the 'n' values are the frequencies and the 'x' values are the ratings, so,

$$\text{Mean} = \sum_{i=1}^{6} \frac{n_i x_i}{6}$$

This can be generalised to:

$$\text{Mean} = \sum_{i=1}^{n} \frac{n_i x_i}{n}$$ where n_i is the frequency of that value of x_i summed over the range 1 to n.

The process is just the same when we have grouped date. For example, suppose the age distribution of purchasers of a particular product is given in Table 18.

We can treat the percentages just like frequency data, with the total, ie n, as 100. The complication comes because we do not know how the ages are distributed through the

Table 18 Purchasers

Age categories	Percentage of purchasers
20–29	15
30–39	60
40–49	25
Total	100

categories. So, we make an assumption that they are distributed evenly through the categories and take the mid-point as our x_i value. The midpoint of the $20-29$ category is $(20 + 29) \div 2 = 24.5$, $30-39$ category is 34.5 and so on. Therefore:

$$\text{Mean} = \frac{15 \times 24.5 + 60 \times 34.5 + 25 \times 44.5}{100}$$

$$= 35.5$$

The average, or mean, is fairly familiar to most of us. We can use it, if we wish, following on from our previous examples to compare the sales of two or more different products over a period of time, or the effectiveness of different training programmes.

The mean is a useful way of comparing two sets of data provided that the data has a symmetric distribution. If the distribution of the data is not symmetric but is bunched up at one end or the other, it is said to be **skewed**. When data is skewed it is helpful to use another measure of location, the median, to help with our comparison.

Median

The **median** is probably the second most commonly used measure of location after the mean. It is the value falling in the middle when the data items are arranged in an array of either ascending or descending order. If there is an odd number of items, the median is the value of the middle item. If there is an even number of items, the median is obtained by taking the mid-point of the two middle items, ie calculating the mean of the two middle points.

Let us look at an example, suppose the results of a skills test for a group of engineering trainees are as shown in Table 19 (the trainees have been listed in order of lowest to highest results):

Table 19 Test results

Trainee	Score on skills test out of 100
1	10
2	15
3	65
4	65
5	70
6	70
7	75 ← MEDIAN
8	75
9	75
10	80
11	80
12	85
13	90
Total	855
Mean	855/13 = 65.8

If you look at the mean figure of 65.8, this suggests reasonable performance on the part of the trainees – however, if you scan the individual scores it is quite clear that the majority of trainees have in fact done very well, 11 out of 13 achieving scores of over 65 and over half achieving scores of 70 or above. The median score of 75 gives a much better flavour of the overall performance. The mean score is being affected by two very low scores – the distribution of scores is skewed towards the top of the range.

We could also use this method to compare the competitiveness of the salaries in different organisations. Let us set out the salary data for each organisation in an array of ascending order, as shown in Table 20.

Using the median as a way of comparing the competitiveness of salaries in the three organisations, Organisation 1 with a median of £11,200 ((10,900 + 11,500) ÷ 2) is the most attractive compared with £10,115 for Organisation 2 and £8,450 ((8,200 + 8,700) ÷ 2) for Organisation 3. To refine this comparison further we can calculate the **upper** and **lower quartiles** and use these together with the medians to make further comparisons between the three organisations. The upper quartile is that

Table 20 Comparison of salary data

Organisation 1 £		Organisation 2 £		Organisation 3 £	
6,000		7,145		3,260	
6.475		7,300		3,365	
6,900		7,465		3,704	
7,125		7,533		5,703	
7,436	◀ Lower quartile 7,968	8,400		5,900	
8,500		8,950	◀ Lower quartile 8,950	6,104	
9,636		9,104		6,236	◀ Lower quartile 6,236
9,700		9,636		7,000	
10,500		9,745		7,124	
10,900	◀ Median 11,200	9,800		7,236	
11,500		10,115	◀ Median 10,115	7,438	
12,000		11,651		8,000	
12,265		11,832		8,200	◀ Median 8,450
12,500		12,014		8,700	
12,600	◀ Upper quartile	12,125		8,715	
12,600	12,600	12,446	◀ Upper quartile 12,446	9,300	
13,000		12,608		9,816	
13,700		13,032		10,230	
14,500		13,500		11,363	
17,343		13,700		12,140	◀ Upper quartile
		13,950		12,500	12,140
				12,600	
				12,716	
				12,999	
				13,200	
				14,600	

value, in an array of numbers, above which one-quarter of the values fall and three-quarters fall below. The lower quartile is the value, in an array, above which three-quarters of the values fall and one-quarter of the numbers fall below. The upper and lower quartiles give us information about the upper and lower parts of the data, as opposed to the middle part. Using the median, the upper quartile and the lower quartile we get three benchmarks with which to compare the salaries (or any other data we wish to compare) in the three organisations. In our example:

	Organisation 1 £	Organisation 2 £	Organisation 3 £
Lower quartile	7,968	8,950	6,236
Median	11,200	10,115	8,450
Upper quartile	12,600	12,446	12,140

Does this tell us anything more? What it does show is that the salaries of Organisation 2 are the best or most competitive at the lower levels (the lower quartile) with the salaries of Organisation 3 trailing well behind at that level. The salaries of Organisation 1 are the best at the middle levels and, while Organisation 1 and Organisation 2 are both more competitive than Organisation 3 at the upper levels, there is little to chose between them at this level. Published salary surveys use medians and quartiles to present their information.

We can if we wish take this measure of location further – by looking at **percentiles** and **deciles**. Percentiles divide the range of data in the array into 100ths. Expressed in this way the median is the 50th percentile, the upper quartile in an ascending array is the 75th percentile and the lower quartile is the same as the 25th percentile. Deciles are simply percentiles ranged in groups of ten. The first decile in an ascending array has 10 per cent of the values below it and 90 per cent above it. The second decile has 20 per cent of the values below it and 80 per cent above it, and so on. Quartiles, deciles and percentiles are all measures of location that tell us about different parts of the data set, other than the middle area.

Mode

The final measure of location that we shall consider is the **mode**. This is another measure of the middle area of the data. The mode is the term given to the value that occurs with the greatest frequency in our data set. In the switchboard example given in Chapter 10, the most commonly occurring number of calls is '70' with 16 occurrences, so this is the mode for that data set.

So, by using the mean (average), median, quartiles, percentiles, deciles and mode we can compare the data on different organisations or machines or anything else we care to choose, and locate the benchmarks for our comparisons with as much precision as we like. One final thing to remember about the mean, median and the mode is that, when the distribution of the data is symmetric, they are the same for all practical purposes. It is only when the distribution is skewed that they differ.

MEASURES OF DISPERSION

When we have obtained our data it is sometimes important to know how variable or dispersed the data values are. Take a simple example – you are a manufacturer and have a machine which is vital to your production process. You have a choice of two service agents, both of whom say that, on average, they will repair a machine breakdown in four hours. You have been caught by these vague statements before so, with the benefit of having read this book, you ask for evidence of their actual repair times for, say, a sample of the most recent 20 call-outs. The data you receive is as follows:

Table 21   **Repair times**

Agent A	Repair time (hours)	5, 4, 3, 4, 3, 5, 4, 4, 4, 5, 3, 4, 3, 3, 4, 4, 4, 5, 5, 4.
Agent B	Repair time (hours)	3, 4, 5, 5, 2, 7, 5, 4, 3, 5, 4, 2, 6, 4, 4, 5, 3, 4, 3, 2.

By substituting these values in our formula we can calculate the mean for each data set

$$\text{Mean, } \bar{x} = \sum_{i=1}^{n} \frac{x_i}{n} = \sum_{i=1}^{20} \frac{x_i}{20} = \frac{80}{20} = 4$$

(Remember $\sum_{i=1}^{20} x_i$ is simply the sum of all the 20 values of x_i ie the repair times.)

So neither agent is breaking the trades description legislation and we have nothing to choose between them based on the mean. However, when we set out the data as histograms (see Chapter 10), the results are shown in Figures 23 and 24.

Now, we can distinguish between the service provided by the two agents. If we look at Agent B, while it may be useful to have our machine repaired in two hours on 15 per cent of occasions it might be totally unacceptable to have to wait for six hours for 5 per cent of the time and seven hours for 5 per cent of the time. So, Agent A is the one for us. It

Figure 23   Histogram of repair times for Agent A

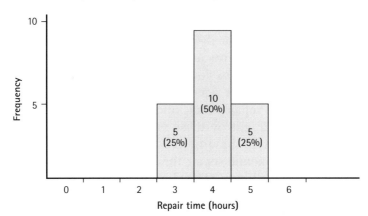

Figure 24   Histogram of repair times for Agent B

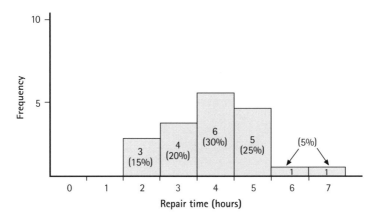

is the dispersion of the data that has allowed us to differentiate between the two agencies.

The simplest measure of dispersion is the **range**. The range for a set of data is the arithmetic difference between the highest and the lowest value. In our example above the range of repair times for Agent A is 5 − 3 = 2 hours. The range of repair times for Agent B is 7 − 2 = 5 hours. The data for Agent B is dispersed over a wider range than that of Agent A and, apart from allowing us to decide which service best suits our needs, the significance of a wide or narrow range of data will be discussed later. We will come back to it in Chapter 13 when we cover sampling and the drawing of inferences. Another similar measure of dispersion is the **inter-quartile range** – the arithmetic difference between the upper and lower quartiles – which gives an indication of the spread of the mid-50 per cent of the data set.

The range is a perfectly adequate measure of dispersion for many purposes but falls down as a vehicle to assess our data when, for example, there are *rogue* values at the top or bottom of the range which are some distance removed from the other values. In these cases the measures of dispersion called the **variance** and **standard deviation** are much more useful than the range.

Both of these are measures of how *dispersed the data is about the mean*. To calculate them we work through the following steps:

1. First find the *mean* of the data set in the usual way by adding up all the values in the data set and dividing this by the number of values (N for a population and n for sample). For Agent A and Agent B above the mean is the same, $80 \div 20 = 4$.

2. Subtract each value from the mean to get the *deviation* from the mean.

3. Then *square* the deviations to get rid of the minus signs as we are only interested in the size of the deviation and not whether it is positive or negative.

4. Add together the squares and divide the sum by the number of values in the case of a population (N) and by the number of values minus 1 for a sample (n − 1). We are finding the *average of the squared deviations*. In our example we divide the sum by $20 - 1 = 19$, as it is a sample. We now have the *variance* of the data.

5. As we had previously squared the deviations we now take the *square root* to obtain the *standard deviation*.

Expressed as a formula, where $x_1 \ldots x_N$ are the values of the population and μ the population mean:

Variance of a population, usually referred to as σ^2,

$$= \sum_{i=1}^{N} \frac{(x_i - \mu)^2}{N}$$

Standard deviation of a population, referred to as σ,

$$= \sqrt{\sum_{i=1}^{N} \frac{(x_i - \mu)^2}{N}}$$

Similarly the formulae for a sample set, where $x_1 \ldots x_n$ are the values of the sample and $\bar{x}$ the sample mean:

Variance of a sample, usually referred to as s^2,

$$= \sum_{i=1}^{n} \frac{(x_i - \bar{x})^2}{n-1}$$

Standard deviation of a sample, referred to as s,

$$= \sqrt{\sum_{i=1}^{n} \frac{(x_i - \bar{x})^2}{n-1}}$$

These variances and standard deviations are not hard to calculate but to do it by hand is rather time consuming and tedious. However, you will pleased to hear that most well-known statistical packages will do the calculations for you, almost at a press of a button. In Chapter 19, we describe how you can use a spreadsheet package, Microsoft Excel™, to calculate a range of descriptive statistics including the mean, median, mode, variance and standard deviations for a data set.

Returning to our example of the two repair agents, the results look like this: the standard deviation for A is 0.73 and 1.34 for B. So, we could say the data on Agent B is about twice as dispersed as that for Agent A.

The standard deviation will be put to further practical use when we come to Chapters 12, 13 and 14 when we cover sampling and hypothesis testing. In our example above, we could have come to the conclusion that B is more dispersed than A, simply by inspecting the data. However, when we have hundreds or thousands of items of data, or a large number of comparisons to be made, we need a calculation to reduce the problem to a single numerical value, hence our use of the standard deviation.

CONCLUSION

In this chapter we have started to get to grips with some of the number crunching. We have also met our first Greek letters. We have looked at measures of location (mean, median, mode, quartiles, deciles and percentiles) and measures of dispersion, (range, inter-quartile range, variance and standard deviation) and seen how they can be used to compare different sets of data. We will see that the standard deviation is very useful in many statistical techniques and will return to it in several of the following chapters.

EXERCISES

11.1 An organisation has carried out an employee satisfaction survey. Staff were asked to rate their satisfaction on a scale of one to 100 on three aspects:

- interesting and stimulating work

- opportunities for training and development

- effectiveness of their manager.

The results for two departments and the organisation as a whole is as follows:

	Department A	Department B	Whole Organisation
Interesting and stimulating work	Mean: 50 Standard deviation: 15	Mean: 75 Standard deviation: 4	Mean: 63 Standard deviation: 9
Opportunities for training and development	Mean: 65 Standard deviation: 6	Mean: 60 Standard deviation: 11	Mean: 67 Standard deviation: 8
Effectiveness of their manager	Mean: 58 Standard deviation: 4	Mean: 68 Standard deviation: 5	Mean: 60 Standard deviation: 9

Comment on the results.

11.2 A small chain of fashion shops has done a survey of its customers' incomes. The results for the three shops in the chain are set out below.

	Shop Suzi £	Shop Cecile £	Shop Marie £
Lower quartile	9,540	6,150	14,330
Median	12,660	12,220	17,500
Upper quartile	15,630	18,430	22,600

Comment on the results and the implications for the business.

12 Introduction to probability and probability distributions

INTRODUCTION

The word **probability** usually strikes fear into the hearts of the bravest non-mathematicians/statisticians. However, it is a concept of vital importance to the manager/specialist and one which he or she will use knowingly or unknowingly almost every working day. We are faced all the time with the need to make decisions that involve uncertainty (see Chapter 1). Situations regularly crop up such as:

- Should we invest in a new factory, and what is the likely effect on profitability?

- What is the likelihood that our employees will settle for a 7 per cent wage increase?

- What is the likelihood that a price decrease will boost sales?

Probability is a measure of uncertainty – a measure of the chance or likelihood that a particular event may occur. It is expressed on a scale of zero to one. If the probability is close to zero then the event is very unlikely to take place; if it is close to one then it is very likely to take place. If the probability is 0.5 then the event is equally likely or unlikely to take place.

We will also talk about **probability distributions**, however only to introduce you to the **normal distribution**, which is key to our understanding and ability to use sampling approaches.

EXPERIMENTS AND OUTCOMES

To get information on probabilities we carry out experiments or, in the business world, activities such as market research. Let us stay for a while with the concept of an experiment. An experiment will have outcomes and here are some examples:

Experiment	*Outcome*
Toss a coin	Head, tail
Throw a dice	1, 2, 3, 4, 5, 6
Make a sales call	Sale, no sale
Inspect a product	Perfect, imperfect

An outcome is often referred to as a **sample point** and all possible outcomes are the **sample space**. Take the example of tossing the coin:

Sample space: head, tail
           ↑   ↑
    sample point sample point

Now consider a more complex example, where we toss a coin twice. A graphical way to help us think about this is a **tree diagram**:

Figure 25　Tree diagram – tossing a coin twice

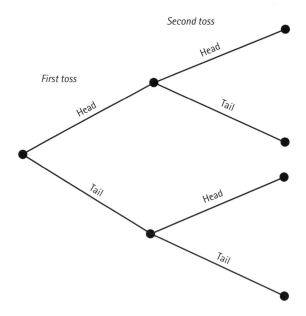

Outcomes, or sample points, of this experiment are:

      head, head
      head, tail
      tail, head
      tail, tail

These four sample points form the sample space.

The basic *rules of probability* are as follows:

• Probability values lie between zero and one.

• The sum of all the probability values associated with the outcomes of an experiment must be one.

EXPERIMENTAL OUTCOMES AND THEIR PROBABILITIES

Associated with each experimental outcome is the probability of it occurring. There are three basic methods of assigning a probability to an experimental outcome, namely: the classical method; the relative frequency method and the subjective method.

The classical method

The **classical method** is based on the assumption that each outcome is equally likely. Good examples of this are tossing a coin and throwing a dice. When tossing a coin the probability of getting a head or tail is equally likely and as there are only two possible outcomes the probability is ½, or 0.5, of getting a head or a tail. With the dice there are six outcomes, each equally likely. Therefore the probability of getting a particular number is ⅙, or 0.17. In our experiment of tossing a coin twice there are four outcomes and therefore the probability of getting a particular outcome is ¼ or 0.25.

The relative frequency method

The **relative frequency method** is based on conducting an experiment or test to assess probable values. For example, suppose you are testing a product to see if it is perfect or defective. Suppose we take a sample, say 100 items chosen at **random**, test them and find that 90 are perfect and 10 are defective. (By random, we mean chosen such that every member of the population is equally likely to be a member of the sample, independently of which other members of the population are chosen; more of this in Chapter 13.) The proportion of defective items in the sample is 10/100, or

0.1. If the ratio of defective to perfect items in the sample is the same as in the overall population then we could infer that the probability of finding defective items overall is 0.1.

The subjective method

The **subjective method** is, as the name suggests, where you make a best guess, based on examining the available information. Thus, the probability of a horse winning a race might be assessed as having a probability of 0.5 by one punter, but 0.4 by another reader of the form book. The subjective method reflects the individual's beliefs or expertise.

EVENTS AND THEIR PROBABILITIES

An *event* is a collection of outcomes or sample points. For example, an event would be the probability of getting at least one head showing in two tosses of a coin. Looking back at our tree diagram in Figure 25 the event, obtaining at least one head, would include the following outcomes:

head, head
head, tail
tail, head

but not tail, tail as this outcome contains no heads.

The probability of a particular event is equal to the sum of the probabilities of the sample points in the event, that is:

the probability of getting at least one head in two tossings of the coin
= the probability of getting head, head (that is, ¼)
+ the probability of getting head, tail (that is, ¼)
+ the probability of getting tail, head (that is, ¼)
= ¼ + ¼ + ¼
= ¾ or 0.75.

So, if we toss a single coin there is the probability of 0.5 that it will come down heads. By doubling our chances, that is, by tossing the coin twice, we increase the probability of achieving one head to 0.75 – doubling the chance only increases the probability by 50 per cent. Can you think of a practical example of this principle? What about having a night watchman whose two states are to be awake or asleep and these are equally likely. If we need a watchman awake more than 50 per cent of the time we have the probability of a watchman being awake for 75 per cent of the time if we employ two watchmen each night. (There are undoubtedly better ways of ensuring an awake watchman but we won't go into them just now!) Let's look at a more realistic example. Suppose as a company we have a 50 per cent chance of winning any contract – perhaps we have only one other competitor, which is of similar capability to ourselves. If we tender for two contracts we would have a 75 per cent chance of winning one.

RANDOM VARIABLE

A **random variable** is a numerical description that defines the outcome of an experiment or test. For any experiment, a random variable can be defined such that each possible outcome generates one, and only one, value of the random variable. Examples of random variables are:

Experiment	Random Variable	Possible Values of Random Variable
Test a production run of 100 cars	Number of defective cars found	0, 1, 2, ... 100
Observe length of a queue	Number of people in the queue	0, 1, 2, etc
Measure times of a production activity	Length of time taken to carry out production activity	2 mins 50 secs, 3 mins, 4 mins, etc

A random variable can be described as discrete or continuous depending on the sort of numerical values it takes on. A **discrete random variable** is one that takes on a finite number of values (say, 1 to 5) or an infinite sequence (say, 1, 2, 3, etc). Examples are number of units sold, numbers of customers, etc. A **continuous random variable** can take on an infinite number of values in an interval, for example percentages, time, weight, distance. Let's look at the specific example of the random variable of employees' heights. An interval could be defined as all heights between 200 and 220 cm. As an individual's height can theoretically be measured to a very high degree of accuracy, for example, 210.679438 ... cm, then we can see (we hope) that there is an infinite number of values in this interval.

PROBABILITY DISTRIBUTIONS

A **probability distribution** for a random variable describes how the probabilities are distributed or spread over the various values that the random variable can assume. Probability distributions provide the bedrock to the theory and understanding of the vitally useful process known as **statistical inference**, and in particular estimation and significance testing. These are covered in the next two chapters.

Let's look at a simple example to help you understand what a probability distribution is. Suppose we are interested in having information on the number of times per month people eat out in a restaurant. Perhaps we are contemplating opening a restaurant in the area and our bank manager wants some evidence on local trade before giving us a bank loan. Let's assume we selected 200 people at random and interviewed them to obtain this data. The results of our survey are set out in Table 22.

The table below describes a probability distribution of a discrete random variable – in other words, a **discrete probability distribution** and it can be shown diagrammatically, as in Figure 26.

Table 22 Probability distribution for eating out

Random variable (No. of times eaten out in a restaurant during last month)	Frequency (No. of people who ate out this number of times)	Probability (of people eating out this number of times)
0	20	20/200 = 0.10
1	80	80/200 = 0.40
2	50	50/200 = 0.25
3	40	40/200 = 0.20
4	10	10/200 = 0.05
	200	1.00

Figure 26 Probability distribution for dining out in a restaurant in a month

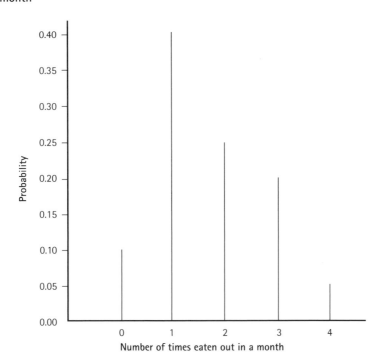

It is quite straightforward to calculate measures of location and dispersion of random variables. It is very similar to the work we did in the chapter on numerical methods where we were manipulating data. If we take the values of a random variable as x_1, x_2, x_3...x_n, with the associated probabilities as $p(x_1)$, $p(x_2)$, $p(x_3)$...$p(x_n)$ then:

Mean of a random variable x (often referred to as the *expected value*)

$$= x_1\, p(x_1) + x_2\, p(x_2)...x_n p(x_n)$$

$$= \sum_{i=1}^{n} x_i\, p(x_i)$$

Variance of a random variable x

$$= (x_1 - \text{mean})^2\, p(x_1) + (x_2 - \text{mean})^2\, p(x_2)...$$
$$(x_n - \text{mean})^2\, p(x_n)$$

$$= \sum_{i=1}^{n} (x_i - \text{mean})^2\, p(x_i)$$

which can be simplified to:

$$= \sum_{i=1}^{n} x_i^2 \, p(x_i) - \text{mean}^2$$

The standard deviation = √variance

Using our previous example:

Mean value of the random variable (the number of times people eat out each month)

$$= (0 \times 0.10) + (1 \times 0.40) + (2 \times 0.25) + (3 \times 0.20)$$
$$+ (4 \times 0.05) \text{ (from Table 22)}$$
$$= 0.4 + 0.5 + 0.6 + 0.2$$
$$= 1.7$$

In other words, on average people eat out 1.7 times each month. However, eating out is a discrete random variable as we can't actually eat out 0.7 or 1.7 times per month. The people in our sample actually eat out on average between once and twice per month.

Using our earlier example again and our simplified formula:

The variance of the random variable (the number of times people eat out each month):

$$= (0^2 \times 0.10) + (1^2 \times 0.40) + (2^2 \times 0.25) + (3^2 \times 0.20) + (4^2 \times 0.05) - 1.7^2$$

(Take note of where the figures in the above equation have come from. The probabilities 'p' came from the Table 22 and the mean 1.7 came from the earlier calculation.)

Continuing with the calculation:

Variance   = 0 + 0.4 + 1.0 + 1.8 + 0.8 − 2.89
           = 1.11

Standard   = √variance
deviation   = √1.11
           = 1.054

There are a number of discrete probability distributions, for example, the binomial distribution. However, we will not cover these here but move onto the next type of probability distributions – those for continuous random variables.

CONTINUOUS PROBABILITY DISTRIBUTION

A continuous random variable may assume any value in an interval, for example, weight, distance, time, etc. All of these can take on values of infinite numbers of decimal points, depending on how accurately you wish to measure them. When we talked about a discrete random variable we defined the probability distribution as something which told us the probability of the random variable assuming a particular value. The equivalent expression for a continuous random variable is a **probability density function** for reasons which will become clear later in this section.

In order to illustrate the concept of a continuous probability distribution, we will use the simple example of a **uniform distribution**. Suppose you have a delivery lorry which travels from London to Cardiff. Assume that the journey time can take any value between 150 minutes and 200 minutes. If the probability of a journey time falling in any one-minute interval is the same, that is, it is equally likely to fall between 160 and 161 minutes, or between 174 and 175 minutes, and so on, then it is said to have a uniform distribution. Since there are 50 one-minute intervals, all of which are equally likely, then the probability of the journey time falling in any one-minute interval is 1/50. Now let us look at this distribution in graphical form as shown in Figure 27.

What is the probability of the journey time falling between 150 and 175 minutes? Intuitively, since this falls halfway

Figure 27 Uniform probability density function for journey times

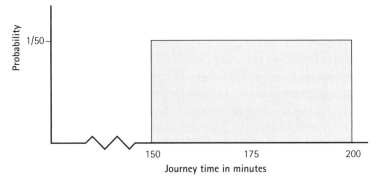

along the total range, we feel that the probability might be ½. Alternatively, as budding statisticians we can use the probability formula from page 148:

The probability of an event = the sum of the probabilities of the constituent outcomes

Probability of a journey time between 150 and 175 minutes p(150–175)

$$= p(150–151) + p(151–152)$$
$$+ p(152–153)...$$
$$+ p(174–175)$$
$$= 25 \times \frac{1}{50}$$
$$= \frac{1}{2} \text{ (just as our intuition suggested)}.$$

Another approach is to take the area of the graph contained within the intervals 150 and 175.

Here, area = height × width
$$= \frac{1}{50} \times 25$$
$$= \frac{1}{2}$$

Similarly, let's work out the probability of the journey time falling between 160 and 180 minutes. Look at the graph again in Figure 37.

Area = height × width
$$= \frac{1}{50} \times 20$$
$$= 0.4$$

Therefore, to find the probability of the journey time falling between 160 and 180 minutes we take the area of the graph

Figure 28 Shaded area gives the probability of journey time falling between 160 and 180 minutes

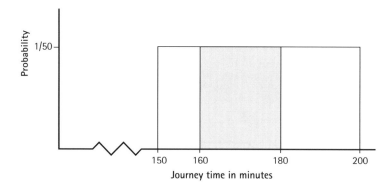

bounded by the interval 160 to 180 minutes. Hence, we calculate the probability of the random variable falling in a particular interval by calculating the area bounded by the density curve over that interval. That is why the distribution of a continuous random variable is called a probability density function.

We now move to the very important continuous distribution, the normal distribution.

THE NORMAL DISTRIBUTION

We mentioned the normal distribution in Chapter 10. We said then that statisticians love the normal distribution because it allows them to make assumptions about the way data will behave in their calculations. It is almost certainly the most important of the distributions that you will come across. It is vital to the theory of sampling which we cover in the next chapter. In order to understand some of the key concepts associated with sampling it is important to make sure you understand what a normal distribution is, together with its principal features.

We will not trouble you with the formula that describes the normal curve, the graphical representation of the density function of the normal distribution – it is sufficient for our purposes to know that it is bell-shaped and has the principal

Figure 29 **A typical normal probability distribution**

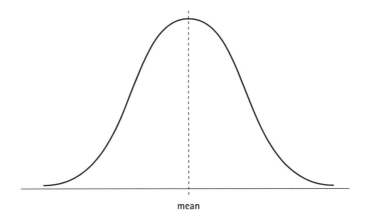

mean

features set out in the next paragraph. The curve itself looks like Figure 29.

The principal features of a normal distribution are as follows:

- The highest point of the normal curve occurs at the mean. The mean is also the mode and the median for the normal curve (see Chapter 11).

- The mean of the distribution can be any value, positive, negative or zero.

- The curve is symmetrical about the mean with tails extending infinitely in both directions and, theoretically, never touching the horizontal (x) axis.

- The spread of the curve determines the standard deviation, that is, the flatter the curve the larger the standard deviation for the same mean (see Figure 30).

- The total area under the curve is 1. (This is true for all continuous probability distributions.)

Figure 30 Two normal distributions with mean μ, but different standard deviations

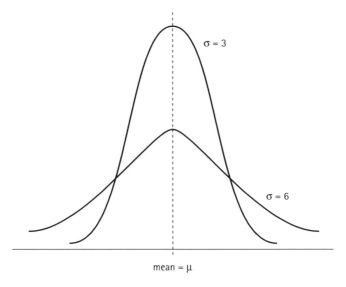

σ = 3

σ = 6

mean = μ

• It has the very important feature that applies to all normal distributions, whatever their mean (μ) or standard deviation (σ), that:

> 68.26 per cent of the time, a *normal random variable* assumes a value within plus or minus one standard deviation of its mean, that is between $\mu \pm 1\sigma$.

> 95.44 per cent of the time, a normal random variable assumes a value within plus or minus two standard deviations of its mean, that is $\mu \pm 2\sigma$

> 99.72 per cent of the time, a normal random variable assumes a value within plus or minus three standard deviations of its mean, that is $\mu \pm 3\sigma$.

In other words, a random variable with a normal distribution falls in the interval of $\mu \pm 1\sigma$ for about two-thirds of the time, and nearly all the time in the interval of $\mu \pm 3\sigma$. We will make good use of this feature when we come to sampling in Chapter 13.

You may at some time come across the **standard normal distribution**. This is a normal distribution with the particular features of a mean of zero and a standard deviation of one. In fact *all* normal distributions can be expressed in terms of the standard distribution very simply. Tables have been developed for the standard normal distribution which statisticians find very useful!

CONCLUSION

We hope that you now understand what a random variable is and that you feel at home with the concept of a probability distribution. We have introduced the fascinating and very important normal distribution. The next two chapters will go on to show how we apply all that we have learned so far to the subject close to the hearts of all statisticians, sampling and hypothesis testing.

EXERCISES

12.1 An engineering company is considering expanding its factory which will enable it to manufacture a new range of products. The MD must decide whether to go for a small scale or large scale project. There is uncertainty about the likely level of demand for the new range of products, which has been categorised as low, medium and high. It has been estimated that the probability for each level of demand is 0.2, 0.6 and 0.2 respectively. The Finance Director has developed a series of profit forecasts for both options:

Demand	Small Scale Project (£000s)	Large Scale Project (£000s)
Low	100	0
Medium	300	250
High	500	800

Which option should the MD choose to maximise the expected value of profit?

Which option might be chosen to minimise risk or uncertainty?

12.2 A railway company states in its printed timetable that the journey time from Atown to Btown is 2 hrs 10 mins. Since the timetable was printed, problems with the track have caused journey times to be uniformly distributed between 2 hrs 15 mins and 2 hrs 30 mins.

What is the probability that the train will be not more than 10 mins late?

What is the probability that the train will be more than 20 mins late?

13 Sampling, estimation and inference

INTRODUCTION

We move on now to talk about the statistical technique, sampling, and the part it can play in providing information for management decision-making. You may first want to ask 'Why take samples at all?' Well, the purpose of sampling is to produce information about a large **population** from a small portion of that population – a **sample**. When the sample is chosen using statistically correct methods we can draw valid conclusions about the larger population by the process of **statistical inference**. Being able to draw these conclusions from a smaller sample than the whole population generally ensures the process will be quicker and less costly than if we were to survey the whole population. By approaching the sampling exercise correctly we will have these early, less costly results without compromising the accuracy too much. However, it is not always helpful to take a sample. If the population is relatively small in size or the list of the population, the **sampling frame**, is readily accessible, for example, the pay of employees from the payroll file on the computer, it may be easier to work with the population as a whole.

One of the most frequent and well-known statistical sampling exercises takes place before our General Elections and tells us how we are going to vote on the day! Other sampling exercises conducted on a regular basis tell us which of the political parties have the strongest support from the voters at that time and even give us details about the popularity of the various party leaders. They are often used to seek views on controversial issues, such as on the fox hunting debate. Clearly, the pollsters do not interview the whole population of Great Britain to give us these eye-catching results; they interview a small, statistically-valid sample of the population.

Most respectable polls give an indication of the size of their sample and sometimes how those people interviewed were selected. The figures can be quite dramatically small. A sample of just over 1,000 people, properly selected, can give a good indication of how the rest of us 26 million voters intend to vote.

Examples of sampling in the business world are:

* In market research, to find out information, for example, about peoples' attitudes or their purchasing habits.

* In manufacturing, to test the life of, say, batteries. A sample of 100 batteries would be taken from production and tested to see how long, on average, they last. (This is an example where there is no alternative to sampling – since we do not want to use up all our products in the tests!)

* In retailing, to try out and test shoppers' reaction to a new product. Suppose we own a chain of 1,000 stores. We may be interested in seeing how well the new product, for example, an exotic fruit, will sell. We could try it in a small sample of the stores, say 20. If we tried the product out in all our stores and it failed, we could have the expense and embarrassment of a lot of rotting exotic fruit!

The sample results provide **estimates** of what the results might be if the whole population was surveyed. The estimate is unlikely to be exactly the same as the true value for the population as a whole and one of the things we will want to know is how good our estimate is, that is, how close it is to the true value for the population.

We will first look at how we choose a sample. We will then go on to discuss point estimates. To help us answer the question of how good our estimate is, we need to understand a little about sampling distributions. We examine in detail the sampling distributions of two important types of estimate – the *sample mean* and the *sample proportion*. From these sampling distributions, we are then able to define confidence limits for these estimates. Finally, we explain how to calculate sample size and talk briefly about how to cope with small samples.

HOW TO CHOOSE YOUR SAMPLE

There are several different methods we can use to select a sample and our choice between these methods will depend on a number of factors as we will explain later in this chapter. We start with the most common method, simple random sampling. We then go on to discuss systematic sampling, stratified random sampling, cluster sampling and finally a range of non-probabilistic methods such as quota sampling, focus groups, convenience sampling and snowball sampling.

Probabilistic sampling

Simple random sampling

First let us consider the case where we have a *finite* population, that is, we know the size of the total population. A **simple random sample** of size 'n' from a population size 'N' is selected in such a way that every sample of size 'n' has the same probability of being selected.

Let us consider a simple example. Suppose we are a small business with six vans and we want to know with a reasonable degree of accuracy what the petrol consumption figures are; but, we do not have the resources to monitor all six vans and decide to monitor two of them. How many different pairs of vans (samples) could we pick from the six vans (the population). Let us set out all the possibilities, labelling the vans A to F, inclusively:

AB, AC, AD, AE, AF
BC, BD, BE, BF
CD, CE, CF
DE, DF
EF

There are 15 different samples we can choose.

You could write each of these 15 samples on a card and put them in a large hat. Pull out a card and, since each card has an equal probability of being picked, that is, one in 15, then it is a random sample. Now clearly, if our population size was very large – then the number of different samples we could pick would also be very large and the method we have used above to select the sample would be too laborious. Instead, to help us the statisticians have prepared what are called *random number tables*, and a section is given in Table 23.

Table 23 Extract from random number tables

98554	52502	11780	04060	56634	58077	02005	80217	65893	78381
89725	00679	28401	79434	00909	22989	31446	76251	17061	66680
49221	37750	26367	44817	09214	82674	65641	14332	58221	49564
31783	96028	69352	78426	94411	38335	22540	37881	10784	34658
51025	72770	13689	21456	48391	00157	61957	11262	12640	17228
*10581	30143	89214	52134	76280	77823	61674	96898	90487	43998
51753	56087	71524	64913	81706	33984	90919	86969	75553	87375
96050	08123	28557	04240	33606	10776	64239	81900	74880	92654
93998	95705	73353	26933	66089	25177	62387	34932	62021	34044
70974	45757	31830	09589	31037	91886	51780	21912	16444	52881
25833	71286	76375	43640	92551	46510	68950	60168	26399	04599
55060	28982	92650	71622	36740	05869	17828	29377	01020	90851
29436	79967	34383	85646	04715	80695	39283	50543	26875	94047
80180	08706	17875	72123	69723	52846	71310	72507	25702	33449
40842	32742	44671	72953	54811	39495	05023	61569	60805	26580
31481	16208	60372	94367	88977	35393	08681	53325	92547	31622
06045	35097	38319	17264	40640	63022	01496	28439	04197	63858
41446	12336	54072	47198	56085	25215	89943	41153	18496	76869
22301	07404	60943	75921	02932	50090	51949	86415	51919	98125
38199	09042	26771	15881	80204	61281	61610	24501	01935	33256
06273	93282	55034	79777	75241	11762	11274	41685	24117	98311
92201	02587	31599	27987	25678	69736	94487	41653	79550	92949
70782	80894	95413	36338	04237	19954	71137	23584	87069	10407
05245	40934	96832	33415	62058	87179	31542	18174	54711	21882
85607	45719	65640	33241	04852	87636	43840	42242	22092	28975

Suppose we wanted to pick a sample of, say, 40 cars from a production run of 3,000 cars for testing. We would start by numbering all the cars from 0001 to 3,000. Then, using the line in the table marked with ⋆, we choose numbers in groups of four digits (as there are four digits in the number '3000'): 1058, 1301, (4389 – discarded), 2145, 2134, and so on until we have 40 appropriate numbers, having discarded the numbers with values over 3000.

We can start anywhere in the table and go up, down or across to get our random numbers. The tables are designed in such a way that there is no bias in the selections, for example, the numbers within the range 2001 to 3000 have no better nor worse chance of being selected than any other range of numbers. Using the random number tables we can be confident that the 40 numbers are selected totally randomly. To a large extent, the advent of computers has overtaken the need for random number tables, as simple spreadsheet packages such as Microsoft Excel™ can readily generate random numbers for us.

Systematic sampling

If there is a very large population from which we are taking our sample it may be too laborious to go through and number the whole population so that we can identify the sample members using random numbers. A much simpler alternative way is to use **systematic sampling**.

Let us suppose there is a population of 10,000 from which we have decided to take a sample of 500 – that is a ratio of one sample member for every 20 population members. We choose the first sample member randomly from the first 20 members of the population and then take every 20th population member thereafter until we have our sample of 500.

Stratified random sampling

This is a complicated name for quite a simple but very useful concept. With **stratified random sampling**, we divide our population into *strata* and choose a random sample from each strata. Examples of such strata are geographical locations, age groups, factories, etc. This method has the advantage of ensuring that we can obtain information on the stratum, for example, a particular age group, as well as enabling us to work out overall estimates for the whole sample.

Cluster sampling

Getting our data by taking a simple random sample of the population is much cheaper than carrying out a comprehensive survey of the whole population. However, random sampling and systematic sampling can be very expensive on occasions and **cluster sampling** will sometimes be used to reduce sampling costs by concentrating our sampling in a small area. For example, let us say that we are interested in finding out information about the electorate's view of a particular policy which is due to be implemented by the local authority. The voting population could be over 100,000 and we might be seeking a sample of 500. It could be very expensive to go and interview every 2,000th person on the electoral register who, probably, would live miles apart. Instead we might randomly select several clusters of voters – perhaps by postal districts – and then all the voters within the clusters would form our sample. Another example might be if you were interested in seeking teachers' views on a new aspect of the curriculum. Schools would be the clusters and you would randomly select a number of schools and then survey all the teachers in that school. Multi-stage sampling is an extension of cluster sampling in which the sample is drawn randomly from within the clusters, instead of the whole cluster being sampled. Cluster sampling is often used for very large surveys.

Non-probabilistic sampling

The sampling methods discussed so far are known as probabilistic sampling methods because the sample members have a known probability of being selected for the sample. This enables us to make statements about sampling errors – about how 'close' the sample estimates are to the true population characteristics. There are a number of methods which are described as non-probabilistic. These are often created either to mimic a random method, eg quota sampling, or for 'convenience'.

Quota sampling

Quota sampling is a method often used for consumer market research. Typically, an interviewer would be given quotas for the people he or she must interview, to represent a typical cross-section of the population. Then, the interviewer might stand in a shopping centre and stop people 'randomly', until he or she has fulfilled the quotas.

Focus groups

Focus groups are another method often used in consumer market research. They usually consist of groups of eight to twelve people who are brought together to discuss a particular topic, eg features sought in new cars, attitudes to health provision. They provide more in-depth information on expectations, needs, etc.

Convenience sampling

Convenience sampling is a sample, as the name suggests, which is chosen for convenience, eg volunteers to participate in research on access for disabled people, or a professor might use his lecture class for some research.

Snowball sampling

Snowball sampling relies on existing sample members identifying other sample members. This is sometimes used when it is difficult to get a reliable population list, eg in research on street gangs, or when it may be helpful to make use of the knowledge and contacts of existing sample members, eg selecting hospital consultants, MPs, etc.

With all non-probabilistic methods it is difficult to comment on the accuracy of the estimates, etc.

POINT ESTIMATES

We explained at the beginning of this chapter that the purpose of sampling is to provide information about a population of interest from a small sample of that population. The types of information about the population that we are interested in might be the average value, the proportion or the standard deviation.

For example, suppose as part of a review of a new benefits package, we want information on the profile of employees who use the staff restaurant. We might be interested in the age profile, the salary profile, type of work, as well as information on the usage such as level of spend, preference for different types of food, etc. We might be interested in the age profile to provide information on the targeting and costs of different benefits packages. We might want to know, for example:

• the average age of all the employees using the staff restaurant

• the proportion of users that are, say, under 30

Table 24   Ages of employees

17	42	23	48	29	52	31	59	38	62
63	39	34	57	54	27	23	46	44	19
45	16	22	49	27	54	34	57	62	37
19	45	50	21	27	52	57	34	39	64
62	37	59	33	27	53	47	23	16	43
62	59	54	49	44	19	24	29	34	39
20	45	25	50	30	55	35	60	40	65
26	34	37	42	44	37	33	27	25	28
52	48	47	43	41	40	37	29	29	32
31	34	37	46	44	51	47	33	24	54

- the variation in ages of users, measured by the standard deviation.

We would choose a sample using one of the (probabilistic) methods discussed earlier in this chapter and then work out from that sample the following statistics:

- the sample mean

- the sample proportions

- the sample standard deviation.

These sample statistics will be **point estimates** of the population statistics, that is of:

- the population mean

- the population proportion

- the population standard deviation.

It should be obvious to us that the information gained from the sample is unlikely to give an exact estimate and if we were able to choose other samples, we would probably get slightly different results. To illustrate this point let us take a simple example. Suppose the population is our employees who use the staff restaurant and the characteristic in which we are interested is age – see Table 24.

We will take two samples of 20 employees from our population of 100 employees using the systematic sampling method. For the first sample we will use as our starting point, say, employee number 4 and for the second sample, employee number 1. We pick every fifth employee for our samples, as follows:

Sample 1			Sample 2	
48	38		17	52
57	44		63	27
49	62		45	54
21	39		19	52
33	16		62	53
49	34		62	19
50	40		20	55
42	25		26	37
43	29		52	40
46	24		31	51

We can now calculate the following:

Population mean	= 39.88 years (by adding all the ages in our population and dividing by 100)
Sample mean from sample 1	= 39.45 years (by adding all the ages from sample 1 and dividing by 20)
Sample mean from sample 2	= 41.85 years (by adding all the ages from sample 2 and dividing by 20)

As you can see the sample means give different estimates of the population mean. Usually, of course, we only take one sample and we use it to calculate estimates of the population characteristics of interest to us. Then, what we need to know is how close our estimate is to the population characteristic we are trying to measure. To find this out we must understand a little about sampling distributions. We have covered the groundwork in Chapter 12, so persevere and you will be delighted with the simplicity of the technique.

SAMPLING DISTRIBUTIONS AND CONFIDENCE LIMITS

As usual, it is easier to understand a concept by looking at an example. Let us focus our minds on the population which interests us. Suppose we are a mail order firm and we want to know more about our customers so that we can make our advertising more cost effective. Suppose their income is of particular interest and we want to know:

- the average income of our customers

- the proportion of customers with incomes in excess of £15,000

- the range, or variation, in incomes of our customers.

Clearly, our population of interest is *all* our customers who could number 10,000, 100,000 or even more. How would we go about the exercise? The first step would be to choose a sample, of say 100 customers, and obtain data on their incomes. As we have explained before, we could go on choosing different samples of 100 customers and each time we would get slightly different values for:

- the sample mean

- the sample proportion

- the sample standard deviation.

Let us imagine that we carried out the sampling exercise four times, using the same sampling method, and found that the sample means (in our case, average incomes) were as follows:

Table 25 Sample means from sampling exercises

Sample number	Sample mean (average salary)
1	£9,014
2	£9,450
3	£8,995
4	£9,222

If we took, say 200, of these samples we would find that we could prepare a frequency distribution, as we did in Chapter 9 – see Table 26.

We could then go on to draw a histogram as we did in Chapter 10 (see Figure 31).

Table 26 Frequency distribution of sample means

Mean income (£)	Frequency	Relative frequency	
8,801–8,900	10	0.05	5%
8,901–9,000	22	0.11	11%
9,001–9,100	38	0.19	19%
9,101–9,200	50	0.25	25%
9,201–9,300	44	0.22	22%
9,301–9,400	24	0.12	12%
9,401–9,500	12	0.06	6%
Total	200	1.00	100%

Figure 31 Relative frequency histogram of values of mean income from 200 samples

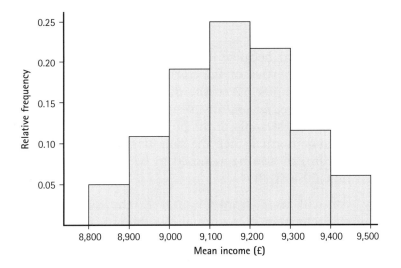

This histogram gives the **sampling distribution** of the sample mean. In other words it describes the way in which the average incomes, calculated from our 200 different samples of 100 customers, varies due to variations in the different samples. We would get a similar distribution, in shape, if we had worked out a sample proportion. Each, in turn, would be the sampling distribution of that sample statistic.

Let us continue with our example of the average income of our customers. Each time we take another sample we are getting another outcome (as explained in Chapter 12) of the sample income. Thus the average income statistic is a random variable (another term from Chapter 12) with a distribution and it will be possible to work out the mean and the standard deviation of the sampling distribution of the random variable average income. So, how does this help us to answer the question 'How good is our estimate?'

A very useful and important theorem in statistics is the **central limit theorem**. This tells us that:

> If simple random samples of size n are drawn from a population with mean μ and standard deviation σ, the sampling distribution of the sample mean, $\bar{x}$, approaches a normal distribution with mean μ and standard deviation $\dfrac{\sigma}{\sqrt{n}}$ as the sample size becomes large.
>
> (Based on Anderson, Sweeney and Williams, 1996)

This is important because it means that we can apply the very useful properties of the normal distribution that we discussed in Chapter 12 to the distribution of the sample mean. In practice, *for any sample of 30 or more*, the Central Limit Theorem can apply. If the population distribution itself is known to be normal, then the sampling distribution of the sample mean can also be assumed to be normal for sample sizes below 30 as well.

Now, you will recall from Chapter 12 the following very useful characteristics of a normal distribution, in particular, that:

1. 68.26% of the time, a normal random variable assumes a value within plus or minus one standard deviation of its mean, that is, 68.26% of the time $\bar{x}$ falls in the range:

$$\mu \pm \frac{\sigma}{\sqrt{n}}$$

2. 95.44% of the time, a normal random variable assumes a value within plus or minus two standard deviations of its mean, that is, 95.44% of the time $\bar{x}$ falls in the range:

$$\mu \pm \frac{2\sigma}{\sqrt{n}}$$

3. 99.72% of the time, a normal random variable assumes a value within plus or minus three standard deviations of its mean, that is, 99.72% of the time $\bar{x}$ falls in the range:

$$\mu \pm \frac{3\sigma}{\sqrt{n}}$$

Let us look rather closer at case 2. This can be expressed a little differently as: there is a 95.44% chance, or 0.9544 probability, that $\bar{x}$ falls in the range $\mu \pm \frac{2\sigma}{\sqrt{n}}$. It is shown by the shaded area in Figure 32.

Figure 32   Normal distribution of $\bar{x}$, with mean μ: standard deviation $\frac{\sigma}{\sqrt{n}}$

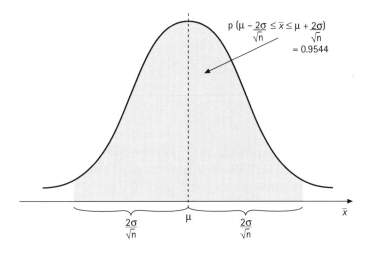

We might find it more convenient to talk in terms of a 95% chance or 0.95 probability of $\bar{x}$ falling in a particular interval. It can be shown that:

there is a 95% chance (rather than 95.44%) or a 0.95 probability of the sample mean $\bar{x}$ falling in the range:

$$\mu \pm \frac{1.96\sigma}{\sqrt{n}} \qquad \text{(1.96 rather than 2)}$$

Similarly:

there is a 99% chance or a 0.99 probability of the sample mean x̄ falling in the range:

$$\mu \pm \frac{2.58\sigma}{\sqrt{n}} \qquad \text{(2.58 rather than 3)}$$

In most cases we will not know the population standard deviation σ and will use our sample standard deviation s to estimate it. (This may be seen as a bit of a fiddle, but please accept that it is quite all right!) Then it can be seen from the above that there is a 95% chance, or a 0.95 probability that x̄ will fall in the range:

$$\mu \pm 1.96 \frac{s}{\sqrt{n}}$$

Intuitively, we can rewrite this relationship as there being a 95% chance, or a 0.95 probability, that μ will fall in the range:

$$\bar{x} \pm 1.96 \frac{s}{\sqrt{n}}$$

(In repeated sampling, each sample generating its own confidence limits, 95% will include μ. Don't worry if you can't see this – just accept our word for it.)

These are known as the 95% **confidence limits** for the population mean, μ. Similarly $\bar{x} \pm \frac{2.58s}{\sqrt{n}}$ are the 99% confidence limits for the population mean, μ.

Let's look at an example. Suppose we have an organisation which sends out a large number of small packages and an important part of its costs is in its distribution system – a courier service. It needs to negotiate terms with the courier service and to do this to establish the average weight of its parcels and the range of confidence limits, be they 95%, 99% or whatever. Assume that we choose a random sample of 30 packages and note the weights as set out in the Table 27:

Table 27 Average package weights (grams)

160	179	188	180	188	195
185	190	162	165	183	199
167	192	186	181	194	172
182	166	187	172	168	181
175	176	195	161	184	172

The sample mean $\bar{x} = \dfrac{\text{sum of the weights}}{30} = 179.5$

We are now going to work out the confidence limits. First we work out the sample deviation, either manually or using the computer (see Chapters 11 and 19):

Sample variance $s^2 = \displaystyle\sum_{i=1}^{n} \dfrac{(\bar{x} - x_i)^2}{n - 1}$ where x_i are the sample points and n = the sample size

$= 122.9$

Sample standard deviation s $= \sqrt{122.9}$

$= 11.1$

Therefore, we can be 95% confident that the population mean lies within the range:

$$\bar{x} \pm 1.96 \, \dfrac{s}{\sqrt{n}}$$

$$= 179.5 \pm \dfrac{1.96 \times 11.1}{\sqrt{30}}$$

$$= 179.5 \pm 4.0$$

$$= 175.5 \text{ to } 183.5$$

Figure 33 95% confidence limits for mean package weights

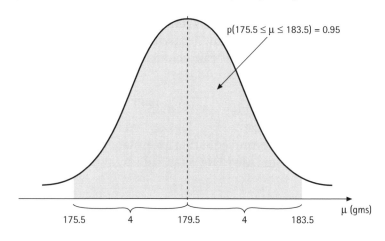

$p(175.5 \leq \mu \leq 183.5) = 0.95$

μ (gms)

175.5   4   179.5   4   183.5

In other words we can be 95% confident that the average package weight will fall within the range 175.5 to 183.5 grams (see Figure 33).

So now, after all that theory, we begin to see the usefulness of understanding the sampling distribution of the sample mean. It enables us to give, *with confidence*, a range around our estimate within which the population mean will fall.

Similarly we can go through exactly the same process for the population proportion p. The 95% confidence limits for the population proportion p are:

$$\bar{p} \pm 1.96\sqrt{\frac{\bar{p}\,(1 - \bar{p})}{n}} \quad \text{where } \bar{p} \text{ is the sample proportion}$$

The formula can also be used for $\bar{p}$ expressed in the form of a percentage as follows:

$$\bar{p} \pm 1.96\sqrt{\frac{\bar{p}(100 - \bar{p})}{n}}$$

CALCULATING SAMPLE SIZE

Now that we have some measure of the accuracy or *precision* of the estimate of our population mean we can go on to look at another very important decision in sampling, the sample size. We can calculate the sample size which is required to give us a certain level of confidence limit.

In our package weight example, we calculated with 95% confidence that the population mean lay within plus or minus four grams of the sample mean of 179.5. Suppose now we decide that we want to be 95% confident that our population mean lies within a range of plus or minus three grams of the sample mean, ie giving ourselves a sampling error of three grams. We can calculate the required sample size as follows:

$$3 = \frac{1.96s}{\sqrt{n}} \qquad \text{(see page 172)}$$

We can manipulate our equation to isolate n by multiplying each side by $\sqrt{n}$ and dividing each side by 3, as follows:

$$\sqrt{n} = \frac{1.96s}{3}$$

$$= \frac{1.96 \times 11.1}{3} \quad \text{(s = 11.1 from page 173)}$$

$$= 7.252$$

Therefore n = 7.252^2 = 52.6.

Rounding this up, it means that we would need a sample size of 53 packages to be 95% sure of this greater precision that the population mean will fall within plus or minus 3 grams of the new sample mean (rather than the sample size of 30 which achieved a precision of plus or minus four grams).

Similarly, we can go on to work out a sample size to achieve a maximum particular sampling error at the 95% confidence level, for a *population proportion*, as follows:

$$n = \frac{1.96^2 \times \bar{p}\,(1 - \bar{p})}{(\text{sampling error})^2}$$

NB All the above formulae for confidence limits and sample sizes depend on calculating the value of the sample standard deviation. The formulae used for these are based on the sample being selected by simple random sampling. If you are using a different method, eg stratified random sampling, the sample standard deviation will be calculated differently – seek advice from a friendly statistician!

CONCLUSION

We hope that you now have a sound understanding of the basic concepts of sampling. Sampling is a vital tool for gathering information. It has enormous power, but must be used with care and understanding. In the next chapter we go on to look at what are called significance and hypothesis tests – they test the significance of our sample results.

EXERCISES

1.31 A survey of student loans based on a sample of 100 final-year students at a particular university showed an average loan of £8,540 and a sample standard deviation of £1,400.

1. Calculate 95% and 99% confidence limits for the population average and comment on the results.

2. What sample size would you need to achieve a confidence interval of $\pm£150$ at the 95% confidence level and explain your result.

13.2 An organisation has surveyed 150 of its customers to find out their views on customer service. 66% commented that the quality of service at the point of sale was excellent and 48% commented that the quality of after-sales care was excellent. You need to report the results back to the MD. The MD may ask for details of how the precision of the results could be improved in later surveys. (This issue is less straightforward than for a sample mean; think about it and then read the answer!)

14 Hypothesis-testing

INTRODUCTION

In the previous chapter we saw how we could draw conclusions about a population from a sample using the technique of statistical inference. We focused our attention on the use of samples for estimating such measures of the population as its mean and proportions of the population possessing a given characteristic. Another major use of sampling is to test hypotheses about the population itself. This technique is frequently adopted in scientific work, for example, testing drugs in pharmaceutical research.

However, hypothesis-testing is also of value in the business world, particularly for quality control. Suppose we have a firm making components, in this case, bolts. It is very important that these bolts are of a particular size or very close to it, let us say three centimetres in length, or they will be rejected by the customer. Let us use again the Greek letter μ to define the mean or average size for the population of all bolts manufactured.

If $\mu = 3$ cm, there is no problem.
If $\mu \neq 3$ cm, there is a problem which the firm will have to address.

NULL AND ALTERNATIVE HYPOTHESES

We tackle this exercise by first defining the **null hypothesis** and the **alternative hypothesis**. The null hypothesis (referred to as H_o) is the tentative assumption about the population characteristic that we are going to test. The alternative hypothesis (usually referred to as H_1) covers all other plausible states of the population characteristic. In our example, above:

H_o: $\mu = 3$ cm
H_1: $\mu \neq 3$ cm

The next step is to choose a sample of, say, 50 bolts and measure them. If the sample results are consistent with the null hypothesis, then we are said to *accept* H_o. However, if the sample results differ *significantly* from the null hypothesis then we *reject* H_o and conclude that H_1, the alternative hypothesis, is true. But what do we mean by the interesting phrase 'differ significantly'?

Before we discuss the interesting and key concept of significance, we need to explain about the different hypothesis tests. There are three types:

1. One type is that already covered in the earlier example, where the item either is the correct size or it is not, ie both oversized and undersized bolts will be rejected by the customer. This type of test is expressed as:

   $H_o: \mu = \mu_V$ Where μ is the mean of the population as
   $H_1: \mu \neq \mu_V$ a whole and μ_V is the specific value you are testing.

2. Another type is where the acceptable limit is greater than or equal to a certain specification and the customer would reject an item which was less than the specification. This type of test is expressed as:

   $H_o: \mu \geq \mu_V$
   $H_1: \mu < \mu_V$

   An example of this type could be a firm making light bulbs which are guaranteed to give 100 hours of life. In order to meet the specification, and not contravene the Trade Description Act, it is important that the light bulbs have an average life of 100 hours or more, that is $\mu \geq 100$. The test would then be expressed as:

   $H_o: \mu \geq 100$
   $H_1: \mu < 100$.

3. The third type is where to meet a specification, an item must not be greater than a certain level. This type of test is expressed as:

   $H_o: \mu \leq \mu_V$
   $H_1: \mu > \mu_V$

An example of this could be in food manufacturing where the level of a certain chemical additive in the product must not be greater than, say, 25 parts per million, that is $\mu \leq 25$ ppm. The test would then be expressed as:

$H_o: \mu \leq 25$
$H_1: \mu > 25$

The first type of test (number one) is called a **two-tailed test** and the other two types of test (numbers two and three) are called **one-tailed tests**. Another set of curious terms you may think, but in fact they refer to the 'tails' of our old friend the normal distribution. The tails are the sections at either end of the distribution covering those extreme values which are distant from the mean. More of this later because we now need to say a few words about the errors involved in hypothesis testing.

Errors

We would like to think that our test of bolts, light bulbs or whatever would always lead us to accept the null hypothesis, H_o, when it is true and reject it when it is false. However, as we are sure you now appreciate, sampling is not an exact science and there are errors involved. The possible situations that can occur are shown as follows:

	Accept H_o	Reject H_o
H_o True	Correct decision	**Type 1 error**
H_o False	**Type 2 error**	Correct decision

As you will see from this simple table, there are two possible types of error:

- Type 1 error – which occurs when we reject H_o even when it is true.

- Type 2 error – which occurs when we accept H_o even when it is false.

In a sense, hypothesis-testing is rather similar to the situation in a criminal court where:

$H_o:$ the defendant is innocent, and,
$H_1:$ the defendant is guilty.

The defendant is considered innocent until proven guilty and we are most concerned to ensure that we do not find an innocent person guilty, that is, not make a Type 1 error. In fact, it is the Type 1 errors that establish the **significance level** of the test.

Traditionally, and we shall follow this convention in this chapter:

α is defined as the probability of making a Type 1 error.
β is defined as the probability of making a Type 2 error.

(Sorry about more Greek letters!)

Two-tailed hypothesis-testing
Let us go back to our example of the firm manufacturing and testing bolts. Our hypothesis test is expressed as follows:

H_0: μ = 3 cms
H_1: μ ≠ 3 cms

We take a sample size of 50 bolts and let us assume the sample average x̄ is 2.95 cm and our sample standard deviation s is 0.25 cm. We decide to set our Type 1 error, α, at 0.05, that is, we are content with a 5 per cent chance of accepting H_0 when it is false. As our sample size is over 30 units, we can assume that our sample mean has a normal distribution and test whether this sample mean comes from a population with the characteristic μ = 3 cm.

Figure 34 Two-tailed hypothesis test, with Type 1 error, α = 0.05

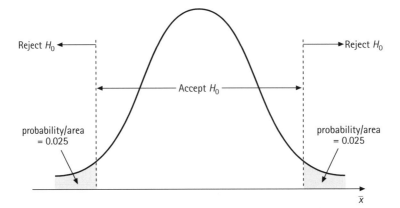

Reject H_0 ← → Reject H_0

Accept H_0

probability/area
= 0.025

probability/area
= 0.025

x̄

If we remember back to the last chapter, we want the confidence interval to be such that there is only a 0.05 probability that it will not include our population mean. Look at Figure 34.

We will reject H_o if the population mean μ falls in the shaded areas, that is, in either of the two tails which each have a probability of 0.025 and which together give a total Type 1 error of 0.05. In other words, we will accept H_o if μ falls in the range:

$$\bar{x} \pm 1.96 \frac{s}{\sqrt{n}} \quad \text{(95\% confidence limits from page 172)}$$

$$= 2.95 \pm \frac{1.96 \times 0.25}{\sqrt{50}}$$

$$= 2.95 \pm \frac{0.49}{7.071}$$

$$= 2.95 \pm 0.07$$

$$= 2.88 \text{ to } 3.02$$

Since the hypothesised population mean of 3 cm lies within this interval we accept H_o, that is, we accept the hypothesis. If, on the other hand the sample mean had been 2.9 cm, the confidence interval would have been 2.83 to 2.97 (2.9 $\pm$ 0.07) and we would have rejected the null hypothesis as the hypothesised population mean of 3 cm lies outside this confidence interval of the sample. From the Figure 34 you will readily see why this is called a two-tailed test! (NB In practice μ is fixed, our confidence interval changes from sample to sample.)

The same principles and approach apply if you want to carry out a hypothesis test on a population proportion. For example, if we set out the test as follows:

$H_o: p = p_V$ (where p_V = the particular population
$H_1: p \neq p_V$ proportion we want to test)

Then, we would accept H_o at the 95% confidence or significance level, that is with a Type 1 error of 0.05, if p_v falls in the range:

$$\bar{p} \pm 1.96 \sqrt{\frac{(1 - \bar{p})}{n}} \quad \text{where } \bar{p} \text{ is the sample proportion and } n \text{ the sample size}$$

We have concentrated on the most useful type of hypothesis test, the two-tailed test. Very similar procedures apply to the one-tailed test – in this case we are only concerned about one tail of the distribution.

STATISTICAL PROCESS CONTROL

The statistical technique described earlier has been developed to provide a very useful mechanism for monitoring quality control – the **statistical process control chart**. This is simply a chart (see Figure 35) that has at its centre line the value of the variable of interest when the *process is in control*. In the example discussed earlier, the process is making bolts and when it is in control the length of the bolt is 3 cm – so the centre line would be set at 3 cm. The two lines labelled UCL (Upper Control Limit) and LCL (Lower Control Limit) set the limits for deciding when the process is out of control. As samples are taken, the average value of the bolts are calculated and logged on the chart. As long as the results are within the limits then there is no need for action. However, if a value falls outside the limits then the process

Figure 35 Statistical process control chart

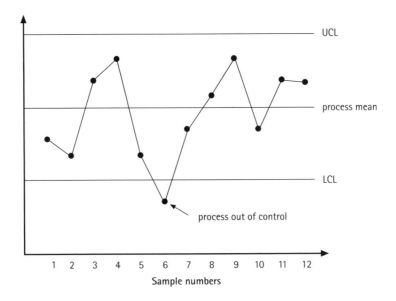

must be examined and adjusted – perhaps the machines reset. As you may have guessed the limits are our old friends the confidence limits of the sample mean and are usually set at the 99.72 per cent level, ie $\pm 3s/\sqrt{n}$ (where s is the sample standard deviation and n the sample size). There are variations on this approach which focus on the range rather than the standard deviation and also where the range of the sample rather than the sample mean is used as the measure of interest.

TWO-POPULATION INFERENCE (INDEPENDENT SAMPLES)

Up until now we have considered only situations which involve one population – in the above examples, the population of all bolts manufactured by the firm. However, in many practical decision-making situations we are dealing with two different populations – usually because we want to compare them with each other. For example, we might want to compare the mean salary for female employees with the mean salary for male employees to test how well our equal opportunities policy is working.

Basically, we follow exactly the same procedure as before, however this time we are interested in the *difference* between the two sample means. Taking our equal pay example, our hypothesis is that there is no difference in male or female salaries and can be expressed as:

$H_0: \mu_1 - \mu_2 = 0$ where μ_1 and μ_2 population means of
$H_1: \mu_1 - \mu_2 \neq 0$ the male and female employees

This is a two-tailed test.

Let us suppose we carry out our test by randomly sampling the male and female populations of employees and get the following results:

Male employees	Female employees
$n_1 = 40$	$n_2 = 45$
$\bar{x}_1 = £8,700$	$\bar{x}_2 = £8,300$
$s_1 = £650$	$s_2 = £600$

This time we will set our probability of a Type 1 error as 0.01. This means that we are willing to accept a one per cent chance of rejecting the null hypothesis even when it's true.

It can be shown (please simply accept our word for this!) that the 99 per cent confidence interval for $\bar{x}_1 - \bar{x}_2$ is

$$(\bar{x}_1 - \bar{x}_2) \pm 2.58 \sqrt{\frac{s_1^2}{n_1} + \frac{s_2^2}{n_2}}$$
$$= (8{,}700 - 8{,}300) \pm 2.58 \sqrt{\frac{650^2}{40} + \frac{600^2}{45}}$$
$$= 400 \pm 2.58 \times 136$$
$$= 400 \pm 350.9$$
$$= 49.1 \text{ to } 750.9$$

Our null hypothesis, H_o, is $\mu_1 - \mu_2 = 0$. As the value of $\mu_1 - \mu_2$ under our null hypothesis (that is, zero) falls outside the range 49.1 to 750.9 calculated above, we reject the null hypothesis. Given the results of our sample, we cannot be sure that our equal opportunities policy is fully effective. One possible explanation or conclusion could be that, as we have only taken this one sample at a single point in time, the equal opportunities policy has not yet worked and we still have some way to go.

The pragmatists among us might have asked what is the point of all these calculations when we could see from the results of the samples (mean salaries for men and women of £8,700 and £8,300 respectively) that men are better paid than women? What we, as statisticians, are interested in is whether the difference between the two sample means is significant. By *significant* we mean: is the difference between the means likely to represent actual differences in the populations of male and female employees or are they errors due to sampling.

Exactly the same procedure can be followed in one-tailed tests, for example, perhaps to test that average profit per acre for wheat on organic farms is greater than for wheat grown on farms using pesticides, etc. Similarly we could use these approaches when dealing with proportions rather than means. For example, continuing our equal opportunities policy testing, perhaps to compare the proportions of males and females at different managerial levels.

So far we have discussed how to set up a hypothesis test by defining null and alternative hypotheses. We discussed the two types of error that can occur, but concentrated on the most important error, the Type 1 error, which is the error of rejecting H_o when it is true. We have shown how to carry out a hypothesis test using the confidence limit approach and discussed the two different types of tests – two-tailed and one-tailed tests. Finally, we looked at the situation where two populations were involved.

All the hypothesis tests covered so far involved testing means and proportions. We are now going to look at two rather different types of hypothesis test.

THE CHI-SQUARED TESTS

These hypothesis tests are as straightforward as the ones we have discussed earlier but are used in different situations. We are going to look at two types of test – **goodness of fit** and **independence tests** – and because they are based on a probability distribution called a Chi-squared (χ^2) distribution, they are called Chi-squared tests.

Goodness of fit
There are 'goodness of fit' tests for different types of populations. However, the most commonly used is the test for what is known as a **multinomial population**. This is a population where each member of the population is assigned to one, and only one, of several classes or categories.

Let us look at an example where you might use a goodness of fit test for a multinomial population. Suppose you are a company which sells cat foods. You are about to embark on a major advertising campaign and you will want to know whether it has a significant effect on your market share of cat food sales. Suppose there are three other major brands of cat food product and your market share before the advertising campaign is as follows:

Your Brand		Competitors' Brands	
Paws	*Yummy*	*Furries*	*Cat-eats*
30%	15%	40%	15%

Following your advertising campaign you carry out a survey of 200 cat owners and ask which cat food they buy. The results are as follows:

Your Brand		Competitors' Brands	
Paws	*Yummy*	*Furries*	*Cat-eats*
80	20	70	30

Your null hypothesis is that the advertising campaign has had no effect and therefore:

$$H_o: p_{PAWS} = 0.3, p_{YUMMY} = 0.15, p_{FURRIES} = 0.4, p_{CAT\text{-}EATS} = 0.15$$

Your alternative hypothesis is that the population has been affected by the advertising campaign and therefore:

$$H_1: p_{PAWS} \neq 0.3, p_{YUMMY} \neq 0.15, p_{FURRIES} \neq 0.4, p_{CAT\text{-}EATS} \neq 0.15$$

The test looks at differences between the observed results or frequencies from the sample and the expected results or frequencies if the null hypothesis is true, ie if the market shares are unchanged. You calculate the expected results by applying the original market share proportions to the sample of 200 cat owners. This gives the following expected results:

Your Brand		Competitors' Brands	
Paws	*Yummy*	*Furries*	*Cat-eats*
200×0.3	200×0.15	200×0.4	200×0.15
$= 60$	$= 30$	$= 80$	$= 30$

It follows that the bigger the differences between the observed and the expected results, the less likely it is that the null hypothesis is true. The statistic χ^2 is computed using the formula:

$$\chi^2 = \sum_{i=1}^{k} \frac{(o_i - e_i)^2}{e_i}$$

where o_i = observed frequencies for class i
         e_i = expected frequency for class i
         k = number of classes

In our example we have four classes (the four brands) and we work out our statistic as follows:

$$\chi^2 = \frac{(80 - 60)^2}{60} + \frac{(20 - 30)^2}{30} + \frac{(70 - 80)^2}{80} + \frac{(30 - 30)^2}{30}$$

$$= \frac{400}{60} + \frac{100}{30} + \frac{100}{80} + 0$$

$$= 6.7 + 3.3 + 1.3$$

$$= 11.3$$

If we took lots of samples and calculated their χ^2 values by comparing their observed results with their expected results as above, the statistic would be shown to have a χ^2 distribution with what is known as k − 1 degrees of freedom. In our case k = 4, so the number of degrees of freedom is three. The only requirement is that generally the minimum class size is five. The chart shown as Table 28 sets out the χ^2 distribution.

Let's see how we use the table. First, as for our earlier hypothesis tests, we must choose our significance level (Type 1 error): let's choose $\alpha = 0.05$. We reject the null hypothesis if the differences between observed and expected frequencies are large, that is, when the value of χ^2 is large. Therefore our rejection area of 0.05 is the upper tail of the distribution. In our case there are four classes (k = 4) and therefore there are three degrees of freedom. From the table we look across row 3 and down column 0.050 and we find:

$$\chi^2_{0.05} = 7.81$$

As our value of χ^2, 11.3, is greater than the value of 7.81 from the table it falls in the shaded area of the χ^2 distribution shown in Table 28 and therefore we reject the null hypothesis. This tells us that the market structure has changed but not how or why. However, from looking at the results, it can be seen that the Paws brand has gained at the expense of both the Yummies and Furries brands, with the Cat-eats share being unaffected. Therefore, it would be

Table 28 Chi–squared (χ^2) distribution

α = area or probability

d.f./α	.250	.100	.050	.025	.010	.005	.001
1	1.32	2.71	3.84	5.02	6.63	7.88	10.8
2	2.77	4.61	5.99	7.38	9.21	10.6	13.8
3	4.11	6.25	7.81	9.35	11.3	12.8	16.3
4	5.39	7.78	9.49	11.1	13.3	14.9	18.5
5	6.63	9.24	11.1	12.8	15.1	16.7	20.5
6	7.84	10.6	12.6	14.4	16.8	18.5	22.5
7	9.04	12.0	14.1	16.0	18.5	20.3	24.3
8	10.2	13.4	15.5	17.5	20.1	22.0	26.1
9	11.4	14.7	16.9	19.0	21.7	23.6	27.9
10	12.5	16.0	18.3	20.5	23.2	25.2	29.6
11	13.7	17.3	19.7	21.9	24.7	26.8	31.3
12	14.8	18.5	21.0	23.3	26.2	28.3	32.9
13	16.0	19.8	22.4	24.7	27.7	29.8	34.5
14	17.1	21.1	23.7	26.1	29.1	31.3	36.1
15	18.2	22.3	25.0	27.5	30.6	32.8	37.7
16	19.4	23.5	26.3	28.8	32.0	34.3	39.3
17	20.5	24.8	27.6	30.2	33.4	35.7	40.8
18	21.6	26.0	28.9	31.5	34.8	37.2	42.3
19	22.7	27.2	30.1	32.9	36.2	38.6	43.8
20	23.8	28.4	31.4	34.2	37.6	40.0	45.3
21	24.9	29.6	32.7	35.5	38.9	41.4	46.8
22	26.0	30.8	33.9	36.8	40.3	42.8	48.3
23	27.1	32.0	35.2	38.1	41.6	44.2	49.7
24	28.2	33.2	36.4	39.4	43.0	45.6	51.2
25	29.3	34.4	37.7	40.6	44.3	46.9	52.6
26	30.4	35.6	38.9	41.9	45.6	48.3	54.1
27	31.5	36.7	40.1	43.2	47.0	49.6	55.5
28	32.6	37.9	41.3	44.5	48.3	51.0	56.9
29	33.7	39.1	42.6	45.7	49.6	52.3	58.3
30	34.8	40.3	43.8	47.0	50.9	53.7	59.7
40	45.6	51.8	55.8	59.3	63.7	66.8	73.4
50	56.3	63.2	67.5	71.4	76.2	79.5	86.7
60	67.0	74.4	79.1	83.3	88.4	92.0	99.6
70	77.6	85.5	90.5	95.0	100.0	104.0	112.0
80	88.1	96.6	102.0	107.0	112.0	116.0	125.0
90	98.6	108.0	113.0	118.0	124.0	128.0	137.0
100	109.0	118.0	124.0	130.0	136.0	140.0	149.0

The χ^2 distribution is a family of distributions where each is distinguished by a single parameter, its *degree(s) of freedom*. Entries in the table give χ^2_α values, where α is the type 1 error or the area/probability in the upper tail of the χ^2 distribution. For example, for α = .050 and with 8 degrees of freedom $\chi^2_{0.05}$ = 15.5.

reasonable to conclude that the advertising campaign has been a success. 'Well', says the cynic, 'we could have told you that by simple observation of the sample results.' 'Possibly', says the statistician, 'but you do not know whether the differences observed in the sample results are merely due to chance errors resulting from the sampling process. Our test enables us to say that the result is significant at the five per cent level.' Hence these tests are often referred to as significance tests – they are testing the significance of the results. You can see where the name *goodness of fit* comes from – because what we are testing is whether our observed (from the sample) results are a good fit with the results we would expect if our null hypothesis is true.

We now go on to look at another application of the χ^2 test, the test of independence.

Test of independence

As the name suggests, a test of independence is a test for checking the independence of two variables. For example, you might want to see whether salary or career progression was independent of the sex of employees. You might wish to check whether consumer preference for, say, free range eggs was independent of age or whether production was independent of the day of the week, etc. Let us take a very simple example. Suppose you wanted to determine whether or not there were differences in preference for full cream milk, semi-skimmed milk and skimmed milk between the different age groups. Let us assume that we are interested in the under-25s, and the 25 and over age groups only.

Our hypotheses are as follows:

H_0: milk preference is independent of whether the milk consumer is under 25 or 25 and over

H_1: milk preference is not independent of whether the milk consumer is under 25 or 25 and over

Our next step is to carry out a survey of, say 300 milk drinkers. The results are as follows:

Consumer	Full cream	Semi-Skimmed	Skimmed	Total
Under 25	20	30	50	100
25 and over	50	80	70	200
Total	70	110	120	300

(A table such as this which sets out all possible combinations of available outcomes is called a **contingency table**.)

These are our observed results. Just as in the test for goodness of fit, we need to work out the expected results if the null hypothesis is true. If there are no preference differences between the two age groups, then we could work out the expected proportions from the total results as follows:

proportion preference
for full cream $\qquad$ = 70/300 = 0.23
proportion preference
for semi-skimmed $\qquad$ = 110/300 = 0.37
proportion preference
for skimmed $\qquad$ = 120/300 = 0.4

If we then apply these proportions to the totals for each age group, we arrive at the following expected frequencies:

Consumer	Full cream	Semi-Skimmed	Skimmed	Total
Under 25	23	37	40	100
25 and over	46	74	80	200
Total	69*	109*	120	300

*due to rounding errors

It is helpful for the arithmetic to combine the observed results and the expected results into one table, as follows (observed values shown first, expected values in brackets):

Consumer	Full cream	Semi-Skimmed	Skimmed
Under 25	20 (23)	30 (37)	50 (40)
25 and over	50 (46)	80 (74)	70 (80)

We then compute a similar statistic as before using the formula:

$$\chi^2 = \sum_i \sum_j \frac{(o_{ij} - e_{ij})^2}{e_{ij}}$$

where o_{ij} = observed result for row i and column j in the contingency table

e_{ij} = expected result for row i and column j in the contingency table

This looks very complicated but all it means is that we are working out our formula:

$$\frac{(\text{observed} - \text{expected})^2}{\text{expected}}$$

and summing over all the classes or entries in our table.

In our example:

$$\chi^2 = \frac{(20 - 23)^2}{23} + \frac{(30 - 37)^2}{37} + \frac{(50 - 40)^2}{40}$$

$$+ \frac{(50 - 46)^2}{46} + \frac{(80 - 74)^2}{74} + \frac{(70 - 80)^2}{80}$$

$$= \frac{9}{23} + \frac{49}{37} + \frac{100}{40} + \frac{16}{46} + \frac{36}{74} + \frac{100}{80}$$

$$= 6.30$$

This statistic can again be shown to have the χ^2 distribution if the null hypothesis is true. The number of degrees of freedom are worked out as follows:

(number of rows $-$ 1) $\times$ (number of columns $-$ 1)

In our example:

$$1 \times 2 = 2$$

We are now ready to test for independence and we again decide to choose the five per cent significance level. As before, we will reject the null hypothesis for large values of χ^2. From Table 28, looking along row two and down column 0.050:

$$\chi^2_{0.05} = 5.99$$

As our computed χ^2, 6.3, is greater than 5.99 we reject the null hypothesis and conclude that the preference for different types of milk is not independent of whether the consumer is under 25 years or over 25 years of age. Again, strictly speaking, we can draw no further conclusions about the relationship. However, observation of the contingency table shows us that a greater proportion of the older age group appears to have a preference for the full cream and semi-skimmed milks, whereas a greater proportion of the younger age group has a preference for skimmed milk.

This is another simple but useful test. The only rules that we have to remember are that the observed results are always expressed as whole numbers – they are frequencies of occurrence – and that the size of each class (for example under 25, 25 and over) should generally be greater than five. If we are dealing with a large number of classes and we are close to this minimum class size, then we may choose to combine some of the classes. Also, we must remember that the test only tells us whether there is independence or not between classes. It cannot and does not tell us anything about the nature or causes of the relationship. However, it is usually quite easy to deduce some simple conclusions about the relationship by looking at the contingency table.

CONCLUSION

We have covered a range of different hypothesis and significance tests to suit quite a wide variety of situations. Although they sound rather daunting at first, we hope we have shown that once you understand the principles, they are in fact very easy and straightforward to carry out.

EXERCISES

14.1 A study of the mean parking times in a multi-storey car park shows that mean length of stay is 175 min. The car park has subsequently been refurbished and the charges increased. The owner would like to find out whether these changes have had any impact on the mean parking time. A random sample of 100 cars showed a mean parking time of 160 min and sample standard deviation of 55 min. Set up the appropriate hypothesis test, using a 5 per cent significance level, and comment on the results.

14.2 A kitchen retailer claims that the mean time from placing an order to completion of the kitchen is 7.8 weeks. An independent researcher wants to check this claim. Set up the appropriate hypothesis test and explain how it can be used to comment on the retailer's claim.

14.3 A survey of employees carried out a year ago showed overall satisfaction levels with the service offered by the Personnel Department as follows:

Very good	Good	Poor	Very poor
21%	45%	30%	4%

In this year's survey of 250 employees the results were as follows:

Very good	Good	Poor	Very poor
55	135	52	8

Use a goodness of fit test to see whether opinions have changed and comment on the results. (Use a significance level of one per cent.)

14.4 Three suppliers provide the following data on defective parts:

Supplier	Good	Minor defect	Major defect
A	90	3	7
B	170	18	7
C	135	6	9

Test for independence and comment on the results.

15 Regression and correlation

INTRODUCTION

'Oh dear', we hear you say, 'not another set of incomprehensible terms!' However, they are easily explained and provide very useful tools for the decision-maker. As a manager/specialist you may often find yourself faced with drawing conclusions or making recommendations based on the relationship between different variables. For example, as a personnel manager you may be interested in looking at whether absenteeism is related to some factor such as age, hours worked, distance from home to work, etc and therefore decide on appropriate measures to tackle the issue. As a marketing manager, you may be interested to see the extent to which sales are related to expenditure on advertising, and use this information to make decisions on the advertising budget, and so on. Regression analysis and correlation are techniques which can help us all in this area of decision-making.

REGRESSION ANALYSIS

Regression analysis is a technique that enables us to describe the relationship between variables using a mathematical equation. In regression analysis there are two types of variables, described as **dependent** and **independent**:

1. The *dependent variable* is the variable being predicted by the relationship; in the above examples, absenteeism and sales would be dependent variables.

2. The *independent variable* is the variable which is being used to predict the dependent variable. For example, age, hours worked and distance from home to work would be independent variables used to predict absenteeism, and money spent on advertising would be an independent variable used to predict sales.

In the first section we are going to look at the simplest form of regression analysis, **simple linear regression**. This is used in situations where there are only two variables – the dependent variable and one independent variable – and the relationship between them can be described as a straight line. Situations involving two or more independent variables are analysed by using **multiple regression** techniques and these will be described briefly in the third section. In the second section we will look at **correlation**. Whereas with regression analysis we are interested in finding a mathematical equation relating two variables, with correlation we are interested in determining the extent to which the variables are related, or the strength of the relationship.

SIMPLE LINEAR REGRESSION

Let us take our usual simple example. Suppose you are a haulier. Up until now, for each tender you have submitted you have prepared detailed figures on the cost of the work. You are now expanding and you want a simple way to work out a cost for a job. You suspect that the most important influence on the cost of the job is the distance to be travelled. You want to test whether or not this is the case and so look back at the last eight jobs and obtain the data shown in Table 29:

Table 29 Comparison of haulage cost against distance

Job	Distance (miles)	Cost (£)
1	20	200
2	25	250
3	35	275
4	37	300
5	48	400
6	60	450
7	75	500
8	80	600

The first step is to present the information graphically, by plotting the jobs on a graph of cost against distance. Traditionally, as we are trying to predict cost, that is, the dependent variable, we put cost on the vertical axis (the y-axis) and the independent variable, distance, on the

Figure 36   Scatter diagram of cost/job against distance travelled

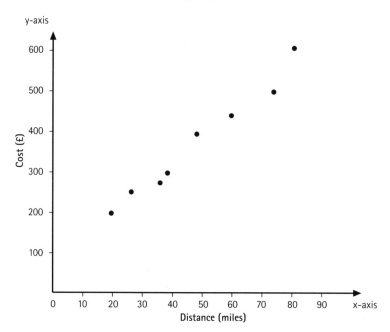

horizontal axis (the x-axis). The above graph, shown as Figure 36, is known as a **scatter diagram**.

The scatter diagram shows us that there does appear to be a linear relationship. A graph showing a straight line or linear relationship between two sets of data can be expressed in the form of a mathematical equation:

$$y = a + bx$$

where:

- 'a' is the intercept where the graph intersects the y-axis (that is, the value of y when x = 0).

- 'b' is the slope of the line (the bigger the value of b the greater the slope, ie the greater the increase in y for a unit increase in x; b can be negative which means that y decreases as x increases).

What we need to do is find the straight line which best fits the points in the scatter diagram. Suppose we define the line of best fit as:

$$y = a_0 + b_0 x$$ (where a_0 and b_0 are the values of a and b associated with the specific straight line.)

Then for a value of $x = x_i$, the predicted value of y_i would be $a_0 + b_0 x_i$

We define the **prediction error** as:

actual value – predicted value

$$y - (a_0 + b_0 x_i)$$

We define our *line of best fit* as one for which:

• The sum of errors is zero (that is the sum of the differences of the points above and below our line), the positive and negative errors, cancel out.

• The sum of these errors squared is minimised; the errors are squared to remove the effect of the +ve and −ve signs.

This is known as the **least squares method** and it can be shown that the line of best fit, $y = a_0 + b_0 x$, is when:

$$a_0 = \frac{\Sigma y}{n} - b_0 \frac{\Sigma x}{n}$$

$$b_0 = \frac{\Sigma xy - \frac{\Sigma x \Sigma y}{n}}{\Sigma x^2 - \frac{(\Sigma x)^2}{n}}$$

where n is the number of observations or points on the scatter diagram.

We can calculate the values of a_0 and b_0 manually. Going back to our example, it is helpful to set out a table with the following computations:

Table 30 Comparison of haulage cost against distance – useful tabulations

Job	Distance x	Cost y	xy	x^2	y^2
1	20	200	4,000	400	40,000
2	25	250	6,250	625	62,500
3	35	275	9,625	1,225	75,625
4	37	300	11,100	1,369	90,000
5	48	400	19,200	2,304	160,000
6	60	450	27,000	3,600	202,500
7	75	500	37,500	5,625	250,000
8	80	600	48,000	6,400	360,000
Total	380	2,975	162,675	21,548	1,240,625
	Σx	Σy	Σxy	Σx^2	Σy^2

NB The y^2 column is not required to calculate the regression line, but is included above as it will be used in a later calculation.

Substituting the values from the table into the formulae above we get:

$$b_0 = \frac{\Sigma xy - \dfrac{\Sigma x \Sigma y}{n}}{\Sigma x^2 - \dfrac{(\Sigma x)^2}{n}}$$

$$= \frac{162,675 - \dfrac{(380 \times 2,975)}{8}}{21,548 - \dfrac{(380 \times 380)}{8}}$$

$$= \frac{21,362.5}{3,498}$$

$$= 6.1$$

(We calculate b_0 first because we need to use the value in our calculation of a_0.)

$$a_0 = \frac{\Sigma y}{n} - b_0 \frac{\Sigma x}{n}$$

$$= \frac{2,975}{8} - \frac{6.1 \times 380}{8}$$

$$= 371.9 - 289.8$$

$$= 82.1$$

Therefore our estimated regression equation is:

$$y = 82.1 + 6.1x$$

This shows that there is a positive intercept on the y-axis (at £82.10) and that the slope is such that cost increases with distance at a rate of 6.1:1. Figure 37 shows our regression line:

Figure 37 Estimated regression line

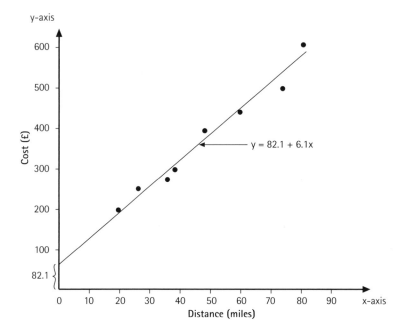

How would we use this equation? Suppose we want to tender, and therefore estimate the cost, for a job which involves a distance of 40 miles? Using our regression equation we get:

$$
\begin{aligned}
y &= 82.1 + 6.1x \\
&= 82.1 + (6.1 \times 40) \\
&= 82.1 + 244 \\
&= 326.1
\end{aligned}
$$

That is, the cost for a journey of 40 miles would be £326.10. We can only be really confident about using the regression equation for predictions of values of x, in this case distance, within the data set that has been used to estimate the equation, ie in this case 20 to 80 miles. If we use it to predict values outside this range then we are making the assumption that the data will continue to behave in the same way. This will not always be the case. For example, we may find that there is a good linear relationship between our yield of potatoes and rainfall – as the rainfall increases so does the yield. However, after a certain level of rainfall the relationship might change significantly – perhaps with the yield even decreasing.

The arithmetic gets somewhat tedious for situations with lots of observations and in practice, you would use a computer package – see Chapter 19. Nevertheless, it is useful to understand what in fact the computer is doing for you. However, the important thing to know is when and how to use regression analysis.

Therefore, we might also want to get some idea of how good a *fit* our regression line is to the raw data. The measure used is called the **coefficient of determination** and is usually denoted by the symbol r^2. It calculates how much of the error $(y - y_0)$ has been reduced by finding the regression line. The coefficient of determination is, in fact, the proportion of the total sum of squares (without using regression) that can be explained using the estimated regression equation, that is:

$$r^2 = \frac{\text{sum of squares explained by regression}}{\text{total sum of squares (before regression)}}$$

The coefficient of determination can be computed by using the following formulae:

Sum of squares explained by regression =

$$\frac{\left(\Sigma xy - \dfrac{\Sigma x \Sigma y}{n}\right)^2}{\Sigma x^2 - \dfrac{(\Sigma x)^2}{n}}$$

Total sum of squares before regression =

$$\Sigma y^2 - \frac{(\Sigma y)^2}{n}$$

You will recognise the same arithmetic terms from before. Using the totals from Table 15.2:

Sum of squares explained by regression

$$= \frac{\left(162{,}675 - \dfrac{380 \times 2{,}975}{8}\right)^2}{21{,}548 - \dfrac{380 \times 380}{8}}$$

$$= \frac{456{,}356{,}406}{3{,}498}$$

$$= 130{,}462$$

Total sum of squares before regression

$$= 1{,}240{,}625 - \frac{2{,}975 \times 2{,}975}{8}$$

$$= 1{,}240{,}625 - 1{,}106{,}328$$

$$= 134{,}296$$

Therefore $r^2 = \dfrac{130{,}462}{134{,}296}$

$$= 0.97$$

Our estimated regression equation has accounted for 0.97 or 97 per cent of the total sum of squares. We would be delighted with a result as high as this in practice, as the closer r^2 is to one (or in explaining 100 per cent of the total sum of squares) the better is the fit of our regression line.

Again in practice we would use a suitable computer package to calculate the coefficient of determination – you do not need to be able to do the calculations. However, we do need to understand what the results tell us.

CORRELATION

There will be many decision-making situations where we are primarily interested in finding out the extent to which two variables are related rather than calculating a linear equation. We use the statistic, the **correlation coefficient**, to establish the strength of the relationship between two variables. The features of the correlation coefficient are:

• The value lies between -1 and $+1$.

• A value of $+1$ means that the two variables are perfectly related in a positive sense, that is, as one increases so does the other. Positive values close to $+1$ show a strong (though not perfect) positive relationship – see scatter diagram in Figure 38.

• A value of -1 means that the two variables are perfectly related in a negative sense, that is, as one increases the other one decreases. Negative values close to -1 show a strong (though not perfect) negative relationship – see scatter diagram in Figure 39.

• Values close to zero show that there is no *linear* relationship – see scatter diagram in Figure 40.

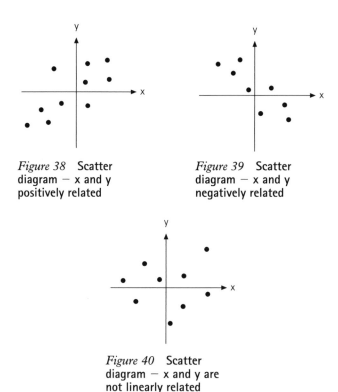

Figure 38 Scatter diagram – x and y positively related

Figure 39 Scatter diagram – x and y negatively related

Figure 40 Scatter diagram – x and y are not linearly related

The correlation coefficient, usually denoted by 'r', is defined by:

$$r = \pm \sqrt{\text{coefficient of determination}}$$

In our example on page 201, $r^2 = 0.97$, therefore:

$$r = \pm \sqrt{0.97}$$
$$= \pm 0.985$$

This shows a strong positive correlation between distance in miles and cost in £s. (From the scatter diagram, it is clear that the relationship is positive.)

There are some very important points that need to be borne in mind when using correlation analysis. In fact caution is the *order of the day* in interpreting our results. We have to be aware that the result on its own tells us little or nothing about the meaning or implications of the relationship other than whether it is strong or not. To explain this point we can use the example of the relationship between cigarette smoking and lung cancer. Originally, the *statistical* evidence was available before the *medical* evidence. The high correlation *suggested* that there was a link between the two but the physical evidence between the two was not available and until the scientists identified the physiological link, the statistical relationship could not be confirmed.

The reason for caution is that it can be quite easy to find examples where two variables are correlated but where it is obvious that changes in the one are not *caused* by changes in the other. Let us take three kinds of examples:

• Each variable may be quite independently related to another third variable, for example, there can be quite a high correlation between the price of washing machines and the price of cars – merely because both are related to a third variable, time.

• The variables may be related via another, intermediate variable. For example, it is likely that there is a high positive relationship between the size of a child's hand and the quality of handwriting. However, there is no direct causal relationship, but the effect of a third variable (age) at work.

• The variables might be linked by sheer chance, sometimes called a nonsense correlation. For example, in the 1930s a *statistical* link was noted between the number of radios in use and the number of suicides. It is possible to test for this chance relationship but we shall not cover it in this book. Readers should simply be aware that the possibility exists.

The final point to be borne in mind is that this chapter has been about testing for a *linear*, that is a straight line, relationship. The two variables could be related in other ways that we will not be covering. Examples of non-linear relationships are curvilinear and exponential, as shown in Figures 41 and 42:

Figure 41   A curvilinear relationship

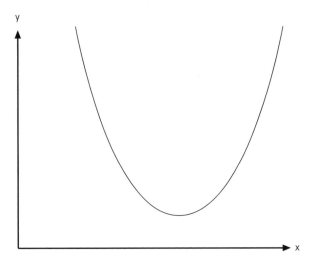

Figure 42 An exponential relationship

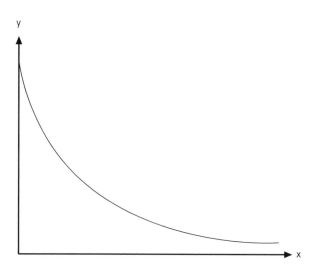

MULTIPLE REGRESSION

Multiple regression sounds a rather grand term for what is really a very simple extension of linear regression. Instead of having only one independent variable, we have two or more. In the real world of business, this is very useful as, by and large, business situations are complex and there may be a number of factors affecting a particular result. For example, if we are launching a new product we might well advertise in newspapers, on television, local radio, etc, and wish to know the impact of each of these forms of advertising on the sales results. Alternatively, we might need to understand what led to a good performance in our sales force – considering factors such as age, years of experience, training, gender, etc.

Explaining how to carry out a multiple regression is beyond the scope of this book. However, we want to tell you enough to recognise when it would be helpful to use this technique and to appraise you of some of its difficulties. There are several computer packages available which will do all the hard work of the calculations – you just need to be aware when the technique might be useful.

First, we must explain the basic concept. Suppose you are trying to examine a particular variable, for example, the sales of a new product and you suspect it is dependent on a number of other variables, x_1, x_2, x_3, etc. In our earlier example, the variables would be the different types of advertising. To start, we set up our equation similarly to the way we did in the linear case:

$$y = a + b_1x_1 + b_2x_2 + b_3x_3 + b_4x_4 \ldots + b_nx_n$$

where y is the dependent variable and x_1, x_2 ... x_n are the independent variables.

Now, from this base we can carry out all sorts of interesting tasks:

• We can calculate the values of b_1 to b_n and hence use our equation to predict values of y from different values of x_1 to x_n. As with the simple linear situation, we can only be confident about such predictions within the respective ranges of each of the variables x_1 to x_n.

• We can find out how good a fit the equation is to our data using r^2, the coefficient of determination.

• We can test whether there is a significant relationship between the dependent variable and independent variables. We can do this as a total and also test each independent variable. Now often, our so-called independent variables are not independent of each other. In our example of the performance of our sales force, age and years of experience might be related. We might find that years of experience is not a significant factor *when* we have age in the equation, although it might be if age was not included. If age proved to be the more powerful influence we would not bother with years of experience in our equation. As far as is possible, it is best to avoid including variables that are highly correlated as it is difficult to separate out the effect of the individual independent variables on the dependent variable.

• We can calculate the importance of each independent variable in explaining the differences in the values of the dependent variable.

It is important to remember again that this technique is based on *linear* relationships. There are lots of other relationships, for example, those that are curvilinear, but here the mathematics becomes a bit more tricky!

CONCLUSION

Well, we hope we hear you say 'that wasn't too bad at all'. Regression and correlation techniques are simple but very powerful statistical tools. However, as we have tried to emphasise the user must beware of trying to draw too many conclusions. We set off with simple linear regression and correlation which are both quite easy to understand, but in practice, it is multiple regression which enables us to cope with more complex situations and which will prove most useful in the business world.

EXERCISES

15.1 A temp agency specialising in clerical staff regularly seeks staff by placing advertisements in the local newspaper. They have been experimenting with the size of the advertisement. The following data shows the number of responses resulting from each advertisement:

Size of advert (column ins)	Responses
1	30
2	42
3	60
4	56
5	82
6	76

A friendly statistician offers to carry out a regression analysis and comes up with the following information:

$y = 23 + 9.9x$, where y = no. of responses and x = size of advert

$r^2 = 0.88$

The agency wants to increase its response to 100 and wants to know what size of advert to select.

Explain with the use of a diagram what this information means and the implication for the business.

15.2 The reservations manager of a major airline wants to estimate the relationship between the number of reservations and the actual numbers of passengers showing up for a specific flight. The manager wishes to use the information to estimate what size of airplane should be used for different reservation levels. For example, what would be the number of passengers with 350 reservations and 425 reservations respectively. Data is gathered over a random sample of 12 different days:

Days	Reservations	Passengers
1	150	210
2	548	405
3	156	120
4	121	89
5	416	304
6	450	320
7	462	319
8	508	410
9	307	275
10	311	289
11	265	236
12	189	170

The research department at the airline supplies the reservations manager with the following information that:

$$y = 57 + 0.64x, \text{ where } y = \text{no. of passengers and } x = \text{no. of reservations}$$

$r^2 = 0.89$

Explain with the use of a diagram what this information means and the implication for the business.

16 Forecasting and time series

INTRODUCTION

This chapter looks at the very useful technique of forecasting; useful in the sense that it can help managers from all professions to focus on what is likely to happen in the future. To be able to predict the future accurately is to be rich beyond comparison and if we were capable of doing this we would need no other business skills at all and most of us would be redundant!

For any organisation, whatever its size, it is vital to plan ahead. Depending on the size and nature of the business, a manager may be required to plan a year ahead or perhaps even twenty years ahead. If you are an operational manager in a manufacturing business you will need to forecast production levels in order to plan for your raw materials, schedule production lines and assess your labour requirements, etc. If you are in retail you will need quite detailed sales forecasts in order to prepare your buying plans, assess your inventory levels, etc. Many large-scale businesses will plan at least five years ahead and sometimes more in order to forecast their requirements for new factories, shops or warehouses and hence their requirements for capital investment.

In Chapter 3 we discussed how our information systems can be used to help in the planning process. This chapter explains some of the statistical techniques we can use to help us plan. However, we must remember that our results will only be as good as the data we use to make the predictions and the extent to which the future is likely to continue along the same lines as the past. Our fallibility in both these respects leaves a place for the manager or specialist to exercise his or her judgement in pursuit of business objectives.

As you will readily appreciate, managers could spend quite a lot of time trying to forecast the future. How is it done? Do they use a crystal ball or, perhaps, the modern equivalent the computerised information system? In fact, there are various ways to approach the challenge of forecasting the future and these fall into two main types: quantitative methods and qualitative methods.

QUANTITATIVE METHODS

Quantitative methods use statistical techniques to analyse the historical data in order to predict the future.

Time series
If we use only historical data relating to the particular item we are trying to forecast, then the forecasting technique is called a **time series** method. For example, if we are a retailer of prams and are trying to forecast sales of prams, then a time series approach would analyse the historical data on pram sales.

Causal approach
If, however, we are going to use historical data relating to other variables, then we use what is called a **causal approach**. In a causal approach to forecasting pram sales we might decide to look at the pattern of births to predict our pram sales. We would use linear or multiple regression techniques to help us.

In this chapter we are going to concentrate on the time series method.

QUALITATIVE METHODS

Qualitative methods usually involve using the judgements of experts as to what the future will hold for us. This is a particularly useful approach if, for some reason, there is no historical data, for example, on the launch of a new product. It is also useful if it is known that something has happened which makes the historical data a poor guide to the future. Examples could be where there has been an advance in technology and the cost of the product drops dramatically, or which affects the demand for a product, or the need for people to produce it. Good examples of this would be the dramatic increase in home computers, the advent of mobile phones, the radical change in our food buying habits from home-prepared to convenience foods, etc. There may be sudden discontinuities caused by new legislation, perhaps on food safety, or unexpected events such as the BSE scare, the collapse of the Asian economies in the late 1990s. We are living in a time of great change, when increasingly perhaps the one certainty is that the future, particularly in the longer term, is unlikely to be the same as the past in many areas. This is putting particular emphasis on qualitative approaches.

Delphi approach

One particular qualitative method used is the **Delphi approach**, which was developed by the Rand Corporation. With this approach a panel of experts are each asked to fill in a questionnaire giving their view of the future for, say, the sales of a product. From the results of the first questionnaire a second is produced which includes the range of opinions of the group. Members of the panel are asked to reconsider their views in the light of the new information from the group. The process goes on until a measure of consensus is reached. The full Delphi approach is a fairly sophisticated technique and it is likely that in many businesses the qualitative method will simply involve a group of people, experts in their areas, sitting around a table thrashing out what appears to be the best forecast for the future.

Other qualitative methods often used, particularly for short-term forecasting, are called **bottom up** or **top down** forecasting (in essence, really the same type of approach).

Bottom up approach

In the bottom up approach, managers at the lowest hierarchical level are asked to make a judgement on what, for example, their sales are going to be and then these forecasts are compiled together. Let us consider the situation in a large retail chain of several stores, with each store consisting of many departments. In the first instance all the department managers in all the stores would be asked to estimate their sales increase for the next year, based on their local knowledge. These departmental estimates would be combined to give the forecast increase for each store and, when the store increases are combined, produce the forecast increase in sales for the whole chain. Top management would then consider the overall result in the light of their knowledge of the wider environment, such as the economic situation, and might accept the overall forecast or vary it according to their assessment.

Top down approach

The top down approach works in the reverse order. Top management will lay down their view of the likely increase in sales overall. This sales forecast will then be allocated across individual stores and the head of each store will allocate the forecast increase across departments.

There are advantages and disadvantages to both approaches. The *bottom up* approach is useful where local conditions can have a significant effect. For example, the sales increase for a store in a rapidly expanding new town is likely to be considerably greater than that for a store in an established area. Also, the approach is considered to be more motivational because those who have to achieve the target forecast have actually been involved in the decision-making for the forecast. The *top down* approach is useful where there are few local variations and the expertise to make the forecasts is concentrated in the head office.

Although qualitative approaches are widely used, we believe that particularly for more short-term forecasting, where it is appropriate and possible to use it, the quantitative approach can produce more helpful results. We are going to concentrate on the quantitative methods for the rest of this chapter and, in particular, the time series approach. Often a combination of approaches may be used – a time series approach to explore the outcomes based on the assumption that the future will continue to be like the past, combined with other more qualitative approaches to look at 'what if' scenarios – what would be the implications of a more rapid increase in demand than the past, what would be the implications of change in leisure habits, etc. It is interesting that in the realms of academia there has been a shift away from relying primarily on quantitative approaches in research to taking a pluralistic approach embracing a wide range of qualitative methods.

STRUCTURE OF A TIME SERIES

A time series is simply a set of results for a particular variable of interest, for example, sales, births, etc, taken over a period of time. In order to try and understand the pattern in a time series of data it is helpful to consider what is known as the structure of the time series. There are four separate elements to consider

- trend

- cyclical

- seasonal

- irregular.

It all sounds a bit technical, but don't worry, it is really very straightforward. Stay with us while we explore each of the above elements in turn.

Trend element

In a set of time series data, the measurements are taken at regular intervals, possibly hourly, daily, weekly, monthly, quarterly, yearly, etc. There will almost certainly be random fluctuations in the data but in some cases the data will exhibit a shift either to lower or higher values over the time period in question. This movement is called the **trend** in the time series and is usually the result of some long term factors such as changes in consumer expenditure, changes in technology, demographic trends, etc.

There may be various trend patterns. Set out in Figures 43 to 46 are some examples comparing sales over time. In our time series graphs, time is always along the x-axis and the variable being measured along the y-axis. Suppose these are sales of consumer products.

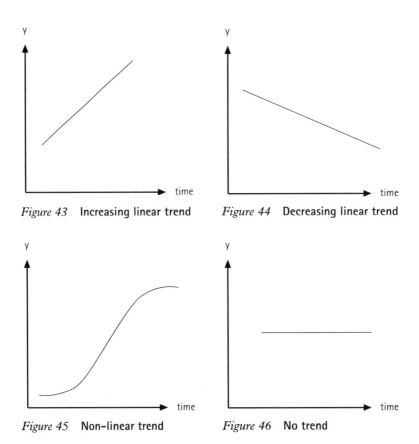

Figure 43   Increasing linear trend

Figure 44   Decreasing linear trend

Figure 45   Non-linear trend

Figure 46   No trend

Figure 43 shows that sales are increasing steadily over time and could represent, say, dishwashers where the market is steadily expanding. Figure 44 shows that sales are decreasing steadily over time. Perhaps this could represent the sales of stand-alone cookers as we move to fitted hobs and built-in ovens. Figure 45 shows a very interesting pattern, a non-linear trend, where sales set off slowly then show a period of rapid growth and finally level off. Students of marketing will recognise this graph as the very common *product life cycle*, where sales of the product are measured from the date of product launch, through its growth period until saturation point is reached and its sales remain steady. Figure 46 shows no trend in sales over time – neither increases nor decreases. This could represent the sales of a basic commodity such as potatoes where, say, with no change in

Figure 47 Cyclical fluctuations

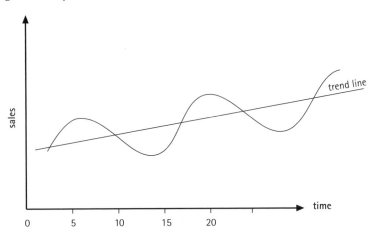

the size of the population, sales might remain quite steady over a long period of time. There may be an occasional *blip* due to, say, a health scare or, alternatively, the promotion of high-fibre jacket potatoes, but there is no overall trend.

Cyclical element

We may have a time series which displays a trend of some sort but in addition will show a cyclical pattern of alternative sequences of observation above and below the trend line. Any regular pattern of observations of this type which lasts longer than a year is called the **cyclical element** of the time series. The graph in Figure 47, displays a cyclical pattern of sales. This is, in fact, a very common occurrence, representing cyclical fluctuations in the economy as evidenced, say, by retail sales.

Seasonal element

Whereas the cyclical pattern is displayed over a number of years, there may be a pattern of variability within one-year periods. For example, the sales of lawnmowers are likely to peak in the second or third quarters of the year, whereas the sales of toys will peak in the pre-Christmas period. The element of the time series which represents variability due to seasonal influences is called, not surprisingly, the **seasonal element**. However, while it normally refers to movements over a one-year period, it can also refer to any repeating pattern of less than one-year's duration. For example, daily passenger figures on the London Underground will show clear *seasonal* movements within the day, with peaks around the rush hour periods of 7.30 am to 9.00 am and 4.30 pm to 6.30 pm, moderate levels during the remainder of the day and a tailing-off in travel during the evening.

Irregular element

Finally we come to the **irregular element** which is that element which cannot be explained by the trend, the cyclical and/or the seasonal elements. It represents the random variability in the time series, caused by unanticipated and non-recurring factors which, by their very nature, are unpredictable.

So let's recap briefly. A time series can show:

• a trend – a long-term shift in the data

• a cyclical pattern – where the measurements show alternate sequences above and below the trend line over periods greater than a year

• a seasonal pattern of movements within a year and, finally

• an irregular element which is the random variability in the data.

In the next section we look first at one of the forecasting techniques called 'smoothing methods', appropriate for fairly stable time series, where there are no significant trends, cyclical or seasonal patterns. We will then go on to look at how to forecast from a time series with a long-term linear trend and finally how to deal with seasonal elements.

SMOOTHING METHODS

Smoothing methods are used to *smooth out* the irregular element of time series where there are no significant trends, cyclical or seasonal patterns. There are two commonly used smoothing methods:

• moving average, and

• exponential smoothing.

We shall discuss only the moving average method in detail as, by and large, it meets most needs. Exponential smoothing is an alternative method, which is a little more complex to calculate, but has the advantage that it requires very little historical data to put it into use. The moving average method involves using the average of the most recent data values to forecast the next period. The number of data values we use to compile our average can be selected in order to minimise the forecasting error – more of this in later pages.

Let us take a simple example of the weekly sales of flour from a supermarket. The data might look like this:

Table 31 Weekly flour sales from a supermarket

Week	Sales (kgs)	Week	Sales (kgs)
1	30	9	31
2	33	10	28
3	29	11	32
4	32	12	35
5	30	13	32
6	32	14	29
7	34	15	31
8	30	16	28

Let us choose to use four data values, that is, base our forecast on a four-week moving average.

Forecast for week 5 = moving average of weeks 1 to 4

$$= \frac{30 + 33 + 29 + 32}{4}$$

$$= 31$$

Since the actual value for week five is 30, the forecast error is said to be $30 - 31$, that is, -1.

We go on with the forecast for week six, dropping the first week's results and including the results for the fifth week as follows.

Forecast for week 6 = moving average of weeks 2 to 5

$$= \frac{33 + 29 + 32 + 30}{4}$$

$$= 31$$

The forecast error is $32 - 31 = +1$.

We go on repeating the calculation and the results are set out in the Table 32 below. The forecast error has been squared to get rid of the minus signs.

Table 32   Weekly flour sales – four-week moving average forecast

Time	Time series	Moving average forecast	Forecast error	Forecast error squared
1	30			
2	33			
3	29			
4	32			
5	30	31.00	−1.00	1.00
6	32	31.00	+1.00	1.00
7	34	30.75	+3.25	10.56
8	30	32.00	−2.00	4.00
9	31	31.50	−0.50	0.25
10	28	31.75	−3.75	14.06
11	32	30.75	+1.25	1.56
12	35	30.25	+4.75	22.56
13	32	31.50	+0.50	0.25
14	29	31.75	−2.75	7.56
15	31	32.00	−1.00	1.00
16	28	31.75	−3.75	14.06
			Totals −4.00	77.86

The results, shown graphically in Figure 48, demonstrate how the moving average *smooths* out the fluctuations in the original series.

We mentioned forecasting error earlier and it would seem that the simple way to work out the overall forecasting error for the series of data would be to take the average of the individual forecasting errors. However, you will see that as some of them are positive and some are negative they tend to cancel each other out. So, instead, we use the average of the squared errors, sometimes referred to as the **mean squared error**. The mean squared error in our example is:

$$\frac{77.86}{12} = 6.49$$

Now, you will remember that we mentioned that we could choose the number of data points to use in our moving average in order to minimise our forecasting error. So, what

Figure 48 Flour sales time series and four–week moving average forecast

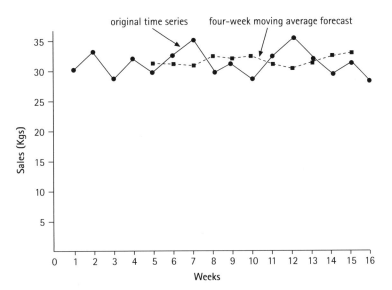

we could do is to repeat the previous calculations for perhaps a three-week or a five-week moving average and see which gives the smallest forecast error. We won't do that here! However, it is very easy to set up the calculations in Microsoft Excel™ – see Chapter 19.

TREND PROJECTIONS

In this section we will look at how we forecast from a time series that shows a long-term linear trend. In fact, we use a technique you are already familiar with – linear regression. Let us consider some of the historical data for the production of toasters set out in Table 33 and shown graphically in Figure 49.

Table 33 Toaster production

Year	Units (000s)	Year	Units (000s)
1	50	6	54
2	52	7	57
3	56	8	60
4	51	9	62
5	48	10	58

Figure 49   Time series of the production of toasters

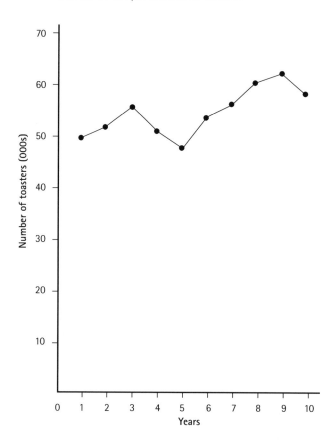

You will recall from Chapter 15 that our linear regression equation linking a dependent variable y and an independent variable x was:

$$y = a_0 + b_0 x$$

In order to emphasise that the independent variable is 'time', we will express the equation as follows:

$$y_t = a_0 + b_0 t$$

where y_t = forecast value of time series in time t
          a_0 = intercept of the trend line
          b_0 = slope of the trend line
          t   = time point.

We can calculate the values of a_0 and b_0 in exactly the same way as we did in Chapter 15 – either manually using the formulae for a_0 and b_0 or using a suitable computer package such as Microsoft Excel™.

We get values of $a_0 = 48.58$ and $b_0 = 1.13$ and therefore the equation can be written:

$$y_t = 48.58 + 1.13t$$

The slope indicates that over the past ten years there has been an increase in production of about 1,130 toasters each year. Figure 50 shows the trend line.

Figure 50   Trend line of the production of toasters – giving forecasts for years 11 and 12

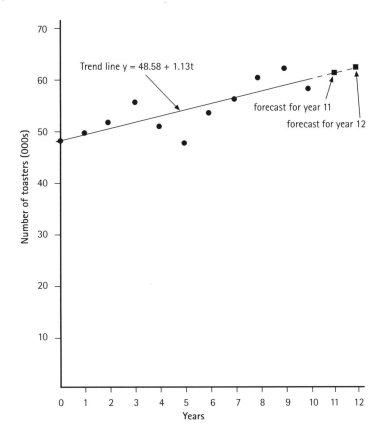

If we wanted to forecast production in years 11 and 12 we would calculate it as follows:

$$y_{11} = 48.58 + 1.13 \times 11$$
$$= 48.58 + 12.43$$
$$= 61.01 \text{ (or 61,010 toasters)}$$

and
$$y_{12} = 48.58 + 1.13 \times 12$$
$$= 48.58 + 13.56$$
$$= 62.14 \text{ (or 62,140 toasters)}$$

and so we could go on.

Remember, this method assumes that we have a linear (straight line) trend and crucially the future will be like the past. As you will remember from our introduction to trends, there are several different types of trend but it is beyond the scope of this book to explain how to deal with non-linear trends.

FORECASTING WITH SEASONAL ELEMENTS

So far we have covered how to forecast a time series where there are no significant trends, cyclical or seasonal elements, using the **moving averages** smoothing method. Then, we looked at how we forecast a time series which displayed a long-term linear trend, using linear regression techniques. Now we are going to explain how to tackle a time series which has both a trend and a seasonal element. (We will not be looking at cyclical elements, as seasonal effects are far more common.) We are going to use what is known, for reasons that will become obvious shortly, as the multiplicative model. There is an alternative approach, the additive model, which we will not pursue here.

The multiplicative approach assumes that the time series value (Y), can be formed by multiplying the trend element (T), the seasonal element (S) and the irregular element (I) as follows:

$$Y = T \times S \times I$$

T is expressed in units of the item being forecast. However, the S $\times$ I factor, referred to as the seasonal factor, is measured in relative terms, with values above one showing a seasonal and irregular effect *above* the trend and values below one showing a seasonal and irregular effect *below* the trend. For example, assume that we have a trend forecast of 100 units for a particular time period and values of S × I equal to 1.08. Then, for that period, the value of the time series is as shown below:

$$Y = 100 \times 1.08$$
$$= 108$$

The first stage in our forecasting procedure is to calculate the seasonal factors. This is a straightforward if lengthy process manually (although very easy to set up on computer using a package such as Microsoft Excel™). It involves smoothing out our time series using the moving averages method described earlier in this chapter. If we assume our seasonal factors are quarterly, then we would calculate our moving averages on groups of four data points. When we are dealing with seasonal elements such as quarters, we need an added step – to work out what are known as *centred moving averages*, which are simply averages of the moving averages. (This is because when we have calculated our quarterly average, say for the first year, we have in effect a figure representing the mid-point of the year, ie between the second and third quarters. Our next moving average will provide an indication of a point between the third and fourth quarters. If we average these two, a centred moving average, we obtain a point against the third quarter.) Dividing our original observations by the equivalent centred moving averages gives us a seasonal factor for each observation. We then take all the seasonal factors shown against the first quarter observations and take an average to obtain the first quarter seasonal factor, and so on for the remaining three quarters (in this way we average out the I effect).

Let us look at a specific example in an area of interest to many professions, that of the energy consumption of a company, measured in gigajoules (a term which allows all energy requirements to be expressed by a common unit regardless of whether they are provided by electricity, coal, gas, etc). The data is set out in Table 34.

Table 34   Energy consumption of a company

Year	Quarter	Energy consumption (000s gigajoules)	Year	Quarter	Energy consumption (000s gigajoules)
1	1	100	4	1	120
	2	80		2	111
	3	70		3	100
	4	90		4	115
2	1	110	5	1	130
	2	93		2	120
	3	98		3	108
	4	100		4	122
3	1	115			
	2	100			
	3	90			
	4	110			

The time series graph of our original observations together with the centred moving averages we have calculated is set out in Figure 51. It shows a clear seasonal influence, with energy consumption being, as one would expect, lowest in the second and third quarters and highest in the first and fourth quarters.

Figure 51   Time series of a company's energy consumption and four-quarterly centred moving average

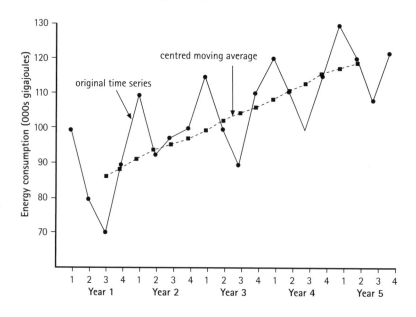

Using the process described earlier we obtain the following seasonal factors:

1st quarter	1.145
2nd quarter	0.983
3rd quarter	0.845
4th quarter	1.027

This shows us, as expected from the graph, that the highest consumption is in the first quarter and is about 14 per cent above the average quarterly value. The lowest level of consumption is in the third quarter and is nearly 16 per cent below the quarterly average. The second and fourth quarters show consumption very close (within 2–3 per cent) to the quarterly average.

We are now ready to go on to the next stage and identify the trend. Let us go back to our model:

$$Y = T \times S \times I$$

Re-write it as:

$$T = \frac{Y}{S \times I}$$

Therefore, it can be seen that the trend element (T) can be calculated by dividing each observation by the appropriate seasonal factor. This process is called **deseasonalising** the time series.

We can now plot the deseasonalised trend line, using the deseasonalised figures rather than using the original observations. Note the difference in Figure 52:

Figure 52   Deseasonalised energy consumption

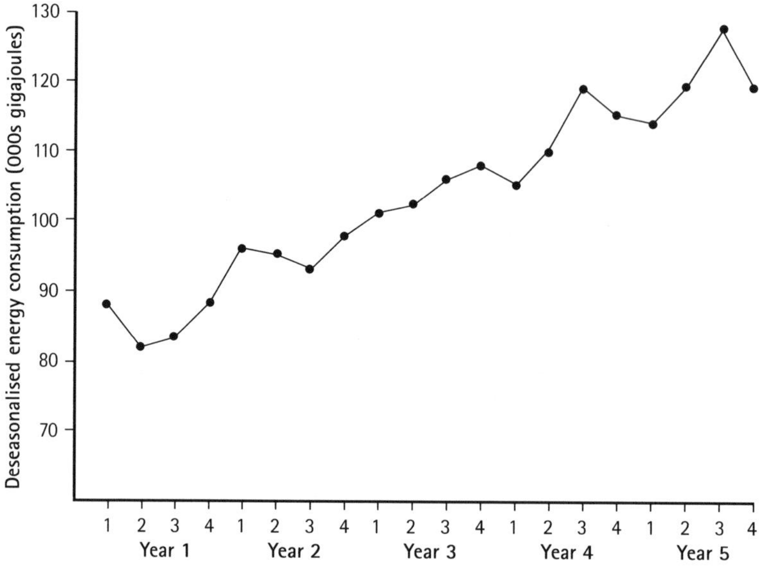

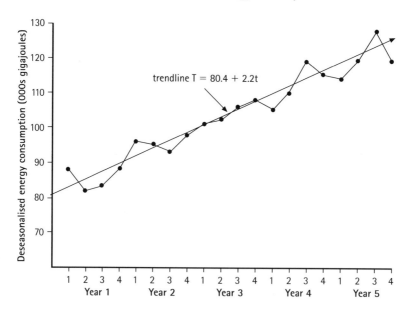

Figure 53   Trend line of deseasonalised energy consumption

Now, although the graph has some fluctuations there is a discernible trend which we can go on to calculate as we did in the previous section, using linear regression. This time, however, we are using the deseasonalised results rather than the original observations. The trend equation can be calculated to give the following:

$$T_t = 80.4 + 2.2t$$

and is shown in Figure 53.

The slope of 2.2 indicates that over the past five years, or 20 quarters, the company has experienced an average deseasonalised increase in energy consumption of 2,200 gigajoules per quarter.

So, if we want to forecast the trend element for the first quarter of year six, that is the twenty-first quarter, we use our trend equation:

$$T_{21} = 80.4 + 2.2 \times 21$$
$$= 126.6$$

We then apply the seasonal factor for the first quarter to get our forecast:

$$Y = 126.6 \times 1.145$$
$$= 145.0$$

In the same way, we can go on to forecast other future quarters.

This may have seemed a rather complex set of calculations. However, it is quite straightforward really – we just need to follow it step by step. First we smoothed the data to identify the seasonal elements for each quarter. We then went on to identify the trend by working out the linear regression equation for the deseasonalised results. We use this trend equation to forecast our trend element and then apply the appropriate quarterly seasonal factor to arrive at our final forecast.

So far we have discussed quarterly data; however, we might have data for a different time interval, where the seasonal effect is, say, monthly. The approach is identical except that a 12-month moving average replaces the quarterly moving average and we go on to identify 12 seasonal factors.

CONCLUSION

So, there you have it – time series analysis and forecasting – all quite straightforward, as we promised. However, all the quantitative methods are critically dependent on the belief that the future will be an extension of the past. Unfortunately for us statisticians, this is not always the case and we must constantly bear this assumption in mind. The further ahead we try and forecast, the less relevant can be the past trends. As ever, in pursuing the statistical technique we must never suspend our professional judgement about the meaningfulness of the results of our calculations and therefore, in the ultimate, the use to which these results can be put.

EXERCISE

16.1 You work for a company that produces lawnmowers and you want to predict the workforce you will require over the next year. You have compiled the following time series data:

Number of people employed

Year	Quarter 1	Quarter 2	Quarter 3	Quarter 4
1	600	1,500	1,000	400
2	1,000	1,800	1,500	700
3	1,400	2,600	2,300	1,200
4	1,900	2,800	2,500	1,800
5	2,200	3,400	2,800	2,100
6	2,400	3,600	3,000	2,000
7	2,800	4,000	3,500	2,700

You handed over the figures to the Company's statistician who provided the following further results and says mysteriously he or she has used the multiplicative time series model.

The seasonal factors are: Quarter 1 = 0.899
Quarter 2 = 1.362
Quarter 3 = 1.118
Quarter 4 = 0.621

The trend equation is:

$$T_t = 633 + 106t$$

Using diagrams, explain the results and their implications for the company. Comment on the method used.

17 Index numbers, published indices and sources of data

INTRODUCTION

Index numbers are used to help understand and present changes in data over time. Rather than simply presenting the data as a series of observations measured over the time it is often clearer and more useful to present them in index number form. This means presenting the data as a proportion or percentage of some base value. For example, suppose we have two factories producing radios and their performance, as measured by the number of radios manufactured, is as follows:

	1995	1996	1997	1998
Factory A	1,500	1,600	1,800	2,200
Factory B	4,000	4,500	4,600	5,000

It is difficult to see which factory has improved its performance most. So, we will express these results as index numbers, using 1995 as the base year. To do this we divide each result by the result for 1995 as shown below. (Alternatively, the index numbers can be presented in percentage form, by multiplying by 100.)

	1995	1996	1997	1998
Factory A	$\frac{1,500}{1,500}$	$\frac{1,600}{1,500}$	$\frac{1,800}{1,500}$	$\frac{2,200}{1,500}$
	= 1.00	= 1.067	= 1.200	= 1.467
Factory B	$\frac{4,000}{4,000}$	$\frac{4,500}{4,000}$	$\frac{4,600}{4,000}$	$\frac{5,000}{4,000}$
	= 1.00	= 1.125	= 1.150	= 1.250

Although Factory B is making 1,000 more radios in 1998 than in 1995, whereas Factory A is making only 700 more, it is clear from using index numbers that Factory A's increase in performance, at 46.7 per cent, is superior to that of Factory B where performance has increased by only 25 per cent.

The usefulness of index numbers becomes even more marked when we are trying to compare unlike items. For example, suppose Factory A makes bottles and Factory B makes cars:

	1995	1996	1997	1998
Factory A (Bottles)	10,000	12,000	13,000	16,000
Factory B (Cars)	500	650	800	900

It is clearly meaningless to try and compare the actual increase in bottles with the actual increase in cars – so, how do you judge an increase of 6,000 bottles against an increase of 400 cars? Well, what about turning them into common units, for example, the money value of production? This could help, but this approach could cause as many problems as it solves! We will look at this suggestion shortly, but first let us look at the increases in terms of an index of units based on 1995. The results are:

	1995	1996	1997	1998
Factory A (Bottles)	1.0	1.2	1.3	1.6
Factory B (Cars)	1.0	1.3	1.6	1.8

Clearly Factory B is increasing production at a faster rate than Factory A.

Let us now look at the example, as suggested earlier, in terms of the value of production. Suppose that the value of a bottle is 25p and the value of a car is £10,000 *and* these values remain constant over time. The results are:

Value of Production (£)

	1995	1996	1997	1998
Factory A (Bottles)	2,500	3,000	3,250	4,000
Factory B (Cars)	5,000,000	6,500,000	8,000,000	9,000,000

We can express this increase in value of production as an index based on 1995. The results are as follows:

	1995	1996	1997	1998
Factory A (Bottles)	1.0	1.2	1.3	1.6
Factory B (Cars)	1.0	1.3	1.6	1.8

Yes, the index numbers are the same as we obtained previously.

However, let us suppose the unit value of the bottle increases as follows:

1995	1996	1997	1998
25p	30p	40p	50p

and the unit value of the car increases as follows:

1995	1996	1997	1998
10,000	11,000	12,000	13,000

Now the value of production (£) is:

	1995	1996	1997	1998
Factory A (Bottles)	2,500	3,600	5,200	8,000
Factory B (Cars)	5,000,000	7,150,000	9,600,000	11,700,000

Expressing these results as index numbers with 1995 as the base year, we get:

	1995	1996	1997	1998
Factory A (Bottles)	1.00	1.44	2.08	3.20
Factory B (Cars)	1.00	1.43	1.92	2.34

The picture has changed: Factory A appears to be performing better, but is it? No, the answer has been clouded by the price increase. Factory A has not increased its productivity more than Factory B, it has merely benefited from a steeper price increase. So we must be very careful, when we make such comparisons, that we understand *what* we are comparing and *what* conclusions can be drawn. In the next section we consider this issue of the changing value of money as we look at one of the most well-known and useful indices, the Retail Price Index (RPI).

RETAIL PRICE INDEX (RPI)

The **retail price index** (RPI) is probably the most important and useful published index. It is also the one most often quoted in the media. After the period of very high price inflation in the 1970s it is now seen as an important economic indicator – of how well the economy is doing. It is probably the only economic indicator that is readily understood and appreciated by the non-economist, as people can see the direct impact on their financial well-being.

So, what does the RPI do? It purports to measure the change in prices over a period of time. The base year is revised at regular intervals to maintain it as a readily understood set of indices. It was revised in January 1974 and again in January 1987. These months then became the base points for subsequent years. (Incidentally, the RPI is presented in the percentage form of the index, ie with 100 for the base period.) The RPI is designed to try and measure changes in prices in an average or representative *basket* of goods and services. The main categories in the current basket and for which separate indices are published are:

- food
- catering
- alcoholic drink
- tobacco
- housing
- fuel and lighting
- household goods
- household services
- clothing and footwear
- personal goods and services
- motoring expenditure
- fares and other travel costs
- leisure goods
- leisure services.

Within each category there is a vast range of individual items – the index covers a selection of more than 600 separate goods and services. Basically a sample of prices is taken from different areas and different types of stores on a monthly basis. From these it is possible to estimate individual indices. How then do we arrive at one figure – one index number? A simple way would be to take a straight average, that is, take all the different index numbers based on the same year, add them together and divide by the number of categories.

So let's take a simplified example. Suppose we have three items (A, B and C) with indices for January 1998 based on January 1995:

$$I_A = 110$$
$$I_B = 130$$
$$I_C = 140$$

$$\text{Simple average} = \frac{110 + 130 + 140}{3}$$
$$= \frac{380}{3}$$
$$= 126.7$$

This would only be appropriate if each of the separate indices was equally important. However, it is quite obvious that changes in housing prices will have a much greater impact on the population at large than changes in tobacco or alcoholic drinks; because people spend very much more on housing than on tobacco or alcoholic drinks. Therefore, in order to arrive at a true average, it is necessary to weight the different components. Going back to our simple example, let us suppose that the average family spends 50 per cent of its income on item A, 30 per cent on item B and 20 per cent on item C.

$$\text{Weighted average} = 110 \times \frac{50}{100} + 130 \times \frac{30}{100} + 140 \times \frac{20}{100}$$
$$= (110 \times 0.5) + (130 \times 0.3) + (140 \times 0.2)$$
$$= 55 + 39 + 28$$
$$= 122$$

Table 35 Retail prices index (all items)

January 1974 = 100

	Annual average	Jan	Feb	Mar	Apr	May	June	July	Aug	Sept	Oct	Nov	Dec
1984	351.8	342.6	344.0	345.1	349.7	351.0	351.9	351.5	354.8	355.5	357.7	358.8	358.5
1985	373.2	359.8	362.7	366.1	373.9	375.6	376.4	375.7	376.7	376.5	377.1	378.4	378.9
1986	385.9	397.7	381.1	381.6	385.3	386.0	385.8	384.7	385.9	387.8	388.4	391.7	393.0
1987		394.5											

January 1987 = 100

	Annual average	Jan	Feb	Mar	Apr	May	June	July	Aug	Sept	Oct	Nov	Dec
1987	101.9	100.0	100.4	100.6	101.8	101.9	101.9	101.8	102.1	102.4	102.9	103.4	103.3
1988	106.9	103.3	103.7	104.1	105.8	106.2	106.6	106.7	107.9	108.4	109.5	110.0	110.3
1989	115.2	111.0	111.8	112.3	114.3	115.0	115.4	115.5	115.8	116.6	117.5	118.5	118.8
1990	126.1	119.5	120.2	121.4	125.1	126.2	126.7	126.8	128.1	129.3	130.3	130.0	129.9
1991	133.5	130.2	130.9	131.4	133.1	133.5	134.1	133.8	134.1	134.6	135.1	135.6	135.7
1992	138.5	135.6	136.3	136.7	138.8	139.3	139.3	138.8	138.9	139.4	139.9	139.7	139.2
1993	140.7	137.9	138.8	139.3	140.6	141.1	141.0	140.7	141.3	141.9	141.8	141.6	141.9
1994	144.1	141.3	142.1	142.5	144.2	144.7	144.7	144.0	144.7	145.0	145.2	145.3	146.0
1995	149.1	146.0	146.9	147.5	149.0	149.6	149.8	149.1	149.9	150.6	149.8	149.8	150.7
1996	152.7	150.2	150.9	151.5	152.6	152.9	153.0	152.4	153.1	153.8	153.8	153.9	154.4
1997	157.5	154.4	155.0	155.4	156.3	156.9	157.5	157.5	158.5	159.3	159.5	159.6	160.0
1998	162.9	159.5	160.3	160.8	162.6	163.5	163.4	163.0	163.7	164.4	164.5	164.4	164.4

Source: *Monthly Digest of Statistics,* Office for National Statistics © Crown Copyright 1999

The weighted average, 122, is less than the simple average, 126.7, reflecting that the price increase in the most important item – Item A – is rather less than the other two items. The government statisticians use the results of another survey, the Family Expenditure Survey, to arrive at the different weighting factors to apply. This survey examines expenditure patterns of a sample of households.

Set out in Table 35 is the Retail Price Index from 1984 to the end of 1998. It can be seen that it provides monthly indices and average annual indices between 1984 and 1998, and that it has been rebased in 1987.

So, how do we work out a particular increase in prices? Let's look at some examples:

• What is the price increase between January 1988 and July 1993?

Index for January 1988 = 103.3
Index for July 1993 = 140.7

We want the July 1993 index based on January 1988, that is, rebasing the index on January 1988 = 100, so we divide each index by 1.033:

Index for January 1988   = $\dfrac{103.3}{1.033}$ = 100.0
(Based on January 1988 = 100)

Index for July 1993   = $\dfrac{140.7}{1.033}$ = 136.2
(Based on January 1988 = 100)

Therefore prices have increased by 36.2 per cent over the period January 1988 to July 1993.

- What is the price increase between 1990 and 1995? Here we use the annual averages and in fact these are probably most frequently used and quoted. The calculations are just the same as before.

Average index for 1990   = 126.1
Average index for 1995   = 149.1

Again, we want the 1995 index based on 1990, that is, when the index in 1990 = 100, so we divide each index by 1.261:

Index for 1990   = $\dfrac{126.1}{1.261}$ = 100.0
(Based on 1990 = 100)

Index for 1995   = $\dfrac{149.1}{1.261}$ = 118.2
(Based on 1990 = 100)

Therefore prices have increased by 18.2 per cent between 1990 and 1995.

- What is the price increase between March 1986 and December 1990?

This is a little trickier as the index was rebased in 1987. The index number for January 1987, with January 1974 as the base year, is 394.5. To get index numbers based on January 1987 as 100 we therefore divide by 3.945. To go the other way, that is, from an index based on January 1987 = 100 to January 1974 = 100, we multiply the index number by 3.945 as follows:

Index for December 1990   = 129.9
(Based on January 1987 = 100)

Index for December 1990   = 129.9 × 3.945 = 512.5
(Based on January 1974 = 100)

Index for March 1986 = 381.6
(Based on January 1974 = 100)

We now have both our indices on the same base, ie January 1974 = 100. Next we calculate March 1986 as our new base point, converting it to 100 by dividing by 3.816:

Index for March 1986 $= \dfrac{381.6}{3.816} = 100.0$
(Based on March 1986 = 100)

Index for December 1990 $= \dfrac{512.5}{3.816} = 134.3$
(Based on March 1986 = 100)

Therefore prices have increased by 34.3% over the period March 1986 to December 1990.

• What is the price increase between 1984 and 1997? Again we are covering a period with a change of base year, so we proceed as in the previous example.

Average index for 1997 = 157.5
(Based on January 1987 = 100)

Average index for 1997 $= 157.5 \times 3.945 = 621.3$
(Based on January 1974 = 100)

Average index for 1984 = 351.8
(Based on January 1974 = 100)

As we want the 1997 index to be based on 1984, we divide each index by 3.518.

Index for 1984 $= \dfrac{351.8}{3.518} = 100.0$
(Based on 1984 = 100)

Index for 1997 $= \dfrac{621.3}{3.518} = 176.6$
(Based on 1984 = 100)

Therefore prices have increased by 76.6 per cent between 1984 and 1997.

So, as we have seen, it is quite simple to manipulate the indices to get the information we want, but how might we use this information?

Use of the Retail Price Index

The Retail Price Index is a vital tool when we want to look at the trend in data over time which is affected by price increases. An obvious example is earnings – suppose we want to look at how the earnings of our workforce have increased after allowing for inflation, or increased in *real* terms, which is the phrase commonly used. Suppose average earnings had moved in actual terms, as follows, and were expressed as an index based on 1990 = 100, as shown in Table 36.

Table 36   Average Earnings Index

Year	Earnings (£)	Index
1990	8,000	100
1991	8,400	105
1992	9,400	118
1993	10,100	126
1994	10,800	135
1995	11,400	143
1996	11,800	148
1997	12,300	154

Over the whole period, earnings have apparently increased in money terms (that is, not adjusted for price inflation) by 54 per cent.

Now let us adjust for price inflation using the RPI. There are two ways of doing this, both basically the same – either express all the earnings at 1990 prices or at 1997 prices. In fact we could express them in any price year, as long as we are consistent. Let's do it in terms of 1990 prices, and choose June 1990 as the base period. We multiply each year's earnings by:

$$\frac{\text{RPI June 1990}}{\text{RPI in June of that year}}$$

The results are shown in Table 37.

Table 37   Earnings adjusted for price inflation

Year	Actual earnings (£)	RPI (June)	Earnings at 1990 prices (£)	Index numbers
1990	8,000	126.7	8,000 × 126.7 ÷ 126.7 = 8,000	100
1991	8,400	134.1	8,400 × 126.7 ÷ 134.1 = 7,936	99
1992	9,400	139.3	9,400 × 126.7 ÷ 139.3 = 8,550	107
1993	10,100	141.0	10,100 × 126.7 ÷ 141.0 = 9,075	113
1994	10,800	144.7	10,800 × 126.7 ÷ 144.7 = 9,457	118
1995	11,400	149.8	11,400 × 126.7 ÷ 149.8 = 9,642	121
1996	11,800	153.0	11,800 × 126.7 ÷ 153.0 = 9,772	122
1997	12,300	157.5	12,300 × 126.7 ÷ 157.5 = 9,895	124

By using the RPI we get quite a different picture. Overall *real* earnings have increased by only 24 per cent in the seven years. In the first year, earnings in real terms, actually declined slightly. This was because although the employees' earnings rose by 5 per cent, inflation rose by 6 per cent (134.1 ÷ 126.7). Then, between 1995 and 1996 in real terms, earnings were virtually static. As you will appreciate, we feel sure, the trade unions will be far keener to talk about real earnings than actual earnings!

Clearly, when you are looking at earnings over a very long period, for example in social research, taking account of price inflation becomes essential. This is well demonstrated in the following extract from the *Independent* reporting on a survey of the lives of children and young people:

> When teenagers started work in 1949, they were paid relatively low wages. On average a man aged under 21 earned 58 shillings and sixpence (£2.92) a week (or £152 per year), which, taking account of inflation, would be an annual wage of £2,872 today. Girls under 18 earned the equivalent of £2,460. The report said: "Even the lowest paid just-out of-school workers would get at least £5,000 a year."
>
> (*Independent*, January 1999)

Let's take another example. Suppose you are the manager of a department store and you measure your performance by sales. However, you are really interested to know how your sales have increased in real terms, or what the *volume* sales increase is (as opposed to the sales *value* increase in actual money terms). This time we will express our sales in terms of the latest year, 1997, and use the average annual indices which we get by multiplying the sales figures by:

$$\frac{\text{RPI in 1997}}{\text{RPI in that year}}$$

Table 38 Sales volumes

Year	Actual sales (£m)	RPI (annual average)	Sales at 1997 prices (£m)	Index numbers
1993	20	140.7	20 × 157.5 ÷ 140.7 = 22.4	100
1994	25	144.1	25 × 157.5 ÷ 144.1 = 27.3	122
1995	27	149.1	27 × 157.5 ÷ 149.1 = 28.5	127
1996	30	152.7	30 × 157.5 ÷ 152.7 = 30.9	138
1997	36	157.5	36 × 157.5 ÷ 157.5 = 36.0	161

Therefore, over the period 1993 to 1997, sales have increased by volume by some 61%.

We hope you have begun to see just how useful is the RPI. The most commonly available source is the *Monthly Digest of Statistics* which, as the name suggests, is published monthly. There are other price indices available, geared towards particular sectors. For example, producer price indices which measure the prices that producers have to pay for inputs such as raw materials and fuel. It is a *producers'* price index rather than a *consumers'* price index like the RPI. As the price of inputs eventually feed through to the finished product and consumer prices, the producer price indices are often seen as an early warning of changes in inflation levels.

STOCK MARKET INDICES

Another set of well-known and regularly quoted indices are those applying to the stock market. Stock market indices tell us the movement over time in aggregate share prices, or the prices of other securities. In Great Britain the most widely used and best known are those published by the *Financial Times*. There are three types – the FT-Ordinary (or 30-Share) Index, the FT-Actuaries Indices and the FT-Stock Exchange 100 Index. Their method of calculation and uses are quite different.

The FT-Ordinary Index was started in 1935 and is the one which gets the most publicity. It is a price index of the shares of 30 premier industrial, financial and commercial companies in the UK. The companies are leaders in their fields and are selected to give a wide coverage of industries together representing a relatively large part of the stock market as a whole. The index of 100 represents this average at the base date of 1 July 1935. The Index is calculated every hour, on the hour, between 10.00 am and 4.00 pm, and at the *close* around 5.00 pm.

The FT-Actuaries Share Indices are designed to measure particular portfolio performance. There are over 30 groups or subsections and they are compiled jointly by the *Financial Times*, the Institute of Actuaries and the Faculty of Actuaries. The Indices' main function is to serve as a reliable measure of portfolio performance. The FT-Actuaries All Share Index represents over three-quarters of the total market value of shares on the stock exchange.

The FT-SE 100 Index was designed to meet the need for an index which would cover options and futures contracts based on the UK market. The basis of calculation of the FT-SE 100 Index is very similar to that of the All Share Index, but based, as the name suggests, on only 100 companies. The Index is recalculated almost continuously throughout the day from 9.00 am to well after the official close. The base level was set at 1,000 at the end of business on 30 December 1983.

There are other Indices published by the *Financial Times* for specific purposes, and by overseas organisations. These latter ones should be used with caution because (you will appreciate this as a student of statistics) they are not all calculated in the same way. One of the best known of the foreign indices is the Dow Jones Industrial Average. This is an unweighted arithmetic average of 30 leading shares on the New York stock exchange.

SOURCES OF DATA

Sources of data are categorised into two main types – primary data and secondary data. Primary data is data that you collect specifically for your own purpose(s). For example, carrying out a survey of staff attitudes to the staff restaurant or asking managers to monitor timekeeping over a period of time. Secondary data is data that has been collected for another purpose which you will then go on to use for your analysis. In simplistic terms there are three types of secondary data:

1. Information within your own organisation. For example, it is likely that you will have access to a wide range of information, eg sales information, information on employees, such as numbers, ages, salary levels, absence data, etc. This information will probably have been collected to monitor performance of the organisation, or for payroll or pension purposes, etc. However, you may want to go on and take this data to analyse productivity, explore absence rates and their relationship to other variables such as age, salary level, etc, ie use it for your own purpose. The advantage of this type of secondary data is that it is usually readily available (assuming your organisation has a well-designed and developed information system – see Part 1). There may be problems of confidentiality and perhaps issues such as the data not quite being in the form that you want it, eg perhaps there has been a reorganisation and it is difficult to track sales and workforce information for a specific department over time, or data from the performance management system are kept as individual records on a manual system and it is a major collation job to look at average performance grades, etc.

2. Information that is in the public domain. We talk in the next section about some of the most useful sources from government statistical publications. The government amasses and publishes information on a wide range of areas – usually in very summary form, for the UK as a whole or particular sectors of industry. There are also sources of published information on individual organisations.

3. Private market research information – which is available at a cost, perhaps through membership of a particular group of organisations or simply by purchasing the results.

Information from within your organisation is essentially the subject of Part 1 of this book. We will go on here to look at the other areas.

GOVERNMENT STATISTICAL PUBLICATIONS

Some of the most commonly used sources are set out below and categorised by type of data. All are available from The Stationery Office, tel: 0870 600 5522.

General Information

General information is set out in the following publications:

- *Monthly Digest of Statistics* – a collection of the main sources of statistics from all Government departments.

- *Annual Abstract of Statistics* – contains more series of data than the *Monthly Digest* and a greater run of years.

- *Social Trends* – includes key social and demographic series of data (annual).

- *Regional Trends* – includes a wide range of demographic, social, industrial and economic statistics at a regional level (annual).

Population and households

Population and household information is available from:

- *Census* – a full census is carried out every 10 years, the last one was in 1991, giving information across a whole range of subjects, for example, household composition, income, transport to work, etc.

- *Family Expenditure Survey* – sets out the income and expenditure in a detailed form by type of household (annual).

- *General Household Survey* – a continuous sample survey of households covering a wide range of social and economic policy areas (annual).

Manpower/earnings/retail prices

Details on manpower, earnings and retail prices are set out in:

- *Department of Employment Gazette* – includes information on employment and unemployment, hours worked, earnings, labour costs and retail prices, etc, (monthly).

- *New Earnings Survey* – relates to earnings from employment by industry category, at April each year. (From the Office for National Statistics, tel. 01633 812 078.)

General economy

General economic statistics are set out in:

- *Economic Trends* – a useful selection of tables and charts on the United Kingdom economy (monthly).

- *United Kingdom National Accounts – the Blue Book* – gives detailed estimates of the national accounts (annual). It is a bit heavy going for most people but beloved of economists.

Industrial production and sales

Details on industrial production and sales are reported in the *Census of Production* (annual) – available by industry and in summary form. Data is included on total purchases, sales, stocks, work in progress, capital expenditure, employment, etc. A useful reference tool is the *Guide to Official Statistics* which provides a comprehensive list of official statistics with a brief description of the data and their availability.

PRIVATE MARKET RESEARCH

There are numerous surveys carried out regularly by private agencies. Some of the ones with which we are most familiar are:

- income and earnings surveys

- public opinion surveys on such topics as the state of the UK political parties, our views on the environment, etc

- surveys aimed at particular industries or products, for example, the *Which* consumer surveys on cars, market reports produced by such organisations as the Economist Intelligence Unit.

ORGANISATION INFORMATION

There are three excellent sources of information on individual organisations:

- The Annual Report and Accounts published by all large companies. Often these are in the form of glossy brochures and, apart from giving the financial information on the company, will give background information on the company's products, workforce, markets, expansion plans, etc.

- Stockbroker bulletins – the City brokers regularly produce bulletins on companies for their investors. Again, although biased towards the investor, they usually provide a very useful appraisal of that company.

- Newspaper articles – particularly from the *Financial Times*, and other quality newspapers – often provide an easy-to-read, potted summary of the company. They are usually produced around the time of the company's results being announced or when there is some particular interest in the company – perhaps there is a takeover bid or the company has diversified in some way. Some large libraries, for example, the City Business Library, carry a very useful reference set of such articles, called McCarthy Cards, indexed by company name.

A growing trend for information in the public domain is to be able to obtain access to it through the Internet.

Finally, a word of caution about all sources of secondary data. It is very important to read the small print – does the data refer to the UK or Great Britain, how does your workforce data deal with part-time workers, does your salary information include bonuses, have there been any changes in the way the data has been collected over time, etc. The great advantage of secondary data is that it is usually much cheaper than collecting your own primary data and often immediately available. Its great downfall is that you need to be sure that it does, in fact, provide you with the information you need.

CONCLUSION

We hope that our discussion of index numbers has given you a feel for this very useful topic. Together with the rich and varied sources of information detailed above, it should help you to get to grips with analysing and understanding organisations and their happenings. If in doubt about sources of information, a good place to start is the research library of your own organisation, where such a facility exists. The IPD's own library is another useful source and, of course, increasingly such information is available through the Internet. Otherwise your local college/university library, or the local public library, will contain a surprising amount of information and have very helpful staff who know where to find it for you.

EXERCISES

17.1 You work for an organisation that makes components for cars. You want to know how productivity has changed over the last five years in a factory which makes a specific component. There was a major upgrade of the machines in Year 4. You have assembled the following information:

Year	Production (000's)	Workforce
1	323	165
2	350	173
3	363	175
4	405	200
5	455	200

Comment on the results.

17.2 Your occupational scheme adjusts its pensions in payment by the rate of RPI (see Table 36) or 5 per cent whichever is the lower. You have been asked by your MD to check the value of pensions since 1991. The average pension in 1991 was £5,000. The MD also wants to know what would have been the value of the average pension if it had been adjusted by the average earnings increases for the company between 1991and 1997. Comment on the results.

The average earnings for your organisation:

Year	Earnings (£)
1991	13,500
1992	14,200
1993	14,900
1994	15,400
1995	16,000
1996	16,600
1997	17,300

18 Decision theory

INTRODUCTION

We talk in Part 1 about the purpose of information systems being to provide information for our decision-making and a little about the decision-making process. **Decision theory** is a rather grand name for what is quite a straightforward approach to decision-making. Decision theory or, as it is sometimes called, decision analysis, is used to arrive at an optimal (best) strategy when faced with a number of alternative strategies or decisions and an uncertain future situation. Take a very simple example, suppose we are a buyer for a clothes shop and we need to decide in the Autumn how much rainwear to buy for the Spring. Clearly if it is a wet Spring and Summer demand will be great, but if the sun shines a lot, the demand will be limited. On the one hand we want to buy enough to meet demand and gain maximum profits – on the other hand we do not want to buy too much and end up having stock on our hands at the end of the season which we have to reduce in price to sell. How do we decide what to buy so far in advance? We cannot know for certain what the weather is going to be like so far ahead. We will look first at a very simple way of structuring such decisions using the technique of pay-off tables and then applying some simple decision criteria. We will then go on to discuss the technique of expected monetary value and the concepts of risk and utility.

PAY-OFF TABLES

The best way to explain decision theory is to use an example. Suppose we are furniture manufacturers and we want to build a new factory. We have the choice between building either a small, medium or large factory. We, therefore, have three decision choices which we will call d_1, d_2 and d_3:

d_1 = build a small factory
d_2 = build a medium size factory
d_3 = build a large factory

Our decision will be based on how we see the future market for our product. In this simple example suppose there are two possible outcomes – a high demand or a low demand for our furniture. If we build our factory too small and demand is high we will lose sales and profit. However, if we build our factory too large and demand is low, then we will have expensive spare capacity on our hands and potential losses. So, let us label our two outcomes o_1 and o_2:

o_1 = low demand
o_2 = high demand

The next step is to estimate the *pay-offs* for each combination of decision and outcome. In this case the pay-off would be measured in terms of profit and we can construct a **pay-off table** for this decision-making problem as follows:

Decision choices	Outcomes	
	Low demand o_1	High demand o_2
Build a small factory d_1	£20,000	£50,000
Build a medium factory d_2	£10,000	£80,000
Build a large factory d_3	−£10,000	£100,000

The figures in the above pay-off table are our best estimates of what the profit might be under the different circumstances. In a commercial situation it is possible that we would have some idea of what the demand might be – in other words we would have a good idea as to how probable it is that there would be a high demand or a low demand. However, let us assume that we have no confidence in our view of the future. In this case, we will need some criteria or some basis on which to make our decision. Let us look at two of these – the **maximin/minimax** criterion and the **maximax/minimin** criterion.

Maximin/minimax

The **maximin** decision criterion is the pessimistic, or conservative, approach to arriving at a decision. As the name suggests, we maximise the minimum possible pay-offs or, in our case, profits. So, first, taking the figures from the table above list the minimum pay-offs for each decision:

Decision Choices	Minimum Pay-off
Build a small factory d_1	£20,000
Build a medium factory d_2	£10,000
Build a large factory d_3	−£10,000

We then choose the decision which gives us the maximum of the minimum pay-offs. In this example we would choose d_1 – to build a small factory.

If our pay-off table was constructed on the basis of costs rather than profit, we would reverse the criterion to **minimax**, that is, we would choose the minimum from the list of the maximum costs related to each decision.

Maximax/minimin

While maximin and minimax offers a pessimistic decision criterion, **maximax** does quite the opposite – it provides an optimistic criterion. Let us take our example again from the pay-off table, but this time list the maximum pay-offs for each decision:

Decision Choices	Maximum Pay-off
Build a small factory d_1	£50,000
Build a medium factory d_2	£80,000
Build a large factory d_3	£100,000

Then we select the decision which gives the maximum pay-off – in this case we would decide to build a large factory. Again, if we are dealing with a pay-off table of costs, we would reverse the criterion and use a **minimin** criterion.

EXPECTED MONETARY VALUE

We will now go on to look at the slightly more complex but more useful technique for making decisions where you have some expectation, or can apply some probability to the outcomes. Suppose we have a number 'n' of decision alternatives:

$d_1 \, d_2 \, \ldots \, d_n$

and a number 'N' of outcomes

$o_1, o_2 \, .. \, o_N$

Suppose also:

> p_1 = probability of outcome o_1 occurring
> p_2 = probability of outcome o_2 occurring
> .
>
> .
>
> .
>
> p_N = probability of outcome o_N occurring

You will recall from the discussion on probability in Chapter 12 that:

> $p_i \geq 0$ for all outcomes, and
> $p_1 + p_2 + \ldots + p_N = 1$

The **expected monetary value** of a decision is the sum of the weighted pay-offs for each outcome, with the weights being the probability of that pay-off or outcome occurring.

Therefore, the expected monetary value (EMV) of decision d_i

> $= p_1 \times$ pay-off for decision i and outcome 1
> $+ \, p_2 =$ pay-off for decision i and outcome 2
> .
>
> .
>
> .
>
> $+ \, p_N \times$ pay-off for decision i and outcome N

Using this formula and our factory example, let us assume that there is a probability of 0.4 that low demand will be the outcome, and a probability of 0.6 that high demand will be the outcome, then:

> EMV of decision d_1 = $(0.4 \times 20{,}000) + (0.6 \times 50{,}000)$
> = £38,000
> EMV of decision d_2 = $(0.4 \times 10{,}000) + (0.6 \times 80{,}000)$
> = £52,000
> EMV of decision d_3 = $(0.4 \times -10{,}000) + (0.6 \times 100{,}000)$
> = £56,000

The criterion for selection is the decision with the highest expected monetary value – in our case, d_3.

If the probabilities are reversed, that is, the probability for low demand is 0.6 and for high demand it is 0.4, then the calculation produces the following EMVs:

$$\text{EMV of decision } d_1 = (0.6 \times 20,000) + (0.4 \times 50,000)$$
$$= £32,000$$
$$\text{EMV of decision } d_2 = (0.6 \times 10,000) + (0.4 \times 80,000)$$
$$= £38,000$$
$$\text{EMV of decision } d_3 = (0.6 \times -10,000) + (0.4 \times 100,000)$$
$$= £34,000$$

Now the decision to be taken is d_2 – to build a medium factory.

So, it can be seen that the choice of decision is critically dependent on the probabilities of the different outcomes occurring. More about this later, but let us now take a look at a way of analysing decision-making problems graphically using a decision tree.

DECISION TREES

You will remember that in Chapter 12 we used a tree diagram to visualise a multi-step experiment of tossing a coin twice. We use a similar diagram here to help in the solution of decision-making problems. We can re-express our furniture factory problem, using a **decision tree**, as in Figure 54.

The tree is made up of nodes:

• decision nodes

• outcome nodes.

and branches:

• decision branches

• outcome branches.

If we now add in the probabilities of the outcomes occurring, being for example, 0.4 for low demand and 0.6 for high demand, then the tree looks like Figure 55, page 254.

Figure 54 **Decision tree of factory problem**

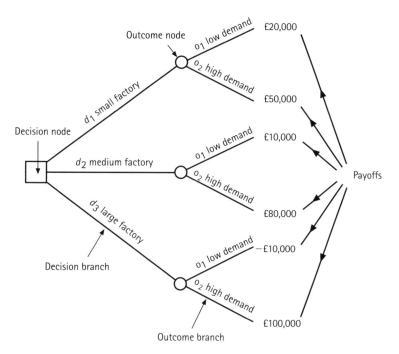

We work backwards through the tree shown in Figure 55 overleaf.

EMV of node 2   = (0.4 × 20,000) + (0.6 × 50,000)
(Same as EMV of d_1) = £38,000

EMV of node 3   = (0.4 × 10,000) + (0.6 × 80,000)
(Same as EMV of d_2) = £52,000

EMV of node 4   = (0.4×−10,000) + (0.6 × 100,000)
(Same as EMV of d_3) = £56,000

We work backwards again and now have the decision tree which looks like Figure 56, page 254.

It can be seen that the best decision is again d_3 – exactly the same as using the expected monetary value criteria and the pay-off table – the decision tree is really just a graphical representation of the pay-off table.

Figure 55 **Decision tree of factory problem showing probabilities of the outcomes**

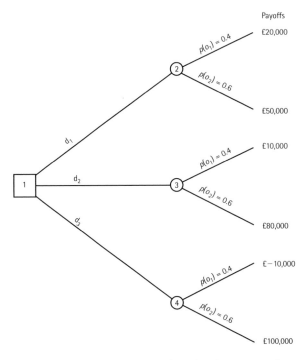

Figure 56 **Decision tree of factory problem showing expected monetary values of the decisions**

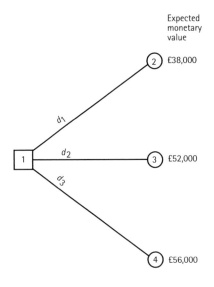

We have noted the importance of the probabilities of the outcomes. How do we arrive at them? Well, there are several ways – for example, we might look at what has happened in similar circumstances in the past or we might carry out a market research survey. It is even possible to work out how much it is worth paying for information on probabilities.

RISK AND UTILITY

Another area of decision-making concerns the decision-maker's attitude to risk. Suppose we are faced with the choice of two investments – investment 'X' will provide us with a definite return of £10,000; investment 'Y' will provide us with a fifty/fifty chance of £30,000 or nothing:

EMV (X) = £10,000
EMV (Y) = (0.5 × 30,000) + (0.5 × 0) = £15,000

Based on our earlier criterion we should choose investment Y. However, it is quite likely that the investor would choose investment X. We see creeping in here the preference of the decision-maker. Investment X is said to have a higher *utility* – utility being a measure of the decision-maker's preference which takes into account not just the expected monetary value but the risks involved.

The concept of utility is particularly useful where there is no strict money value, like profits or costs, associated with an outcome. There are some interesting examples of this in the field of medicine and to demonstrate the contribution that decision theory can make to dealing with such problems, let's look at the very difficult decision which faces older pregnant women. The risk of Down's Syndrome and other disorders increases with age but can be identified prior to birth by using a test called an amniocentesis test. However, there is a small risk that the test will cause a miscarriage. So here we have a classic decision-making situation with known probabilities of the risks. It is impossible to set monetary values on the outcomes – each set of prospective parents will have their own set of utilities, that is, what it would mean to them to have a miscarriage or a handicapped child. A very difficult decision – but one which sometimes can be helped using the decision-analysis technique.

CONCLUSION

So, you have seen that decision theory is quite easy. Although we have tackled it at a simple level, the concepts can be applied widely and to more complex situations. In essence, it is a way of approaching and structuring the decision-making process in a logical and systematic way, using some predetermined criteria. Try using the techniques in some of your everyday situations and see which criterion suits you and what is your attitude to risk and what are your utilities.

EXERCISES

18.1 A company has produced an innovative gadget for cleaning shoes called ShoePerfect. The initial market research has suggested that if the company decides to manufacture and sell the product themselves there are two possible scenarios – high demand, which would result in profits of £300,000, and low demand, resulting in a profit of £50,000. Alternatively, the company has been made an offer of £150,000 to buy out the patent. Given the innovative nature of the project, there is little information on the likelihood of the different scenarios occurring. Structure the problem to help the company in their decision-making.

18.2 You are working in the personnel department of a medium-sized organisation and currently your information costs per employee are £150. You are considering investing in a state-of-the-art Personnel Information System (PIS). There is every likelihood that the organisation will undergo a major expansion. If this expansion goes ahead and you purchase the system the cost per employee will be £100. If you do not purchase the PIS, you are likely to have to sub-contract a lot of the information processing work at a cost of £175 per employee. There is a small chance, estimated at around 20 per cent that the expansion will not take place, in which case the system would result in a cost per employee of £200. Structure the problem so as to help in the discussion with the management team – you have found in the past that a visual approach is useful.

19 Using the computer

INTRODUCTION

Computers can play a very important role in helping the manager, administrator and personnel professional understand, explore, analyse and present data – transforming it into information that will be useful to the organisation. Once the province of the professional statistician, many software packages used for statistical analysis are both relatively inexpensive and also accessible to the layperson. This has provided the layperson with the ability to carry out quite sophisticated statistical processes relatively easily. However, herein lies the potential dual danger of both using an inappropriate statistical approach and misinterpreting the outcomes of the analysis. That is why in this book we have tried to give you an understanding of:

- what the different techniques can be used for

- the logic and rationale behind the techniques – without overwhelming you with too much statistical theory (!) – because we believe that if you understand some of the theory you will be able to make better use of the technique

- some of the pitfalls to watch out for.

There are a number of statistical packages available – ranging from sophisticated packages such as SPSS and Minitab, through smaller packages designed for specific purposes, eg training evaluation, manipulating competency data etc, to general purpose spreadsheets such as Microsoft Excel™, Lotus 1-2-3™, etc which have basic statistical capabilities. If you want to analyse the results of a survey, then a package such as SPSS is designed to handle the quantitative outcomes from questionnaires and produce tabulations, charts as well as more complex statistical techniques. If you want to analyse general data such as sales information and absence rates, then the facilities offered by a package such as Excel™ will meet the majority of needs. Also, Excel™, for example, has very good facilities for producing a wide range of charts quickly and easily. As many readers will have access to a spreadsheet package, in this chapter we will concentrate on the facilities offered by Excel™. We will describe how to use Excel™ to undertake a selection of the statistical processes described in this book. Our aim is not to provide a comprehensive guide, but to demonstrate how straightforward it is to undertake simple statistical analyses using such packages.

Please note that we are not trying to teach you how to use Excel™ and in fact assume that you have some knowledge of the basic commands – such as how to open worksheets, save worksheets, move and copy data, etc. Also bear in mind, as the rate of change and improvement of all software packages is so great that, by the time you come to read this book it is more than likely that some of the details will have changed. As a starting point remember that, like all spreadsheet packages, the basic working document in Excel™ is the *worksheet* which consists of rows and columns that can be used to enter and store data.

FREQUENCY DISTRIBUTIONS

Aim: To produce a frequency distribution, a cumulative frequency distribution and a histogram.

Example: Ages of employees from Chapter 9.

Process:

STEP 1   Input the data – see Figure 57 as rows 4 to 37 of column A.

STEP 2   Identify bins (an Excel term) for the data – the upper limit of the classes, <20, 20–24, 25–29, etc that you wish to use for grouping the data, eg 19, 24, 29 as rows 4 to 13 of column C.

STEP 3   Select *tools* from menu.

STEP 4   Select *data analysis* option.

STEP 5   Select *histogram*.

STEP 6   In the dialogue box, enter in:
          input range: *A4:A37*
          bin range: *C4:C13*
          Select *output range* and enter: *E4* (this identifies
          the upper left-hand corner of the area in the
          worksheet where the frequency distribution will
          appear).
          Select *chart output*.
          Select *ok*.

Figure 57   Frequency Distribution, Cumulative Frequency Distribution and
Histogram

	A	B	C	D	E	F	G	H
1								
2								
3	AGES		BINS					
4	25		19		Bin	Frequency		
5	56		24		19	3		
6	22		29		24	4		
7	53		34		29	5		
8	21		39		34	5		
9	30		44		39	9		
10	30		49		44	3		
11	18		54		49	2		
12	39		59		54	1		
13	43		64		59	1		
14	32				64	1		
15	42				More	0		
16	35							
17	41				Bin	Frequency	Cumulative %	
18	29				19	3	8.8%	
19	35				24	4	20.6%	
20	39				29	5	35.3%	
21	32				34	5	50.0%	
22	37				39	9	76.5%	
23	47				44	3	85.3%	
24	29				49	2	91.2%	
25	38				54	1	94.1%	
26	46				59	1	97.1%	
27	36				64	1	100.0%	
28	17				More	0	100.0%	
29	22							
30	24							
31	16							
32	27					Histogram		
33	37							
34	35							
35	29							
36	62							
37	34							
38								
39								
40								
41								
42								
43								

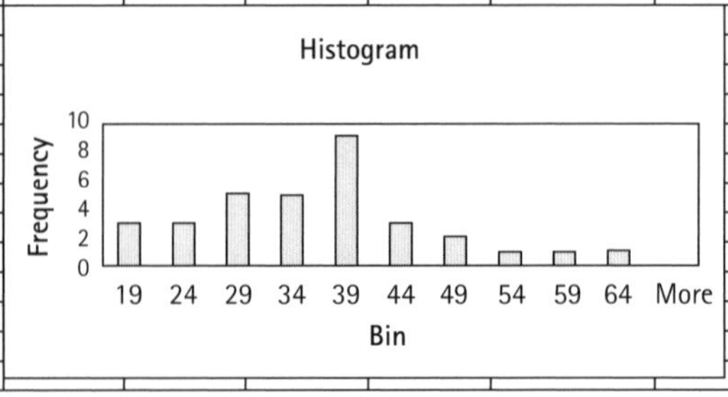

The frequency distribution and accompanying histogram produced by this process is shown on Figure 57. To obtain the cumulative frequency distribution, follow the above steps, but select *cumulative percentage* instead of *chart output*. Remember to choose an output range which is free.

Having produced the histogram it is possible to improve its presentation by resizing, better labelling and scaling of axes, etc using the various chart facilities offered by Excel™.

DIAGRAMMATIC METHODS

Excel™ is excellent at producing all sorts of diagrams and charts.

Aim:	To produce a bar diagram, stacked bar diagram, and pie chart.
Example:	Sales performance from Chapter 10.

Process:

STEP 1	Input data on sales performance – see Figure 58. Select the data table including the row and column labels.
STEP 2	On the tool bar, select the *chart wizard* icon (looks like a bar chart).
STEP 3	You will be offered a range of types of charts – select the appropriate type, eg *column*, *pie chart*. Select the appropriate sub-type by highlighting the appropriate chart. Enter *next*.
STEP 4	The dialogue box will show the highlighted table in the *data range* box. Select the row or column option. Choosing the *row* option for our bar chart would give months along the x-axis, choosing the *column* option would give sales persons along the x-axis. Enter *next*.
STEP 5	Enter the *chart title* and axes labels in *category x axis* and *value y axis* boxes. Enter *next*.
STEP 6	Select whether you wish the chart to be shown as *new sheet*, ie as a separate worksheet, or *object in*,

> ie imbedded in the existing worksheet with the data set (as shown in Figure 58).
> Enter *finish*.

Figure 58 shows a bar chart, a stacked bar chart and a pie chart for January sales.

The Chart Wizard facility offers the opportunity to produce a wide range of different diagrams in all sorts of different

Figure 58 Bar Diagram, Stacked Bar Diagram and Pie Chart

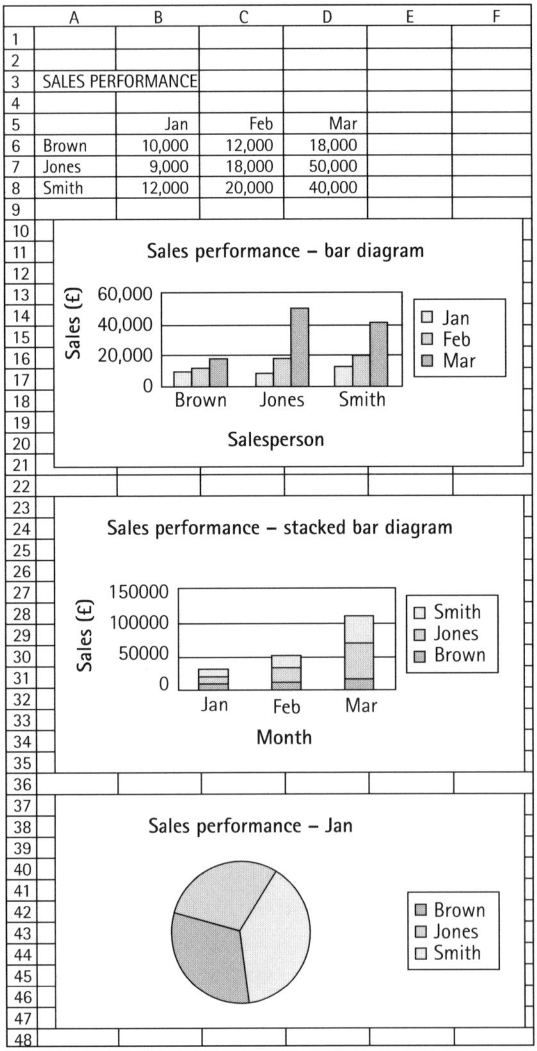

formats. For example, the bar charts and pie charts can be shown three dimensionally. It also offers the facility to produce graphs and scatter diagrams as well as some more unusual charts.

It is very easy to customise the presentation, eg in terms of the font size of the chart titles and axes labels, the scale of the axes, colour and patterns in the bars.

NUMERICAL METHODS

Excel™ has a very useful facility for producing a range of descriptive statistics through operating one function.

Aim:	To produce the mean, median, mode, range, standard deviation and variance.
Example:	Repair times from Chapter 11.

Process:

STEP 1	Input data on repair times for Machine A – see Figure 59.
STEP 2	Select *tools* from menu.
STEP 3	Select *data analysis* option.
STEP 4	Select *descriptive statistics*.
STEP 5	In the dialogue box, enter in: *input range*: *A5:A24* for Machine A Select *output range* and enter: *D3* (this identifies the upper left-hand corner of the area in the worksheet where the descriptive statistics will appear). Select *summary statistics*. Select *ok*.
STEP 6	Repeat above steps for Machine B.

As you will see from Figure 59, we obtain a wide range of descriptive statistics. We have highlighted the statistics of greatest interest. Some of the others are familiar, eg minimum and maximum values of the data set, the sum of all the data values, the number of data values. Some of the other items, eg standard error, kurtosis and skewness, are beyond the scope of this book.

Figure 59   **Descriptive Statistics**

	A	B	C	D	E
1					
2					
3	REPAIR TIMES			Machine A	
4	Machine A	Machine B			
5	5	3		Mean	4.00
6	4	4		Standard Error	0.16
7	3	5		Median	4.00
8	4	5		Mode	4.00
9	3	2		Standard Deviation	0.73
10	5	7		Sample Variance	0.53
11	4	5		Kurtosis	-0.93
12	4	4		Skewness	0.00
13	4	3		Range	2.00
14	5	5		Minimum	3.00
15	3	4		Maximum	5.00
16	4	2		Sum	80.00
17	3	6		Count	20
18	3	4			
19	4	4		Machine B	
20	4	5			
21	4	3		Mean	4.00
22	5	4		Standard Error	0.30
23	5	3		Median	4.00
24	4	2		Mode	4.00
25				Standard Deviation	1.34
26				Sample Variance	1.79
27				Kurtosis	-0.07
28				Skewness	0.29
29				Range	5.00
30				Minimum	2.00
31				Maximum	7.00
32				Sum	80.00
33				Count	20.00

SAMPLING

Aim: To produce confidence intervals for the sample mean.

Example: Package weights from Chapter 13.

Process:

This is a two-stage process:

1. Calculate the sample mean and sample standard deviation.

2. Calculate the confidence limits.

The first stage is accomplished by the process described in the previous section on descriptive statistics.

STEP 1   Input data on journey times – see Figure 60.

STEP 2   Calculate the sample mean and sample deviation as in previous section.

STEP 3	Choose an empty set of cells to record the result.
STEP 4	Select *insert* from menu.
STEP 5	Select *functions* option.
STEP 6	Select function category: *statistical*. Select function name: *confidence*. Select *ok*.
STEP 7	In the dialogue box, enter in: *alpha*: *0.05* (for 95 per cent confidence limits, alpha = 1 − 0.95) *standard dev*: *11.1* (from Descriptive Statistics) *size*: *30* (size of sample) Select *finish*.

NB1 It is possible to calculate the sample mean and standard deviation through using the *functions* wizard – using *average* and *stdev*.

NB2 Within the *descriptive statistics* option is the facility to calculate the confidence level of the mean. However, this is for small sample sizes, ie less than 30.

Figure 60   Confidence Interval for a Sample Mean

	A	B	C	D	E	F	G	H
1								
2								
3	AVERAGE PACKAGE WEIGHTS							
4	160			Descriptive Statistics				
5	179							
6	188			Mean	179.5			
7	180			St. error	2.0			
8	188			Median	181.0			
9	195			Mode	172.0			
10	185			St. dev	11.1			
11	190			Sample V	122.9			
12	162			Kurtosis	−1.0			
13	165			Skewness	−0.2			
14	183			Range	39.0			
15	199			Minimum	160.0			
16	167			Maximum	199.0			
17	192			Sum	5385.0			
18	186			Count	30.0			
19	181							
20	194			Interval		4.0		
21	172							
22	182			Confidence interval		175.5	to	183.5
23	166							
24	187							
25	172							
26	168							
27	181							
28	175							
29	176							
30	195							
31	161							
32	184							
33	172							

REGRESSION AND CORRELATION

Aim: To produce the regression equation, coefficient of determination and chart showing the regression line on the scatter diagram.

Example: Haulage Costs from Chapter 15.

Process:

STEP 1   Input data on haulage costs and distance in Figure 61. Select the data ie columns *B7:B14* and *C7:C14* – make sure the x values (distance data) are in the first column.

STEP 2   On the tool bar, select the *chart wizard* icon (looks like a bar chart).

STEP 3   You will be offered a range of types of charts – select the appropriate type, ie *XY (scatter)*.
Select the appropriate sub-type by highlighting the appropriate chart.
Enter *next*.

STEP 4   The dialogue box will show the highlighted data in the *data range* box.
Enter *next*.

STEP 5   Enter the *chart title* and axes labels in *category x axis* and *value y axis* boxes. Enter *next*.

STEP 6   Select whether you wish the chart to be shown as *new sheet*, ie as a separate worksheet, or *object in*, ie imbedded in the existing worksheet with the data set (as shown in Figure 61).
Enter *finish*.

STEP 7   Select *chart* on the toolbar
Select *add trendline* (to add the regression line to the chart)

STEP 8   In the dialogue box:
Select type by highlighting the appropriate chart.
Select *options*
Select *display equation on chart*
Select *display r^2 value on chart*
Enter *ok*.

Figure 61 **Regression Equation, Coefficient of Determination, Chart showing Regression Line on the Scatter Diagram**

	A	B	C	D	E	F	G	H
1								
2								
3								
4	HAULAGE COSTS AGAINST DISTANCE							
5	Job	Distance	Cost					
6		x	y					
7	1	20	200					
8	2	25	250					
9	3	35	275					
10	4	37	300					
11	5	48	400					
12	6	60	450					
13	7	75	500					
14	8	80	600					
15								
16								
17								
18								
19								
20								
21								
22								
23								
24								
25								
26								
27								
28								
29								
30								
31								

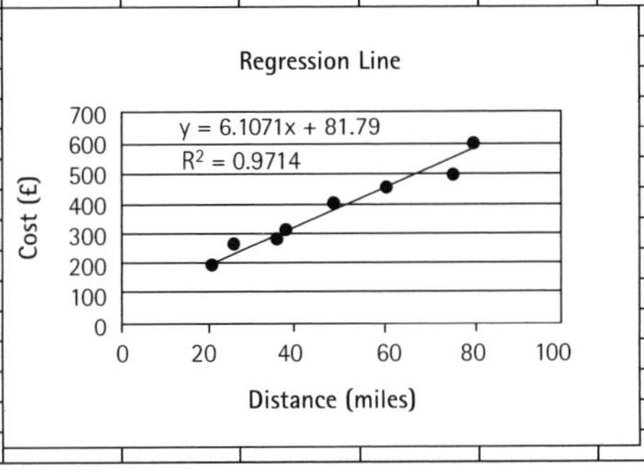

As you can see from Figure 61, the process described above first plots the data on a chart, then draws the regression line on the chart and finally prints out the equation for the regression line and the coefficient of determination (R^2) on the chart. To calculate the correlation coefficient, you simply take the square root of the coefficient of determination.

An alternative process using *tools* from the menu, the *data analysis* wizard, followed by the *regression* option provides output in tabular form but in a more complex format. This output also includes information which allows us to test that the relationship between the two variables is significant and provides confidence limits for the parameters in the regression line – both of which are beyond the scope of this book.

FORECASTING

We cover two of the key techniques – moving average forecast and trend projections.

Aim: To produce a moving average forecast of a set of data.

Example: Flour sales from Chapter 16.

Process:

STEP 1 Input data on flour sales – see Figure 62.

STEP 2 Select *tools* from menu.

STEP 3 Select *data analysis* option.

STEP 4 Select *moving average*.

STEP 5 In the dialogue box, enter in:

input range: *B7:B22* for flour sales

interval: *4* (for a four-weekly moving average)

output range: *D7* (this identifies the upper left-hand corner of the area in the worksheet where the descriptive statistics will appear). It is helpful to choose the appropriate cell which places the forecasts against the correct period.

Select *chart output*.

Select *ok*.

The process in Figure 62 produces a four-weekly moving average forecast and a chart showing the original data set and the moving average (the presentation of the chart can be customised in terms of labelling the axes, adjusting the title, scale, etc). Using the basic spreadsheet facilities, we have gone on to calculate the mean squared error (MSE) of the forecast (Σ(forecast error)^2/12) as a measure of the accuracy of the forecast.

You will recall from Chapter 16 how we commented that you could vary the interval for the moving average in order to minimise the forecasting error. We repeated the process to produce a three-weekly moving average forecast, just altering the input for the *interval* to three instead of four, and again calculated the MSE. You will see that in fact a three-weekly moving average is a better approach to smoothing the data.

Figure 62   Moving Average Forecasts

	A	B	C	D	E	F	G	H
1								
2								
3	FLOUR SALES							
4	Week	Flour	4-week	Forecast	Error	3-week	Forecast	Error
5		sales	moving	error	squared	moving	error	squared
6			average	B – C	(B – C)²	average	B – F	(B – F)²
7	1	30						
8	2	33						
9	3	29						
10	4	32				30.67	1.33	1.78
11	5	30	31	-1	1	31.33	-1.33	1.78
12	6	32	31	1	1.00	30.33	1.67	2.78
13	7	34	30.75	3.25	10.56	31.33	2.67	7.11
14	8	30	32	-2	4.00	32.00	-2.00	4.00
15	9	31	31.5	-0.5	0.25	32.00	-1.00	1.00
16	10	28	31.75	-3.75	14.06	31.67	-3.67	13.44
17	11	32	30.75	1.25	1.56	29.67	2.33	5.44
18	12	35	30.25	4.75	22.56	30.33	4.67	21.78
19	13	32	31.5	0.5	0.25	31.67	0.33	0.11
20	14	29	31.75	-2.75	7.56	33.00	-4.00	16.00
21	15	31	32	-1	1.00	32.00	-1.00	1.00
22	16	28	31.75	-3.75	14.06	30.67	-2.67	7.11
23				*Total*	77.88		*Total*	83.33
24				MSE	6.49		MSE	6.41
25								
26								
27								
28			Four-week moving average forecast					
29								
30		40						
31								
32		35						
33								
34		30						
35								
36		25						
37								
38		20						
39		1 3 5 7 9 11 13 15 17						
40		Weeks						
41								

Aim: To produce trend projections.

Example: Toaster production from Chapter 16.

Process:

If we just want to produce the forecasts, then the following process does this very simply.

STEP 1   Input data on toaster production in Figure 63.

STEP 2   Choose an empty cell to record the output, ie the forecast.

STEP 3   Select *insert* from menu.

STEP 4   Select *functions* option.

STEP 5   Select function category: *statistical*.
Select function name: *forecast*.
Select *ok*.

STEP 6   In the dialogue box, enter in:
X: *11* (the year for which you want your forecast)
Known Ys: *B7:B16* (toaster production data – see Figure 63)
Known Xs: *A7:A16* (years data – see Figure 63)
Select *ok*.

To produce the forecast for any other year, just input the year number into the 'X' box.

If you want to display the regression equation that is the basis for the forecast, then the easiest route is the process described under the section on regression and correlation.

Figure 63 Trend Projections

	A	B	C	D	E
1					
2					
3	TOASTER PRODUCTION				
4	Year	Toaster		Forecast	Forecast
5		production		Year 11	Year 12
6		(000s)			
7	1	50		61.00	62.13
8	2	52			
9	3	56			
10	4	51			
11	5	48			
12	6	54			
13	7	57			
14	8	60			
15	9	62			
16	10	58			

CONCLUSION

We hope the description of how to use a typical spreadsheet package for some of the most common statistical activities will encourage you to explore and experiment with the facilities offered by the computer. These enable us quickly and easily to analyse our data and present the results as useful information. No longer do we have to struggle with the sometimes quite complex arithmetic and algebra, but instead can concentrate on deciding what is the appropriate technique to use, what might be the most helpful way to present the information. We hope that you will find using the computer both an exciting and liberating experience!

This concludes our journey through the statistical techniques that we hope you will find useful in your quest to turn 'numbers into information'. These techniques, together with an understanding of the concepts and applications of information systems covered in Part 1, provide you with the key to managing your information effectively – which in our view is crucial to both individual and organisational success in today's world of accelerating change and ever-increasing technological advances.

Appendix A

FURTHER READING

ANDERSON D. R., SWEENEY D. J. *and* WILLIAMS T. A. *Statistics for Business and Economics.* 6th edn. St Paul/Minnesota, West Publishing Co, 1996.

COHEN M. D., MARCH J. G. *and* OLSEN J. P. 'A garbage-can model of organisational choice', *Administrative Science Quarterly.* Vol. 17, No. 1. 1972.

EDWARDS C., WARD J. *and* BYTHEWAY A. *The Essence of Information Systems.* 2nd edn. London, Prentice Hall, 1991.

HARRY M. *Information Systems in Business.* 2nd edn. London, Pitman Publishing, 1997.

The IPD Guide on Implementing Computerised Personnel Systems. London, IPD, 1997.

LUCEY T. *Management Information Systems.* 8th edn. London, Letts Educational, 1997.

MINTZBERG H. *and* WATERS J. A. 'Of strategies deliberate and emergent'. *Strategic Management Journal.* Vol. 6, pp257–72, 1985.

OFFICE FOR NATIONAL STATISTICS (ONS) (tel. 01633 812 078) publications are available from The Stationery Office, tel: 0870 600 5522.

PEPPARD J. Ed. *IT Strategy for Business.* London, Pitman Publishing, 1993.

QUINN J. B. *Strategies for Change.* New York, McGraw-Hill, 1980.

SHULTHEIS R. *and* SUMNER M. *Management Information Systems – The manager's view.* 3rd edn. London, Irwin, 1995.

SUTHERLAND J. *and* CANWELL D. *Planning and Decision Making.* London, Pitman Publishing, 1997.

Appendix B

Syllabus	*Chapters*
requirements of different organisational functions and activities	1, 7
• Methodologies for systems analysis and design, eg Structured Systems Analysis and Design Method (SSADM)	6
• Current software applications for data processing, report generation, modelling and communications.	3, 5, 7

Section 3 Statistics

• Presentation of statistics	9, 10, 11
Sources of data	17
• Frequency distributions	9
Mean, standard deviation	11
Index numbers	17
Sampling	12, 13
Significance tests	14
Correlation and regression	15
Time series analysis	16
Control charts	14
• Use of current software applications for computation of statistics	19
Simple business calculations.	Chapters 9–19

Appendix C

ANSWERS

Chapter 9

9.1 The relative and cumulative frequency distributions are set below:

Parts/day	Relative Frequency Distribution %	Cumulative Frequency Distribution %
2,001–2,250	13	13
2,251–2,500	3	16
2,501–2,750	33	49
2,751–3,000	42	91
3,001–3,250	5	96
3,251–3,500	3	99
	99*	

*Due to rounding

75% of the operatives are achieving a productivity level of 2,500 to 3,000 parts/day. However, a sizeable minority, 16%, are below this level and 13% are in the 2,001–2,250 band. This might suggest that some operatives are either newly trained and are building up their productivity levels, or that there is some other reason for their below-standard performance. If the training records suggest that this group have not recently been trained, then the following options might need investigating:

- whether some form of retraining is required – particularly if the initial training took place some time ago, or there have been any changes in the process since training

- whether there are any differences in the machinery that is being used by this group or any other external factors, eg closeness to stores for picking up raw materials, that might affect productivity levels

- motivational factors, for example, quality of supervision, absence/sickness records.

8% of the operatives are achieving above standard performances. It may be useful to look in detail at this group and identify possible reasons for this. Also, this group may provide useful coaches for those staff who are underachieving.

9.2 The relative and cumulative frequency distributions for both offices are set out below:

Time (mins)	Frequency Office 1	Relative Frequency Office 1 %	Cumulative Frequency Office 1 %	Frequency Office 2	Relative Frequency Office 2 %	Cumulative Frequency Office 2 %
<5	1	1	1	7	8	8
6–10	6	7	8	40	46	54
11–15	30	37	45	35	40	94
16–20	26	32	77	5	6	100
21–25	10	12	89	0	0	
26–30	9	11	100	0	0	
	82	100		87	100	

There is a marked difference in waiting times between the two offices. In Office 2 most people, 94%, wait 15 mins or less, whereas in Office 1 less than half, 45%, are seen within 15 mins. Just over half, 55%, have to wait more than 15 mins in Office 1 compared to only 6% in Office 2. The sorts of issues that may need to be investigated are:

- how the booking system is arranged – for example, times allowed for appointments, catch-up gaps between groups of appointments

- experience and training of staff – in getting at the information on the client problem, discussing and agreeing solutions, handling the paperwork, time management

- whether there is a difference in the types of client problem being dealt with at the two offices, eg more complex, unusual problems at Office 1.

Chapter 10

10.1 You could use bar diagrams, pie charts or pictograms. Most commonly, bar diagrams are used for this type of data. Also you could present the frequency data, ie the number of delegates commenting in each quality category – the raw data in the table; or the relative frequencies, ie the percentage of delegates commenting in each quality category. If you wanted to compare two tutors, or the same tutor over two programmes, and there were different numbers of delegates commenting, then it would make sense to use relative frequencies so that the results can be directly compared. Also, it is often more powerful to comment in terms of percentages, ie to say 75% of delegates, rather than 15 out of 20.

Knowledgeable

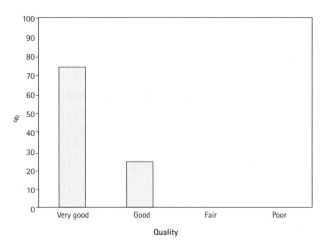

Appropriate pace

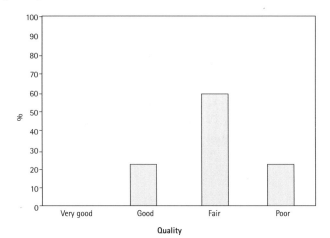

Creates interest

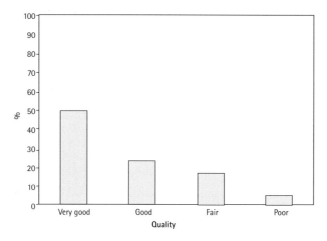

Involves group

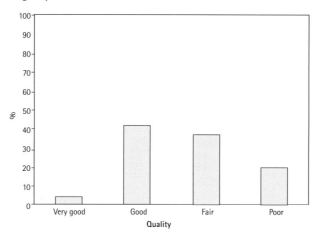

The delegates rated the tutor highly on her knowledge, with 100% rating the tutor very good or good. 75% of delegates commented favourably on the tutor's ability to create interest. The delegates were more mixed on the question of the tutor's ability to involve the group. The weakest area was whether the pace of the course was appropriate – with only 20% of the delegates rating this aspect good, the vast majority, 60% rating it fair and 20% as poor.

10.2 The most eye-catching methods of presentation are pictograms. Be creative. Here are some examples:

Pictogram of number of accidents

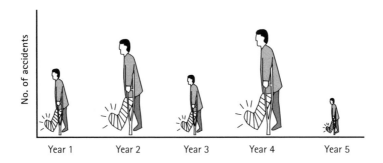

Pictogram of water consumption

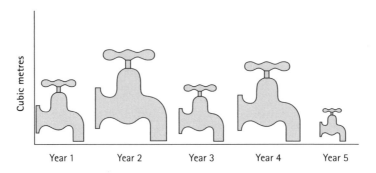

Pictogram of administration costs

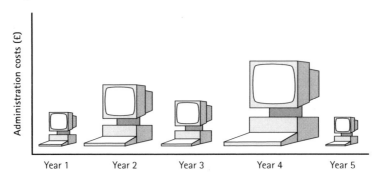

Pictogram of staff turnover

- No. of days lost through accidents. The symbol of a man on crutches gives a humorous indication of the outcome of accidents.

- Water consumption. We have used the symbol of a tap – which is readily understood as the medium for supplying water.

- Administration costs. We have used the symbol of a computer. It might be more appropriate in some organisations to use another symbol, eg a filing cabinet.

- Staff turnover. This is not an easy one for which to identify an appropriate symbol. We have used the idea of people running away (from the organisation!)

In all the above examples the height of the symbol or picture represents the numbers involved and provides the relative scale.

10.3 Set out below are the frequency, relative frequency and cumulative frequency data on the number of hours staff spend at their desks:

Hours at Desk	Frequency	Relative Frequency %	Cumulative Frequency %
< 2	6	24	24
2 < 4	8	32	56
4 < 6	2	8	64
6 < 8	7	28	92
8 < 10	2	8	100
Total	25	100	

Histogram of hours spent at desk

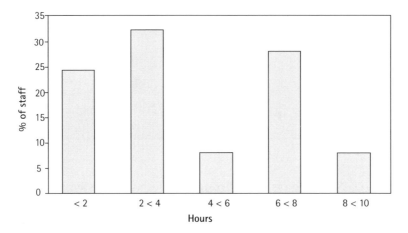

NB The symbol < means less than but not equal to the number following it. So that 2 < 4, includes the values of 2 and 3.

Just over half of the staff spend half their time or less at their desks and nearly a quarter spend less than two hours. 36% of staff spend the greater part of each day at their desk. This suggests that there is the opportunity for 'hot desking' for at least half the staff. Allowing two desks for the six staff who spend less than two hours in this office and four desks for those who spend between two and four hours at their desks, this would give a saving of eight desks overall. Although this would suggest a saving of nearly a third in terms of space, this will partially be offset by the need for the staff sharing desks to have some form of personal space for diaries, pending trays, filing drawers, etc.

Chapter 11
11.1 Department B had a considerably higher than average score for interesting and stimulating work compared to the organisation as a whole. Also, the small standard deviation shows a consistency of views amongst those responding. In contrast Department A scored relatively low in this area and showed a very wide variation in

results. Department B fared well in terms of the effectiveness of their manager – again with a consistency of results. Department A was close to the organisational average, with again only relatively little spread in the results. Interestingly Department B's staff were on average less satisfied than the organisation as a whole with the opportunities for training and development but there was quite a wide disparity of results. This was the best result for Department A – an average close to the organisational average with a consistency of approach.

Particular attention needs to be paid to the nature and content of the work in Department A. Perhaps, initiatives such as job rotation or job enrichment might be considered. In Department B, there needs to be a greater focus on training and development. Given the wide range of views, attention may need to be given to the systems and procedures for identifying training needs. Generally, the scores for the effectiveness of line management look disappointing across the organisation and these were consistent, suggesting that the problem is widespread. There may be a need to carry out a programme of management development.

11.2 The inter-quartile ranges for the three shops are:

	Shop Suzi £	Shop Cecile £	Shop Marie £
Inter-quartile range	6,090	12,280	8,470

Shop Suzi has the smallest inter-quartile range with 50% of customers with incomes between about £9,500 and £15,500. Although Shop Cecile has about the same median customer income as Shop Suzi, there is a much wider inter-quartile range, with the lower quartile well below and the upper quartile well above those of Shop Suzi. Shop Marie has quite a different customer income profile from those of the other two shops, with 75% of customers' incomes above £14,330 and 25% above £22,600.

The results suggest that Shop Marie would benefit from a good range of higher-priced merchandise. Shop Cecile has a very diverse customer income profile and would best be served by a cross-section of the ranges. Shop Suzi's customer profile is clustered closely around the median income of £12,660 and the best approach would be to concentrate on the middle-priced ranges.

Chapter 12

12.1 These are two discrete probability distributions, with the values of the random variable, x and y, being the different profit forecasts associated with each of the three demand options:

Demand	Small Scale Project x (£000s)	Probability p(x)	Large Scale Project y (£000s)	Probability p(y)
Low	100	0.2	0	0.2
Medium	300	0.6	250	0.6
High	500	0.2	800	0.2

The expected value of profits for the small scale project

$$= \sum_{i=1}^{n} x_i\, p(x_i)$$
$$= (100 \times 0.2) + (300 \times 0.6) + (500 \times 0.2)$$
$$= 20 + 180 + 100$$
$$= 300$$

ie the expected value of profits for the small scale project is £300,000.

The expected value of profits for the larger scale project

$$= \sum_{i=1}^{n} y_i\, p(y_i)$$
$$= (0 \times 0.2) + (250 \times 0.6) + (800 \times 0.2)$$
$$= 150 + 160$$
$$= 310$$

ie the expected value of profits for the large scale project is £310,000.

The standard deviation in expected profits for the small scale project

$$= \sqrt{\sum_{i=1}^{n} x_i^2\, p(x_i) - \text{mean}^2}$$

$$= \sqrt{((10,000 \times 0.2) + (90,000 \times 0.6) + (250,000 \times 0.2) - 300^2)}$$
$$= \sqrt{(2,000 + 54,000 + 50,000 - 90,000)}$$
$$= \sqrt{16,000}$$
$$= 126.5$$

ie the standard deviation in expected profits for the small scale project is £126,500.

The standard deviation in expected profits for the large scale project

$$= \sqrt{\sum_{i=1}^{n} y_i^2\, p(y_i) - \text{mean}^2}$$

$$= \sqrt{((0 \times 0.2) + (62,500 \times 0.6) + (640,000 \times 0.2) - 310^2)}$$
$$= \sqrt{(37,500 + 128,00 - 96,100)}$$
$$= \sqrt{69,400}$$
$$= 263.5$$

ie the standard deviation in expected profits for the large scale project is £263,500.

Based on the expected value of the profit, the MD might be tempted to go for the large scale project, as it offered £10,000 additional profits. However, the standard deviation for the larger scale project is more than double that for the medium scale project, suggesting that this is the riskier option.

12.2 As the journey times are uniformly distributed between 2 hrs 15 mins and 2 hrs 30 mins, ie over a 15-minute interval, the probability of the journey time falling in a particular one-minute interval is 1/15. The probability of the train not being more than 10 mins late is represented by the shaded area for the interval 2 hrs 15 mins and 2 hrs 20 mins – see the figure overleaf for a diagrammatic representation of the problem.

Shaded area gives the probability of journey time falling between 2 hrs 15 mins and 2 hrs 20 mins

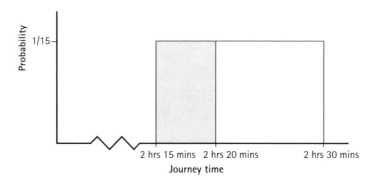

The probability = p(2 hrs 15 mins – 2hrs 16 mins)
of the train being + p(2 hrs 16 mins – 2 hrs 17 mins)
no more than + p(2 hrs 19 mins – 2 hrs 20 mins)
10 mins late = 5 × 1/15
= 1/3

The probability of = p(2 hrs 30 min – 2 hrs 31 mins) + ...
the train being more
than 20 mins late
= 0

Therefore on a 1/3 of occasions it is likely that the train will be 10 mins or less late. On 2/3 of occasions the train will be between 10 and 20 minutes late.

Chapter 13

13.1 1. The 95% confidence limits for the population average student loan:

$$= \bar{x} \pm \frac{1.96s}{\sqrt{n}}$$

$$= 8{,}540 \pm \frac{1.96s \times 1{,}400}{\sqrt{100}}$$

$$= 8{,}540 \pm 274$$

$$= 8{,}266 \pm 8{,}814$$

The 99% confidence limits (see page 172) for the population average student loan:

$$= \bar{x} \pm 2.58 \frac{s}{\sqrt{n}}$$

$$= 8{,}540 \pm \frac{2.58 \times 1{,}400}{\sqrt{100}}$$

$$= 8{,}540 \pm 361$$

$$= 8{,}179 \pm 8{,}901$$

We can be 95% confident that the average loan for final year students falls in the interval £8,266 to £8,814. To increase our level of confidence to 99% widens the interval to £8,179–£8,901.

2. To achieve a confidence interval at the 95% level of ±£150, the sample size would need to be:

$$= \frac{(1.96s)^2}{(\text{sampling error})}$$

$$= \frac{(1.96 \times 1{,}400)^2}{(150)^2}$$

$$= 335$$

To achieve an almost halving of the confidence interval, reducing it from ±£274 to ±£150, would require an increase in sample size of over three times. Given the costs of surveying, it will be important to decide how precise an estimate of the average loan is required.

13.2 It is important to indicate to the MD how precise the results are. You feel that he or she would be comfortable with a 95% level of confidence and so decide to report back with 95% confidence limits.

The 95% confidence limits for the point-of-sales proportion are:

$$= \bar{p} \pm 1.96 \sqrt{\frac{\bar{p}\,(100 - \bar{p})}{n}}$$

$$= 66 \pm 1.96 \sqrt{\frac{66(100 - 66)}{150}}$$

$$= 66 \pm 1.96 \times \sqrt{0.15}$$

$$= 66 \pm 7.6$$

$$= 58.4\% \text{ to } 73.6\%$$

The 95% confidence limits for the after-sales proportion are:

$$= \bar{p} \pm 1.96 \sqrt{\frac{\bar{p}\,(100 - \bar{p})}{n}}$$

$$= 48 \pm 1.96 \sqrt{\frac{48\,(100 - 45)}{150}}$$

$$= 48 \pm 1.96 \times \sqrt{16.6}$$
$$= 48 \pm 8.0$$
$$= 40\% \text{ to } 56\%$$

Between 58% and 74% of customers feel the customer service at point of sale was excellent. However, only between 40% to 56% expressed the same view about the quality of the after-sales service.

The confidence interval varies with the proportion likely to occur. For example, it was greater for the 48% statistic than with the 66% statistic. It is at its highest at 50%. (If you look at the formula, the variation comes from the $\bar{p}(100 - \bar{p})$ part – this is greatest at $50 \times 50 = 2,500$, and lowest at the low/high proportions eg $99 \times 1 = 1 \times 99 = 99$.) To improve the precision of the results to a maximum of $\pm 5\%$ would require a sample size of:

$$= \frac{1.96^2 \times \bar{p}(100 - \bar{p})}{5^2}$$

$$= \frac{1.96^2 \times 50 \times 50}{5^2} \qquad \text{(worst case option)}$$

$$= \frac{9,600}{25}$$
$$= 384$$

Chapter 14

14.1 As the owner is interested in whether there has been any change in mean parking time, then the appropriate hypothesis test would be:

H_0: $\mu = 175$ min
H_1: $\mu \neq 175$ min

We will reject H_0 if the population mean μ falls in the shaded areas of the figure opposite, that is, in either of the two tails which each have a probability of 0.025 and which together give a total Type 1 error of 0.05. In other words, we will accept H_0 at the 5% significance level if μ falls in the range:

$$\bar{x} \pm 1.96 \frac{s}{\sqrt{n}}$$

$$= 160 \pm \frac{1.96 \times 55}{\sqrt{100}}$$

$$= 160 \pm \frac{107.8}{10}$$

$$= 160 \pm 10.8$$

$$= 149.2 \text{ to } 170.8$$

Two–tailed hypothesis test for mean packing times, type 1 error, $\alpha = 0.05$

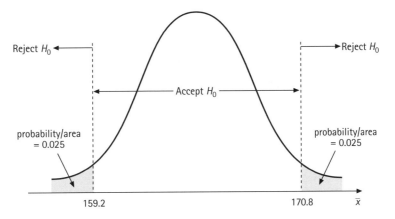

The population mean of 175 falls outside this range, therefore we reject the null hypothesis and conclude that there has been a change in the mean parking time. We are confident that there is only a 5% probability of rejecting the null hypothesis if it is true.

14.2 The researcher is interested only in whether the average time from order to completion of a kitchen is longer than that claimed, 7.8 weeks, so he or she will be setting up a one-tailed test, with the following hypotheses:

H_0: $\mu \leq 7.8$
H_1: $\mu > 7.8$

The researcher will reject the null hypothesis, H_0, if μ falls in the shaded area in the figure below, that is in the lower tail. If you are using a 5% significance level, then the probability/area of the tail will be 0.05.

One-tailed hypothesis test for kitchen-order completion times, type 1 error, $\alpha = 0.05$

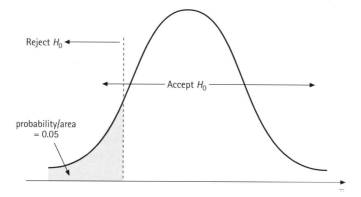

14.3 As we are interested in whether there has been a change in opinion, the null hypothesis is that there has been no change:

H_0: $p_{VG} = 0.21$, $p_G = 0.45$, $p_P = 0.3$, $p_{VP} = 0.04$

Then, the alternative hypothesis is:

H_1: $p_{VG} \neq 0.21$, $p_G \neq 0.45$, $p_P \neq 0.3$, $p_{VP} \neq 0.04$

The expected results based on the null hypothesis being true would be:

Very good	Good	Poor	Very poor
52.5	112.5	75	10

The statistic,

$$\chi^2 = \sum_{i=1}^{n} \frac{(o_i - e_i)^2}{e_i}$$

$$= \frac{(55 - 52.5)^2}{52.5} + \frac{(135 - 112.5)^2}{112.5} + \frac{(52 - 75)^2}{75}$$

$$+ \frac{(8 - 10)^2}{10}$$

$$= \frac{6.25}{52.5} + \frac{506.25}{112.5} + \frac{529}{75} + \frac{4}{10}$$

$$= 0.12 + 4.5 + 7.05 + 0.4$$

$$= 12.07$$

The χ^2 distribution has 3 degrees of freedom (no. of classes − 1).

$\chi^2_{0.01} = 11.3$ (from Table 28)

As our value of χ^2, 12.07, is greater than the value of 11.3 from the table, it falls in the shaded are of the distribution as shown in Table 28 and therefore we reject the null hypothesis. This tells us that the employees' opinions have changed and from looking at the results they suggest that employees' perceptions of the service offered by the Personnel Department have shifted downwards – they feel that the service has deteriorated.

14.4 Our null hypothesis is that there is no difference between the profile of defects between the suppliers:

H_0: the proportion of defects is independent of the supplier

And our alternative hypothesis is that the proportion of defects varies with supplier:

H_1: the proportion of defects is not independent of the supplier

The observed results are:

Supplier	Good	Minor defect	Major defect	Total
A	90	3	7	100
B	170	18	7	195
C	135	6	9	150
Total	395	27	23	445
Proportion of total	395/445 = 0.89	27/445 = 0.06	23/445 = 0.05	

The expected results if the null hypothesis is true are derived by applying the overall proportions for each state of defect to the totals of parts from each supplier, eg 0.89 (proportion of good parts) × 100 (total of parts for supplier A) = 89† in the first column in the next table:

Supplier	Good	Minor defect	Major defect	Total
A	89†	6	5	100
B	174	12	10	196*
C	134	9	8	151*

*rounding errors

We now compute:

$$\chi^2 = \sum_i \sum_j \frac{(o_{ij} - e_{ij})^2}{e_{ij}}$$

$$= \frac{(90 - 89)^2}{89} + \frac{(3 - 6)^2}{6} + \frac{(7 - 5)^2}{5} + \frac{(170 - 174)^2}{174}$$

$$+ \frac{(18 - 12)^2}{12} + \frac{(7 - 10)^2}{10} + \frac{(135 - 134)^2}{134}$$

$$+ \frac{(6 - 9)^2}{9} + \frac{(9 - 8)^2}{8}$$

$$= 0.01 + 1.5 + 0.8 + 0.09 + 3 + 0.9 + 0.01 + 1 + 0.13$$

$$= 7.44$$

This χ^2 distribution has 4 degrees of freedom (2 × 2), ie (number of rows −1) × (number of columns −1).

$$\chi^2_{0.050} = 9.49 \text{ (from Table 28)}$$

As our value of χ^2, 7.44, is less than the value of 9.49 from the table, it falls in the non-shaded area of the distribution as shown in Table 28 and therefore we accept the null hypothesis. This tell us that there is no significant difference between the suppliers in terms of defective parts provided.

Chapter 15

15.1 The business is interested to find out whether and to what extent the response rate to their adverts is affected by the size. The scatter diagram and regression line shown in the figure opposite indicates that there is a linear relationship with a positive trend, ie as advert size increases so does the response. The equation of the regression line tells us:

- that the line of best fit crosses the y-axis at the value of y of 23, ie when x = 0, y = 23

- the slope of the line is 9.9, ie for every increase of one column inch, then the response increases by 9.9.

Scatter diagram and regression line of responses against advertisement size

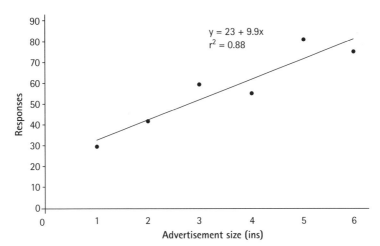

The coefficient of determination r^2 indicates how well the regression line fits the data: r^2 can vary between 0 and 1, the closer to 1 the better the fit. An r^2 value of 0.88 indicates that the regression line reduces the error by 88 per cent, suggesting a strong relationship between the two variables advert size and level of response and therefore that the regression line would provide a good means for predicting response levels from the size of the advert.

If the agency wishes to achieve a response level of 100, then you calculate the advert size by putting y = 100 in the regression equation:

y = 23 + 9.9x
100 = 23 + 9.9x
100 − 23 = 9.9x
or 9.9x = 77
x = $\dfrac{77}{9.9}$
= 7.8

The agency would need an advert of 8 column inches to achieve a response level of 100. It is important to emphasise that the regression line is reliable for predicting values within the data set of 1 to 6 inches. However, there are no grounds for thinking that the relationship would change for values of x above 6 inches in this example.

15.2 The reservations manager wants to find a way of predicting the number of passengers from the reservations made. This is to try and ensure optimal take-up of seats on the airplane and avoidance of disappointed customers who cannot get a seat on the flight they wanted. The scatter diagram and regression line shown in the figure below indicates that there is a linear relation with a positive trend, ie as reservations increase so does the actual number of passengers. The equation of the regression line tells us that:

• the line of best fit crosses the y-axis at the value of y of 57, ie when x = 0, y = 57

• the slope of the line is 0.64, ie for every increase of one reservation, then the actual number of passengers increases by 0.64.

The coefficient of determination r^2 indicates how well the regression line fits the data: r^2 can vary

Scatter diagram and regression line of passengers against reservations

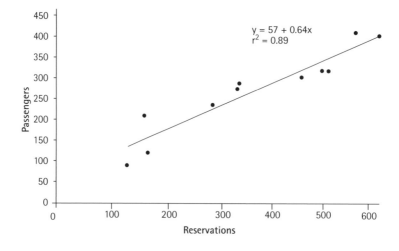

between 0 and 1, the closer to 1 the better the fit. An r^2 value of 0.89 indicates that the regression line reduces the error by 89%, suggesting a strong linear relationship between the number of reservations and passengers and therefore that the regression line would provide a good means for predicting the number of passengers from reservations made.

To predict the number of passengers from a reservation level of 350, you put x = 350 in the regression equation:

y = 57 + 0.64x
y = 57+ (0.64 × 350)
y = 57+ 224
y = 281

With 350 reservations, the airline should expect 281 passengers to actually show up for that specific flight. As the value of x = 350 lies within the range of data used to calculate the regression line, then one can be confident in the result.

To predict the number of passengers from a reservation level of 425, you put x = 425 in the regression equation:

y = 57+ 0.64x
y = 57+ (0.64× 425)
y = 57 + 272
y = 329

With 425 reservations, the airline should expect 329 passengers to actually show up for that specific flight. As the value of x = 425 lies outside the range of data used to calculate the regression line, one has to be cautious in using the result – we are assuming that the relationship is maintained beyond the range. In this case the value of x = 425 is quite close to the end of the data range and there are no grounds for thinking that the relationship might change.

Chapter 16

16.1 The figure below shows a plot of the original observations and the trend line. From the diagram, it can be seen that there is both an upward trend, ie the workforce is gradually increasing over the years and a strong seasonal effect, ie the results vary considerably but in a consistent manner between the four quarters. The statistician had analysed the time series using the following model:

$$Y = T \times S \times I, \text{ where T is the trend element, S the seasonal element and I the irregular element.}$$

She has calculated the seasonal factors, the S × I element, using this model. The seasonal factors support the visual information from the graph, in that the workforce peaks in the second quarters of the year when it is on average about 36% higher than the quarterly average. It remains above average in the third quarters – at 12% above the quarterly average. It falls significantly in the fourth quarter, when it is 38% below the quarterly average and is still well below the quarterly average in the first quarter. These results also

Time series of workforce and trend line

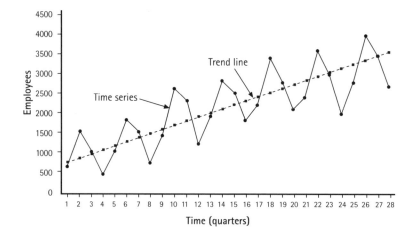

make common sense in that given the nature of the product – the demand for lawnmowers is likely to be highest in the summer quarters, particularly in the early summer, and tails-off significantly in the first winter quarter. Sales and hence production needs will begin to pick up in the first quarter as customers begin to think about their grass cutting requirements prior to the main grass cutting season in Spring. The workforce is likely to mirror this demand.

The results have then been deseasonalised by dividing the original observations by the respective seasonal factors and linear regression analysis carried out on these deseasonalised results. The equation of the trend line has been calculated as:

$$T_t = 633 + 106t, \text{ where t is the time period}$$
$$\text{expressed in quarters}$$

The trend line demonstrates that there has been a steady increase in workforce over the seven years at an average of 106 employees per quarter.

To predict next year's workforce, you first calculate the trend element from the trend line.

Year 8, Quarter 1, t = 29

$T_{29} = 633 + 106 \times 29$
$T_{29} = 633 + 3,074$
$T_{29} = 3,707$

You then apply the seasonal factor (S $\times$ I) for the Quarter 1, ie 0.899

Predicted workforce in Year 8, Quarter 1 = 3,707$\times$ 0.899 = 3,323

In a similar way, you can predict the other three quarters as follows:

Year 8, Quarter 2, t = 30

$T_{30} = 633 + 106 \times 30$
$T_{30} = 633 + 3,180$
$T_{30} = 3,813$

You then apply the seasonal factor (S × I) for the Quarter 2, ie 1.362

Predicted workforce in Year 8, Quarter 2 = 3,813 × 1.362 = 5,193

Year 8, Quarter 3, t = 31

$T_{31} = 633 + 106 \times 31$
$T_{31} = 633 + 3,286$
$T_{31} = 3,919$

You then apply the seasonal factor (S × I) for the Quarter 3, ie 1.118

Predicted workforce in Year 8, Quarter 3 = 3,919× 1.118 = 4,381

Year 8, Quarter 4, t = 32

$T_{32} = 633 + 106 \times 32$
$T_{32} = 633 + 3,392$
$T_{32} = 4,025$

You then apply the seasonal factor (S × I) for the Quarter 4, ie 0.621

Predicted workforce in Year 8, Quarter 4= 4,025× 0.621= 2,500

These predictions are based on the assumption that the future will continue like the past. Given that we are only predicting one year ahead and there are no reasons to believe that there are major changes on the short-term horizon that might affect the results, the predictions for the workforce should provide a reasonable basis for the company's manpower plan.

In the longer term technological advances, for example, the concept of robot mowers may have a significant effect on demand for this type of product. Another possible long-term factor that could affect demand is changes in climate, eg global warming.

Chapter 17

17.1 The productivity figures for each year can be calculated by dividing the production level by the workforce for that year:

Year	Productivity (components/ employee 000s)	Index Based on Year 1 = 100
1	323/165 = 1.958	100
2	350/173 = 2.023	103
3	363/175 = 2.074	106
4	405/200 = 2.025	103
5	455/200 = 2.275	116

Productivity increased steadily but at a low level for the first three years. However, in Year 4 there was a downturn and productivity dropped back to about the level in Year 2. This was at a time when production levels were increasing and so was the workforce. Then, productivity recovered significantly in Year 5. This suggests that the upgrade in machinery caused some disruption in the production schedules during the year of implementation, however, there was a significant productivity gain in the following year suggesting that the new machinery was having an impact.

17.2 To calculate the adjustment to the pensions, we take the annual RPI between 1991 and 1997 and rebase it on 1991 = 100. We also have to check whether any of the increases year on year have been greater than 5%, in which case the increase is pegged at 5%.

Year	RPI* (1987 = 100	RPI (1991 = 100)	Year on year increase
1991	133.5	133.5 ÷ 133.5 = 100.0	
1992	138.5	138.5 ÷ 133.5 = 103.8	3.8%
1993	140.7	140.7 ÷ 133.5 = 105.4	1.6%
1994	144.1	144.1 ÷ 133.5 = 107.9	2.4%
1995	149.1	149.1 ÷ 133.5 = 111.7	3.5%
1996	152.7	152.7 ÷ 133.5 = 114.4	2.4%
1997	157.5	157.5 ÷ 133.5 = 118.0	3.2%

*See Table 35.

It can be seen that in no year has the RPI hit the 5% ceiling so the average pension would have been revalued by the RPI as follows:

Year	Pension(£)
1991	5,000 × 1.000 = 5,000
1992	5,000 × 1.038 = 5,190
1993	5,000 × 1.054 = 5,270
1994	5,000 × 1.079 = 5,395
1995	5,000 × 1.117 = 5,585
1996	5,000 × 1.144 = 5,720
1997	5,000 × 1.180 = 5,900

To calculate the effect of revaluing the pensions based on the increase in average earnings, calculate an index for average earnings as follows:

Year	Earnings (£)	Index numbers
1991	13,500	13,500 ÷ 13,500 = 1.00
1992	14,200	14,200 ÷ 13,500 = 1.052
1993	14,900	14,900 ÷ 13,500 = 1.104
1994	15,400	15,400 ÷ 13,500 = 1.141
1995	16,000	16,000 ÷ 13,500 = 1.185
1996	16,600	16,600 ÷ 13,500 = 1.230
1997	17,300	17,300 ÷ 13,500 = 1.282

Apply these index numbers to the average pension as follows:

Year	Pension(£)
1991	5000 × 1.000 = 5,000
1992	5000 × 1.052 = 5,260
1993	5000 × 1.104 = 5,520
1994	5000 × 1.141 = 5,705
1995	5000 × 1.185 = 5,925
1996	5000 × 1.230 = 6,150
1997	5000 × 1.282 = 6,410

Comparing the two sets of pension figures:

Year	Actual Pension (£)	Pension (£) based on increase in average earnings
1991	5,000	5,000
1992	5,190	5,260
1993	5,270	5,520
1994	5,395	5,705
1995	5,585	5,925
1996	5,720	6,150
1997	5,900	6,410

In the period 1991 to 1997 the pension actually increased by 18%. If pensions had kept pace with average earnings they would have increased by 28% and be at a value of £6,410 compared to £5,900. To bring the average pension in line with average earnings would cost the pension fund an additional £510 per pensioner in 1997 and onwards.

Chapter 18

18.1 First set out the problem in the form of a pay-off table:

Decision choices	Outcomes	
	Low demand o_1	High demand o_2
Manufacture and sell the product d_1	£50,000	£300,000
Sell the patent d_2	£150,000	£150,000

If the company adopts a pessimistic or conservative approach, they would use the maximin criteria – which maximises the minimum possible pay-offs.

The minimum pay-offs for each decision are:

Decision choices	Minimum pay-off
Manufacture and sell the product	£50,000
Sell the patent	£150,000

The company would then choose the decision that gives them the maximum of the minimum pay-offs, ie the company would choose to sell the patent.

If the company adopts a more optimistic approach it

would use the maximax criteria – which seeks to maximise the maximum pay-offs:

Decision choices	Maximum pay-off
Manufacture and sell the product	£300,000
Sell the patent	£150,000

In this case the company would choose to manufacture and sell the product.

18.2 A decision tree is a useful way to lay out the decision-making problem in a visual way – see the figure below.

Decision tree of personnel information system problem

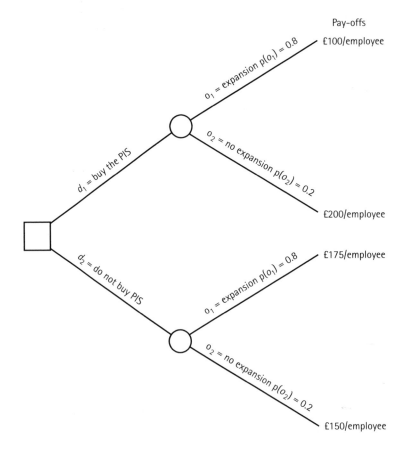

Pay-offs

o_1 = expansion $p(o_1)$ = 0.8 — £100/employee

o_2 = no expansion $p(o_2)$ = 0.2 — £200/employee

d_1 = buy the PIS

d_2 = do not buy PIS

o_1 = expansion $p(o_1)$ = 0.8 — £175/employee

o_2 = no expansion $p(o_2)$ = 0.2 — £150/employee

The Expected Monetary Value for the 'buy' decision = (0.8 × 100) + (0.2 × 200) = £120

The Expected Monetary Value for the 'not to buy' decision = (0.8 × 175) + (0.2 × 150) = £170

As these are costs, then selecting the lowest EMV would lead to a decision to buy the personnel information system.

Appendix D

TABLE OF STATISTICAL TECHNIQUES AND EXAMPLES OF THEIR USES

TECHNIQUE	USES
Tabulations	The essential first steps in any summary or analysis of data are structuring it in tabular form. Examples are analysis of salary surveys, production costs, sales performance.
Diagrammatic methods	These describe how data can be presented in diagrammatic or graphical form. Useful for illustrating reports and presentations.
Numerical methods	Used for summarising and highlighting key aspects of information – for example, using averages or medians to compare costs, salary levels, production output.
Probability	Deals with uncertainty in decision-making – for example, calculating the likely effect on profitability of investing in a new factory, the likelihood of a sales call being successful, a product being defective.
Sampling	Used to obtain data and information on a large population more quickly and at less cost than surveying the whole population – for example, market research into people's voting intentions, customer attitude towards new products.
Hypothesis-testing	Used to test hypotheses about a population from a sample – for example, testing the specification of a product or the effect of an advertising campaign.
Regression and correlation	These measure the existence and strength of relationships between different variables – for example, whether staff absenteeism is related to age, or production costs to factory size. They also enable us to describe the relationships using mathematical equations.
Time series and forecasting	These are techniques used to forecast future events – for example, level of sales, production, markets.
Index numbers	These are a useful way to measure changes over time by presenting the data as a proportion or percentage of a base figure and are particularly useful in comparing unlike elements. Examples are comparing changes in sales against changes in staffing, changes in product performance in different industries. Use of published indices such as the Retail Price Index (RPI) enables us to compare sales or salaries, etc, over time, taking out the effects of inflation.
Decision theory	These techniques help to structure a decision-making problem and can be used in a variety of situations – for example, investment decisions, new product decisions, medical decisions.

Glossary of Statistical Terms

Alternative hypothesis The alternative hypothesis covers all other plausible states of the population characteristic, other than the null hypothesis, for which the test is being carried out.

Array *in ascending order* An array is where the data is set out in order of value, either increasing or decreasing in size. An array in ascending order puts the lowest value first and the highest value last.

Bar diagram A bar diagram is a graphical representation of a frequency distribution where the horizontal axis shows non-numerical data, for example, sales representatives, factories, etc.

Bottom up *forecasting* Bottom up forecasting is a qualitative technique whereby mangers at the lowest level are asked to give their view of the future for their area of responsibility. The forecasts are then put together to provide a forecast for the overall business. It is particularly used in short-term forecasting.

Causal approach *to forecasting* The causal approach to forecasting involves the use of historical data thought to explain or cause changes in the variable being forecast.

Central limit theorem The central limit theorem allows the application of the very useful properties of the normal distribution to the sampling distributions of the sample mean and the sample proportion.

Classical method of assigning probabilities This is a method of assigning probabilities to experimental outcomes which assumes that each outcome is equally likely.

Cluster sampling In cluster sampling, the population is divided into separate groups called clusters. A simple random sample of the cluster is then taken and the elements within the sampled clusters form the sample. Multi-stage sampling is an extension of cluster sampling in which the samples are drawn randomly from within the clusters, instead of the whole cluster being sampled.

Coefficient of determination The coefficient of determination is a measure of how good a fit the regression line is to the data.

Confidence limits Confidence limits provide a range within which a population characteristic, such as a mean, is expected to fall and with which is associated a probability or level of confidence.

Contingency table A contingency table is a table which sets out all the possible combinations and contingencies associated with an experiment or test. It is used in the test of independence.

Continuous random variable A continuous random variable is a random variable that can take on an infinite number of values in an interval, for example, time, weight and distance.

Convenience sampling A sample, which as the name suggests, is chosen for convenience, eg using volunteers, or a lecture class. This is a non-probabilistic sampling method.

Correlation coefficient The correlation coefficient measures the strength of the (linear) relationship between two variables.

Critical path The critical path in a network is the longest path and, therefore, one where any delay is critical to the completion of the project.

Cumulative frequency distribution In a cumulative frequency distribution the data is summarised in tabular form, showing the frequency or number of items with values less than or equal to a particular data point or upper limit of a class.

Cyclical element The cyclical element in a time series is a regular pattern of alternative sequences of observations above and below the trend line which lasts longer than a year.

Data set The set of data of interest.

Decision theory Decision theory or analysis is a technique used to arrive at an optimal (best) strategy when faced with a number of alternative strategies or decisions and an uncertain future situation.

Deciles Deciles are markers in an array which subdivide it into ten equal parts.

Decision tree A decision tree is a graphical representation of a decision problem.

Delphi approach *to forecasting* The Delphi approach to forecasting is a qualitative technique where a panel of experts give their view of the future and these views are refined until consensus is achieved.

Dependent variable The dependent variable is the variable being predicted by the relationship with the independent variables.

Deseasonalising Deseasonalising is the term given to the technique of removing the seasonal element from a time series.

Discrete probability distribution This is the probability distribution of a discrete random variable.

Discrete random variable A discrete random variable is a random variable that takes on a finite number of values (say, one to five) or an infinite sequence (say one, two, three, etc). Examples are numbers of units sold, numbers of customers etc.

Estimates The sample results provide estimates of what the results might be if the whole population was surveyed.

Event An event is a collection of outcomes or sample points.

Expected monetary value   Expected monetary value is a decision criteria based on the sum of the weighted pay-offs for each outcome of a decision, where the weights are the probability of that pay-off or outcome occurring.

Finite *population*   A finite population is one where the size of the total population is known.

Focus groups   A non-probabilistic sampling method that uses small discussion groups to collect in-depth information.

Frequency distribution   In a frequency distribution, the data is summarised in tabular form showing the frequency, ie the number of occurrences, of the data at each data point, or reference point, or in each class.

Frequency polygon   A frequency polygon is a graphical representation of a frequency distribution where the class intervals are shown on the horizontal axis and the frequencies are plotted as points against the mid-points of the classes.

Goodness of fit test   A goodness of fit test is a hypothesis test based on the Chi-squared distribution, used to determine whether a hypothesised probability distribution provides a good fit for a population.

Histogram   A histogram is a graphical representation of a frequency distribution of quantitative data, where the class intervals are shown on the horizontal axis and the frequencies are plotted against the vertical axis in the form of rectangles.

Independence test   An independence test is a hypothesis test based on the Chi-squared distribution, used to test the independence of two variables.

Independent variable   An independent variable is a variable which is being used to predict the dependent variable.

Index numbers   Index numbers are used to measure changes in data over time by presenting the data as a proportion or percentage of some base value.

Inter-quartile range   The inter-quartile range is a measure of dispersion and is the difference between the lower and upper quartile values in a data set.

Irregular element   The irregular element in a time series is that element which cannot be explained by the trend, the cyclical and/or seasonal elements. It represents the random variability in the time series caused by unanticipated and non-recurring factors.

Least squares method   The least squares method is a technique used to find the straight line which provides the best linear approximation for the relationship between two variables.

Maximax/minimin   Maximax/minimin are decision criteria which seek to maximise the maximum pay-off (maximax) or minimise the minimum pay-off (minimin).

Maximin/minimax   Maximin/minimax are decision criteria which seek to maximise the minimum pay-off (maximin) or minimise the maximum pay-off (minimax).

Mean (or average)   The arithmetic mean (or average) is the most commonly used measure of location for the middle of a data set and is obtained by adding together all the individual items of data and then dividing by the number of items in the data set.

Mean squared error   The mean squared error is one measure of the accuracy of a forecasting model and is based on the average of the squared differences between the forecast values and the actual values of a time series.

Measures of dispersion   Measures of dispersion tell us how variable or dispersed is the data in the set. Examples are range, variance and standard deviation.

Measures of location   Measures of location are ways of defining particular points in an array of data. The most common are those relating to the middle of the array, the average or mean, the median and the mode. Others are percentiles, deciles and quartiles.

Median   The median is a measure of location which divides an array of data, so that half of the data items are smaller and half are greater in value than the median.

Mode   The mode is the item in a data set which occurs with the greatest frequency.

Moving average   A method of forecasting or smoothing a time series by averaging a successive or 'moving' group of data points.

Multinomial population   A multinomial population is a population where each member is assigned to one, and only one, of several classes or categories.

Multiple regression   Multiple regression is the technique used in situations where two or more independent variables are used to predict the dependent variable.

Normal distribution   The normal distribution is a continuous probability distribution which is bell-shaped and has the characteristics set out in pages 156–7.

Null hypothesis   The null hypothesis is the tentative assumption made about the population characteristic to be tested.

Ogive   An ogive is a graph of the cumulative frequency distribution, or cumulative relative frequency distribution.

One-tailed test   A one-tailed test is a type of hypothesis test where the alternative hypothesis is for a value either greater or smaller than that of the null hypothesis.

Pay-off table   A pay-off table sets out the pay-offs for the different decisions or strategies of a particular decision problem.

Percentiles   Percentiles are markets within an array which divide the data into 100 numerically equal parts. For example, the seventeenth percentile is the value such that 17 per cent of the data items fall below it and 83 per cent above. The median is the fiftieth percentile.

Pictogram   A pictogram uses the device of relevant pictures, for example '£' signs representing money, as an eye-catching way of presenting information. The size of the pictures represents the value of the item being depicted.

Pie chart A pie chart is the graphical representation of a frequency distribution in the form of a 'pie' or circle. Slices of the pie represent categories of data and are proportionate to the percentage of the whole pie that each category occupies.

Point estimates A point estimate is a single value estimate of a population characteristic such as a mean or a proportion.

Population In statistics, the population is defined as the collection of all items of interest for a particular purpose.

Prediction error Prediction error is the difference between the actual value and the predicted value.

Probability Probability is a measure of uncertainty. It is a measure of the chance or likelihood that a particular event will occur.

Probability density function The probability density function is the equivalent expression for a continuous random variable of the probability distribution of a discrete random variable.

Probability distribution A probability distribution for a random variable describes how the probabilities are distributed or spread over the various values that the random variable can assume.

Quartiles (upper/lower) The upper quartile is a marker in an array above which one quarter of the items fall, and below which fall three-quarters. The lower quartile is a marker in an array below which fall one quarter of the items and above which fall three-quarters.

Quota sampling A sampling method where an interviewer would be given 'quotas' against which to select the sample, but where the samples are not chosen truly randomly. This is a non-probabilistic sampling method.

Random See **simple random sample.**

Random variable A random variable is a numerical description that defines the outcome of an experiment or test.

Range The range is a measure of dispersion and is the difference between the lowest and highest values in the data set.

Raw data Raw data is data as originally recorded, in its original state – 'uncooked', ie not manipulated or tampered with in any way.

Regression analysis Regression analysis is a technique which enables us to describe the relationship between variables using a mathematical equation.

Relative frequency distribution In a relative frequency distribution the data is summarised in tabular form showing the relative frequency – that is, the proportion of the total number of items at each data point or in each class of the data.

Relative frequency method of assigning probabilities This is a method of assigning probabilities to experimental outcomes by conducting experiments or tests.

Retail price index (RPI) The RPI is a published index that measures changes in consumer prices over time.

Sample A sample is a portion of the population selected to represent the whole.

Sample points Sample points are the individual outcomes of an experiment.

Sample space Sample space is the set of all possible sample points, that is, outcomes of an experiment.

Sampling distribution A sampling distribution is the probability distribution of a sample statistic.

Sampling error The sampling error is the magnitude of the difference between the estimate and the actual value of the population statistic of interest.

Sampling frame A sampling frame is a list of the whole population being surveyed.

Scatter diagram A scatter diagram is a graph with the independent variable on the horizontal axis and the dependent variable of the vertical axis and showing a plot of the data points.

Seasonal element The seasonal element in a time series is a regular pattern of alternative sequences of observations above and below the trend line all the features of which appear in a year of less.

Significance level The significance level is the maximum probability of a Type 1 error that the user will accept when carrying out a hypothesis test. It is a measure of confidence in the result.

Simple linear regression Simple linear regression is the technique used in situations where there are only two variables, one independent and one dependent, and the relationship between them can be described as a straight line.

Simple random sample A simple random sample selected from a population is a sample selected in such a way that every sample of that size has the same probability of being selected.

Skewed Data is said to be skewed when the distribution of the data is not symmetrical about the mean.

Smoothing methods Smoothing methods are used to smooth out the irregular element of time series.

Snowball sampling A sampling method that relies on existing sample members to identify other sample members. Often used when it is difficult to get a population list, eg for research on street gangs. This is a non-probabilistic sampling method.

Standard deviation Standard deviation is a measure of how dispersed the data is about the mean. It is the square root of the variance.

Standard normal distribution The standard normal distribution is a normal distribution with the particular features of a mean of 0 and a standard deviation of 1.

Statistical inference Statistical inference is the process of making estimates or drawing conclusions about a population from a sample.

Statistical process control chart This is a chart used for monitoring quality control in manufacturing processes. It has a central line which represents the target for the variable being monitored and lines representing upper and lower control limits. Samples are taken and the results logged on the chart. If a result falls outside the limits this indicates that there is a need for action.

Stratified random sampling In stratified random sampling the population is divided into strata, eg age groups, geographical areas, and a random sample is chosen from each strata.

Subjective method This is a method of assigning probabilities to experimental outcomes using one's judgement.

Systematic sampling Systematic sampling is a method of taking a sample from a large population whereby the first sample member is selected randomly and the remainder selected at regular intervals, until the sample size is achieved.

Time series *method of forecasting* The time series method of forecasting uses a sequence of values of a variable at successive points or periods of time to forecast what will happen to that variable in the future.

Top down *forecasting* Top down forecasting is a qualitative technique whereby top management sets out its view of the future. The forecasts are then broken down to lower level forecasts. It is particularly used in short-term forecasting.

Tree diagram A diagrammatic representation showing the sample points or outcomes of a series of experiments.

Trend The trend in a set of time series data is the long-term movement or shift in the values observed over the time period in question.

Two-tailed test   The two-tailed test is a type of hypothesis test where the values of the alternative hypothesis are both greater than and smaller than that of the null hypothesis.

Type 1 error   A Type 1 error occurs when the null hypothesis is rejected even when it is true.

Type 2 error   A Type 2 error occurs when the null hypothesis is accepted even when it is false.

Uniform distribution   A uniform distribution is a continuous probability distribution where the probability that the random variable will assume a value in any interval of equal length is the same for each interval within the range of values for which distribution is defined.

Variance   Variance is a measure of how dispersed the data is about the mean. It is the square of the standard deviation.

Index

The People and Organisations series and Core Management studies

The only route to a professional career in personnel and development is through the achievement of the IPD's professional standards. One of the three fields that make up these standards, the new Core Management standards define the essentials for competently managing and developing people. They are compatible with an N/SVQ at Level 4 in management.

IPD Publications has five new books in the *People and Organisations* series as textbooks for the new Core Management standards. The texts of these five books and their titles will closely follow the Core Management syllabus. The titles of the books are:

Managing Activities	Michael Armstrong
Managing Financial Information	David Davies
Managing in a Business Context	David Farnham
Managing Information and Statistics	Roland and Frances Bee
Managing People	Jane Weightman

Managing Financial Information
David Davies

Managing Financial Information is a practical explanation of the interface between the finance and HR functions in organisations. It analyses thoroughly many areas that managers may find daunting, and includes test questions and work-based exercises to assist competent learning.

It examines:

- balance sheets
- trading and profit and loss accounts
- budgeting
- costing.

David Davies is a principal lecturer in financial management at the University of Portsmouth. A qualified accountant with a Masters degree in management from Henley Management College, he previously spent 17 years in the private and public sectors. He currently lectures on post- and undergraduate courses, as well as undertaking consultancy work.

June 1999
£13.95
0 85292 782 7
Paperback
240 pages approx.
246 × 177mm format

Managing in a Business Context
by David Farnham

Managing in a Business Context illustrates the framework in which businesses are working in Britain today. Beginning with the nature of strategy and how strategy can be converted into practice, it then considers the issues of wider concern to HR practitioners and business managers in general.

It examines:

- economics, politics and political systems, and their effect on the workplace
- social and legal structures, and how they impinge on the private and public sectors
- the technological revolution and its effect on working practices
- business ethics and the impact of an international climate.

Professor David Farnham holds the chair in Employment Relations at the University of Portsmouth. He has also written *Employee Relations in Context*, published by the IPD.

July 1999
£15.95
0 85292 783 5
Paperback
256 pages approx.
246 × 177mm format

Managing People
by Jane Weightman

Managing People is an approachable introduction to working with people and to understanding how people work. It discusses the psychology of the workplace, including its fundamental characteristics, differences between individuals, and how people learn. *Managing People* also studies issues of central concern to all managers, such as performance management, and training and development.

It examines:

- how to motivate your employees
- differing work patterns and their implications for the workplace
- how to manage work-related stress.

Jane Weightman is a psychologist and has been associated with UMIST since 1980. She has carried out research into a wide range of management-related topics and has written widely in a range of journals. Her books include *Competencies in Action* and *Managing People in the Health Service*, both published by the IPD.

May 1999
£15.95
0 85292 784 3
Paperback
240 pages
246 × 177mm format